REBEL SENATOR

The Senator at work, with his legislative assistant, Sam Stilwell

by Alberta Lachicotte

REBEL
SENATOR

Strom Thurmond of South Carolina

New York 1967
The Devin-Adair Company

TO MY HUSBAND
Who patiently endured the author
throughout the writing of this book

Table of Contents

Acknowledgments

A biographical account of this nature, by necessity, is a composite of the contributions of many people. Without the willing assistance of personages in Washington's official circles and of citizens all over South Carolina, the author could not have written this book. Her deep appreciation is extended to all who helped.

First and foremost, I am grateful to Senator Strom Thurmond himself for his gracious, full cooperation in answering questions and in making his records available. Second, I am grateful to the many present and former members of the Senator's staff for their various courtesies and for sharing their recollections of the Senator and his deceased wife Jean. Their assistance was invaluable.

Third, I extend appreciation to the Crouch family—Mr. and Mrs. Horace J. Crouch of Elko, S.C., Mrs. David Kennedy of Williston, S.C. and Dr. Robert Crouch of Frederick, Md.—for their cooperation in supplying material on Jean Thurmond.

In addition, appreciation for their recollections of Jean Thurmond is extended to Senators Sam Ervin of North Carolina, Lister Hill of Alabama, Spessard Holland of Florida, the late Olin D. Johnston of South Carolina, Stuart Symington of Missouri, Herman Talmadge of Georgia and John J. Williams of Delaware; and to Representatives William C. Cramer and Paul G. Rogers of Florida.

I acknowledge with appreciation, also, the valuable assistance of the Congressional wives who knew Jean Thurmond, especially Mrs. Gordon Allott of Colorado and Mrs. Richard Nixon, wife of the former Vice President of the United States. Others contributing were: Mrs. Clifford P. Case of New Jersey, Mrs. Carl Curtis of Nebraska, Mrs. J. Allen Frear, Jr. of Delaware, Mrs. Barry Goldwater of Arizona, Mrs. Frank J. Lausche of Ohio, Mrs. Herman Talmadge of Georgia and Mrs. John J. Williams of Delaware; Mrs. John F. Baldwin of California, Mrs. Richard Lankford of Maryland, Mrs. John McMillan of South Carolina and Mrs. Eugene Siler of Kentucky.

Further appreciation is extended to Mrs. Robert LeBaron of Washington and to Mr. Cedric Foster of Washington for their contributions. I wish to thank, too, Captain Leonard H. Ballard of the Capitol Police for his material.

Unfortunately, space does not permit listing the names of all in South Carolina who so kindly shared their impressions and memories of the Strom Thurmonds, because so many people responded. I do want, however, to make special acknowledgment to the exceptionally helpful information given by the following persons:

In Columbia—Miss Gertrude Thurmond, Mr. William D. Workman, Mrs. Robert McC. Figg, Mr. N. Heyward Clarkson, Jr., Mrs. Harry Ernst, Mr. James H. Hammond, Mrs. W. Lewis Spearman, Miss Faith Clayton and Mr. Robert S. Galloway;

In Aiken—the Rev. Dr. and Mrs. W. Austin Roberts, Mr. Robert Penland, Mrs. Frank B. Norman, Mrs. Arthur J. Slayton, Mrs. J. Noland Parker, Mrs. Audley Ward and Mrs. Charles Simons;

In Greenwood—Mrs. W. G. Bishop, Mr. Thurmond Bishop, Dr. and Mrs. Boyce M. Grier, Mrs. W. A. Byrd and Mrs. N. Gist Gee;

In Greenville—Dr. Bob Jones, Mr. Roger C. Peace and Mr. L. M. Glenn;

In Spartanburg—the Hon. C. C. Wyche and Mrs. Neville Holcombe;

In Anderson—Mr. and Mrs. Fred Pearman and Mr. M. T. O'Neal, Jr.;

In Edgefield—the Hon. James O. Sheppard and Mrs. J. F. Byrd;

In Orangeburg—the Hon. and Mrs. T. B. Bryant and Mrs. Marshall B. Williams;

Also—Mr. and Mrs. Paul Quattlebaum of Charleston, Col. and Mrs. J. F. Risher of Bamberg, Mrs. R. F. Poole of Clemson, Mr. W. R. Symmes of St. Matthews, Mr. J. E. McTeer of Beaufort and Mr. Peter A. Mitchell of Laurens;

In addition, these college classmates of the late Jean Thurmond—Mrs. Charles E. Neal of Norfolk, Va., Mrs. Carlisle H. Barr of Wilmington, Del., Mrs. Louis G. McCullough of Columbus, Ohio, Mrs. Harry C. Wannamaker III, of Orangeburg, S.C., Mrs. J. O. Burroughs of Conway, S.C., and Mrs. Gary F. Bass, Jr., of Winnsboro, S.C.

I further acknowledge with gratitude the typing assistance of my sister, the late Mrs. Lewis B. Middleton of Charleston, as well as Mrs. George A. Whetsell of Charleston, who typed the final draft of the manuscript.

The kindness of everyone who contributed toward this book made it possible, and of that fact I expect to remain ever mindful and ever grateful.

A. L.

I

The Governor Wins a Bride

FRIDAY, November 7, 1947, was an unseasonably warm autumn day, and almost as an omen of the sun and shadows of the future, the sky alternated between patches of sunlight and a gray cover of clouds. Occasional puffs of breeze rustled through the towering trees releasing flutters of dying red, yellow and brown foliage to the meticulously manicured grounds of the Governor's Mansion in Columbia. Finally the sky decided on a light overcast. Before midafternoon rain would fall, but the symbolism would be lost on the happy gathering inside.

Within, the mansion had never known a more festive day. It had been refurbished especially for this occasion because at noon the Governor of South Carolina was to be married here. Although the wedding of a governor is always of more than ordinary interest, there were about this one so many unique aspects, that it had captured the attention of the national press, and some thirty or more reporters and photographers milled around near the front entrance waiting for admittance. They represented state newspapers, national wire services, newsreel companies and magazines. The event was historic, and nothing about it was to go unrecorded.

Governor James Strom Thurmond, a 44-year-old bachelor, was taking as his bride a 21-year-old girl, Jean Crouch. The ceremony would be a simple one witnessed only by the immediate families and a representative of the press.

The wedding was the first of a South Carolina governor to take place in this house, the home of State chief executives since 1868. Before and during the Civil War, the structure was the officers quarters for Arsenal Academy. It was the only one of the Academy buildings to escape burning by Union troops as they set fire to the city in 1865. It had been the scene over the years of countless glittering affairs, but only once had anything approached such gaiety, and that was the mansion wedding many years ago of a governor's daughter.

The imminent marriage of James Strom Thurmond and Jean Crouch was the culmination of an unlikely romance between a middle-aged man and a college girl, and it did not have the whole-hearted endorsement of the citizenry. Despite a "friendly press" glad for something warmhearted and romantically appealing to feed its readers and despite the couple's blissful mood, there were many in South Carolina who looked upon the marriage with open disapproval. They had written in aggravatingly substantial numbers to the Governor; and, lest the bride-elect should feel neglected, to her also.

"What in God's name is the man thinking about?" people wanted to know. Letters told Governor Thurmond that, in short, he was a horrid old man, a corrupter of young womanhood, a middle-aged fool. What did he mean by marrying that child, a mere schoolgirl and placing her in the mansion with the responsibilities of the First Lady of South Carolina? He had lost his balance completely. The marriage would be nothing but a source of embarrassment to the

State. The prospective groom, whose skin had been pummeled by politics into alligator-hide thickness, was able to laugh off his critics, but the sudden glare of publicity surrounding her engagement was a new experience to the Governor's fiancée, and so was criticism. Some of her mail was startling, even disturbing. She was told quite bluntly that she was not in love with the Governor but with the governorship. With so many younger men around, how could she possibly be sincerely interested in a 44-year-old man? The charm had to be his position. Such open quest for status was shameful, the letters repeated. Jean reacted philosophically, even with amusement, except to occasional remarks that were too sharp not to hurt.

"They just don't understand," she commented frequently on opening her mail, adding almost plaintively, "Everybody's doubtful about this marriage but Strom and me."

The blue-eyed, blond, militarily-erect man with the up-country dialect—the man Jean Crouch had fallen in love with, over a score of others her own age—had proved himself a forceful personality to be reckoned with in South Carolina. He had won over ten other candidates to become Governor in January 1947. He was noted for energy, boldness, toughness and hard-driving ambition, and his political ascent had been steady.

"Thurmond is as courageous as men come—and as goodhearted; he would give you the shirt off his back if you were in need. The man has a real soft side to him if you can get beneath that exterior," observed an acquaintance once on the subject of the Governor, "but, lord, once he sets his mind about something, nothing on earth can change it. He's as stubborn as the very devil! Maybe that's what it takes."

Born in Edgefield, South Carolina, December 5, 1902, Strom, as he preferred to be called (in later years he dropped the James entirely), was second oldest in a family of three sons and three daughters. He was named for his

maternal grandfather. The Thurmond children grew up in
politically conscious Edgefield, a beautiful, proud up-country
town of ante-bellum vintage that since 1816 had produced
more governors and more political activists than any other
place in the State. Their mother, Eleanor Gertrude Strom,
came from a well-known Edgefield family and was the
daughter of a physician. She united two old families of the
vicinity when she married John William Thurmond, a prom-
ising young lawyer who was solicitor of that circuit. He
previously had been a state legislator and in later years
served as a United States attorney. He was described by
State Chief Justice Eugene S. Blease as "the ablest all-round
lawyer who ever appeared before the Supreme Court of
South Carolina."

Will Thurmond, as people called Strom's father, was a
tall, heavily-built man with a personality as commanding
as his physical bearing. Strom's mother, on the other hand,
was small, almost fragile in appearance, but there was nothing fragile about her spirit. Both parents were strong, forceful personalities.

The family attended Edgefield's Baptist church regularly, and lived by a strict code of ethics, having no tolerance
for compromise between right and wrong. The Thurmonds
were noted for their hospitality and generosity. They made
a habit of inviting to dinner or for the night all acquaintances who came through town, and country kin took Thurmond hospitality for granted.

Both his mother and his father exerted major influences
over the formation of Strom Thurmond's character. He was
always close to his mother and wrote to her regularly each
week throughout her lifetime, but it was probably his father
who more than any other one person shaped the boy's
personality. All through public life, Strom was to quote Will
Thurmond and to reveal an obvious admiration for his
father.

When he graduated in 1923 from Clemson College at
the age of twenty with a major in Agricultural Science and

English, these words appeared beneath Strom's picture in the college annual: "One cannot always be a hero, but one can always be a man." For the next five years he taught agriculture in the small towns of McCormick, Edgefield and Ridge Spring. Then his mind turned toward advancement. He ran in 1928 for the office of Edgefield county superintendent of education—and won—at the age of twenty-five. The venture marked his first success in politics, rekindling an interest in public service he had shown as a small boy.

Not long after his first election to office, Strom decided to enter the legal profession. He studied law at night under his father's tutorage (a method of preparation chosen because he felt he could progress more rapidly than under the more impersonal, prescribed law school routine) and finished a three-year law course in about one year. The home-taught lawyer was told by an examiner following the three-day bar examination that he had tied for first place with a graduate of Harvard Law School. Strom Thurmond was admitted to the South Carolina Bar in 1930. In 1933 he was elected state senator from Edgefield county, and, with this step in the political world, was on his way. He served in the senate until elected a circuit judge in 1938 by the General Assembly. The young politician's interest in education, meanwhile, had resulted in his election in 1936 to the board of trustees of the State's college for women, Winthrop. Later a classroom building there was named Thurmond Hall in his honor.

At various times along his way to the top, Thurmond had been South Carolina's youngest agriculture teacher, youngest superintendent of education, youngest state senator, youngest college board member and youngest circuit judge. He was far too occupied with his career to think about any one woman, much less to entertain notions of marriage, and was often known to keep his date of the evening waiting while he cleared important papers from his desk after office hours.

As a judge he was exempt from active duty in the armed

services, but Strom had not the slightest intention of missing
anything, and on the day Congress declared war against
Germany, he volunteered for Army service.

Actually, the young circuit judge had a habit of not
missing out on danger. Just the year before, for instance,
Strom Thurmond strode into one of the wildest affairs in
the history of his native Edgefield County. It was the bloody
climax to a feud between two old, well-established Edgefield families, the Timmermans and the Logues, whose bad
feeling for one another claimed a total of nine lives.

An ordinary mule belonging to Davis Timmerman in the
autumn of 1940 triggered the tale of horror by squeezing
through a neighboring fence and kicking to death Wallace
Logue's prized bull which had charged the mule. Wallace
Logue went to Timmerman's country store to demand pay-
ment for the bull. After the two, who already were on the
"outs" over another matter, argued about compensation for
a while, Logue leaned across the counter and grabbed Timmerman by the shirt front. The latter promptly reached for
a pistol beside the cash register and killed Logue. On March
2, 1941, a jury acquitted Timmerman on the grounds that
he shot in self-defense.

The victim's widow, Sue Logue, and her brother-in-law,
George Logue, immediately began plotting revenge, taking
into their plan a devoted sharecropper, Fred Dorn. A few
weeks later Timmerman's Negro hired hand was killed without warning by a single rifle shot. The killer was never
identified.

Taken about this time into the plot for revenge was
another member of the family, Sue Logue's nephew, Joe
Frank Logue, only recently cited as an outstanding officer
of the Spartanburg city police force. Sue gave her nephew
$500 to hire a man to kill Davis Timmerman. Logue found
his man in the person of Clarence Bagwell. While Bagwell
went into the store to pump four bullets into Timmerman's
back, Joe Frank hid under a coat in the back of the automobile outside.

An offer of reward brought forth an informer who implicated Bagwell. After his arrest, Bagwell then implicated Joe Frank Logue, who confessed his own role and, in turn, implicated both Sue and George Logue.

On Sunday morning, November 16, 1941, Edgefield County sheriff, Wad Allen, a cousin of the Logues ironically enough, drove out with his deputy, W. L. Clark, to the Logue farm to arrest Sue and George. Sheriff Allen went unarmed to his relatives. The two officers were admitted to the house only to be ambushed by George Logue and Fred Dorn, the sharecropper. Sheriff Allen fell dead under a hail of bullets from George Logue's pistol, while Deputy Clark reeled with fatal wounds inflicted by charges from both barrels of Dorn's shotgun. Clark drew his pistol and felled Dorn before staggering outside to be carried by a passing motorist to Edgefield. He died shortly thereafter in an Augusta, Georgia, hospital.

Clark's return to Edgefield with accompanying news of the latest episode in the Logue tragedy occurred during church hour. The word spread as church ended.

Strom Thurmond was among those who heard the news at the conclusion of the service at Edgefield's Baptist church, and he was disturbed at the potential for further violence in the public reaction to the popular sheriff's slaying. The 38-year-old circuit judge drove immediately to the Logue home some ten miles from town. With the sheriff dead, the deputy dying and the coroner-undertaker occupied with the earlier carnage, there was no law enforcement official in the county to take charge.

When Thurmond arrived, there was already before the farmhouse a large gathering of local citizens armed with rifles and shotguns. It was apparent, too, that there were people of different sympathies inside the house. Thurmond removed his coat, turned his pockets inside out to indicate he was unarmed and proceeded alone across "no-man's land" to the dwelling's front entrance. Asked what he wanted by a voice behind the closed door, the judge identified

himself and asked to talk with Sue and George Logue. Told
that George was not at home and that Sue was not feeling
well, Thurmond insisted on speaking to Sue and finally was
instructed to go to the back door. At the back door he came
face-to-face with the business end of a shotgun in the hands
of a Logue friend. After a tense few minutes Thurmond
managed to talk his way into the house. He learned that
George Logue had, in truth, already left the house and that
the body of Dorn had been removed. In the interest of
avoiding further bloodshed and with assurances of safe
conduct through the crowd, the judge persuaded Sue Logue
to surrender and to leave the house.

Thurmond went back to the yard and arranged for Aiken
County sheriff, J. C. Howard, and another out-of-county
officer who had arrived on the scene to come to the house
with him. He then went back inside and escorted Sue Logue
through the still blood-spattered living room and through
the sullen, armed crowd inside the building to the porch.
From there the judge and the peace officers escorted Sue
Logue through another sullen, armed crowd on the grounds
to a waiting car that spirited the woman to the State penitentiary at Columbia.

Sue and George Logue and Clarence Bagwell all received
death sentences and were executed. Joe Frank Logue, who
testified for the State, finally was given a life sentence.

The hero of that hour, Strom Thurmond, has been walking into one "no man's land" or another ever since.

After joining the Army following American entrance into
World War II, Thurmond became a civil affairs officer. Yet
he managed to get himself attached to the 82nd Airborne
division for the European invasion and made his way to
France on what proved to be one of the most dangerous of
all conveyances—the troop glider. His damaged glider crash-
landed behind enemy lines in Normandy on D-Day injuring
a number of occupants, including Thurmond (though not
seriously). The unit then fought through two days' isolation

to link up with advancing American forces. Thurmond subsequently participated in five battles of the First Army, which fought through France, Belgium, Holland, Luxembourg, Czechoslovakia and Germany. At the end of the war in the European theater, Thurmond was transferred to the Pacific, serving in Hawaii, the Johnston and Marshall Islands, Guam and in the Philippine Islands before the Japanese surrender. During those years, he was awarded the Legion of Merit, the Bronze Star Medal with "V" device, the Army Commendation Ribbon, the Purple Heart, the Presidential Distinguished Unit Citation, a bronze arrowhead, five battle stars, the French Croix de Guerre avec Etoile de Vermiel, the Belgian Cross of the Order of the Officer of the Crown, and eight lesser awards and citations.

Upon discharge from service in January 1946 with the rank of lieutenant-colonel, Strom resumed his duties as circuit judge, but not for long. With ten other hopefuls, he decided to throw his hat into the political ring for Governor. All eleven geared for the August 1946 Democratic primary, which with South Carolina's one-party system, was tantamount to election. With so many candidates in the field, a man had to latch on to an attention-getting issue to make himself stand out from the herd. Moreover, he had to have a certain amount of pure political savvy going for him. Thurmond had both.

For his main issue, Thurmond chose domination of the State's political life by the "Barnwell Ring," and he stayed with it like a bulldog with a bone. The "Barnwell Ring," to which he referred constantly, was composed of State Senator Edgar A. Brown, president pro tempore of the state senate and powerful chairman of its finance committee, and Solomon Blatt, speaker of the state house of representatives. Both were Barnwell county men. By primary election day on Tuesday, August 20, the State was steeped with ringing denunciations of the "notorious Barnwell Ring" and the electorate gave Strom Thurmond the highest number of votes.

The nearest runner-up was Dr. James C. McLeod, a physician from Florence, South Carolina. A run-off election took place two weeks later on September 3rd. Thurmond emerged the winner to become the tenth South Carolina governor from Edgefield County.

Choice of the "Barnwell Ring" as a campaign issue paid off in votes, but it did not endear the Governor-elect to the two most powerful men in the General Assembly. The election and ensuing squabbles led Senator Brown many years afterward to say in a newspaper story when asked whom he considered the worst South Carolina governor in modern times, "Strom Thurmond. He always wanted his own way."

Inauguration of the new Governor took place on the steps of the capitol in Columbia on Tuesday, January 21, 1947. That day the State's first bachelor governor since 1897 moved into the Executive Mansion, taking with him a sister, Gertrude, to serve as hostess. At the age of forty-four, Strom Thurmond was one of the most eligible bachelors in Carolina. His pre-war public service coupled with an outstanding war record were in themselves impressive. The governorship was the final touch of glamour. Even so, hardly anyone envisioned for him a bride of twenty-one.

The girl destined to become the next First Lady of South Carolina turned twenty-one on July 14, 1947, only three months before announcement of her engagement, yet she had already achieved a measure of distinction and political success.

Jean Crouch was the youngest of four children, two sons and two daughters. Her mother, the former Inez Breazeale, was from an old Anderson County family. She had married her teacher, Horace J. Crouch, an Edgefield County native, who had been teaching in her community school and boarding at her parents' home. After their marriage the Crouches lived in Greenville, South Carolina, for a year and then settled at Elko, a farm village in Barnwell County, where they built a large, two-story, columned home and established permanent residence. In this lower-state village Jean was born and reared. She could tussle, climb trees, bicycle-ride or swim with just about anybody her age. In fact, a rare spanking was administered once for turning somersaults on her bed with such abandon that she kicked out a bedroom window pane. Despite this tomboyishness, she loved music and learned to play the piano, violin and saxophone.

As she entered Williston-Elko high school and began stretching up to her eventual five feet seven inches (at one point she had been so small that others nicknamed her Tiny), her fancy turned to basketball. It was characteristic of her to put heart and soul into whatever interested her and this she did with basketball. One year she captained her team to a district championship. And once after the Williston-Elko team lost an important game by two points Jean smiled at her teammates as if they had won and gave each a cheerful word, but as soon as she got home, collapsed in a big chair and sobbed in disappointment. A friend, having noticed her show of nonchalance after the game, was completely taken aback.

"Why are you crying?" she asked in bewilderment.

"You just don't understand how I feel," was the tearful reply. "We were supposed to win."

Jean Crouch never knew what it was to give second best to any cause. Even when her energy was misdirected, she went full speed ahead with varying results. One day she led a group of her fellow-pupils off the school grounds on an April Fool's Day prank. On their return, the principal took the future First Lady of South Carolina aside for a lecture. Recognizing her qualities of leadership, he suggested firmly that hereafter she use them for more constructive purposes.

By the time of her high school graduation, she had taken this advice seriously. She had become president of the senior class, received an award as the most outstanding student at Williston-Elko, was voted "Miss Hi-Miss" for superior leadership, was class valedictorian, president of the school's scholastic organization called the Beta Club, winner of the Daughters of the American Revolution Medal for Good Citizenship, and winner of the Solomon Blatt Medal for Expression. Following news of Jean's engagement several years later, her father could not resist teasing her about that Sol Blatt Medal. It was a never-ending joke that Governor Thurmond's wife had once been the recipient of an award from a member of the "Barnwell Ring," target of continuous harassment during Strom's gubernatorial race. Said Jean, with a grin before her marriage, "I don't think Daddy should have let that slip!"

Jean entered Winthrop College at Rock Hill in the fall of 1943, majoring in Commerce with the intention of teaching secretarial studies. Analyzed feature by feature, Jean Crouch had her physical defects, but she had a knack for accentuating her positive features. Her large, blue eyes, set off by brown, wavy hair, sparkled with warmth, vivacity, enthusiasm and humor, and a broad smile lighted her whole face, but she never lost sight of what she regarded as her weak points, particularly her Roman nose and her legs. After her marriage she remarked to someone while showing a childhood photograph, "Look at that. There isn't anything pretty about me. I'm bowlegged and knockkneed at the same time, and that takes some doing! Now that I'm First Lady, people say I'm pretty."

In college Jean worried because she seemed to make friends with men more quickly than with women. She felt this was a lack of balance, a fault in need of correction. The knowledge that many a girl would have exchanged places did not relieve her mind. Not until the spring of 1946 when she was elected president of the rising senior class did she learn that her anxiety was groundless. She was exuberant over the highest compliment that classmates could pay her at a woman's college.

Even as a freshman, the girl from Elko had entered with characteristic vigor into campus life. She took special interest in the dramatics club and in the Baptist Student Union, though the two groups seemed poles apart. As a matter of fact, she soon involved herself so deeply in the church that one Sunday during October she presided at a Sunday school general assembly in the main auditorium of Rock Hill's downtown Baptist church. Jean put such fervor into her talk that her brother, Bob, there on a week-end visit, panicked for fear his sister was becoming overly religious. As soon as they got outside, Bob scowled in brotherly fashion and decreed, "You've got to stay out of that pulpit, and that's all there is to it!" Jean grinned. "I thought I was right brave to get up there," she told him.

In the meantime she had not been neglecting her social life. While she dated college men frequently, Strom Thurmond began playing an increasingly important role in shaping her destiny during her last year at college.

The couple had first met in the fall of 1941 when Judge Thurmond of the 11th judicial circuit was holding court in Barnwell. Jean went with her high school junior class to observe a session of court. Horace Crouch, county superintendent of education, called his daughter up to meet the judge, who, in making conversation, told the teenager she had pretty eyes, a compliment the girl remembered always. Strom did not see her again until the spring of 1946 and then only briefly at a function at Winthrop. That autumn as Governor-elect he stopped one day at Elko to talk with Mr. Crouch about various state school problems. Spotting a girl's picture on the wall, he asked who it was.

"That's my daughter, Jean, whom you met some years back at court in Barnwell," the educator replied. "She's a senior at Winthrop."

"What is she taking?" inquired the Governor-elect, eyeing the photograph more closely.

"Commerce."

"Do you think she might be interested in coming to work in the Governor's office after graduation?"

"She's to be in Columbia soon at some kind of education meeting. Maybe you can talk with her then," replied father as the conversation drifted to other topics.

As soon as he returned to his Edgefield office, Strom Thurmond busied himself learning all about the Columbia meeting and decided that it was important for him to attend a November gathering of the coordinating council of the South Carolina Education Association to make a talk. Various college students were to be there and were scheduled to say something about the teaching profession. Among them were Jean Crouch, who planned to teach in Sumter, South Carolina, the next year, and a classmate who wanted to avoid teaching. The most memorable statement Jean made was an off-hand comment that "I think many young girls don't enter the teaching profession because they are afraid they won't get married, but I am not going to be an old maid." That day she was asked to think over the possibility of working for the new Governor and to forget about teaching for a while.

Soon the Winthrop senior, who had caught Thurmond's attention, received a "Glad-to-have-seen-you" postcard from him during his attendance at the Southern Governors conference in Miami, Florida. On returning to South Carolina, Strom deemed it wise to follow up a bit on the crucial matter of office help. With studied casualness he suggested to Winthrop President Henry R. Sims that some of the student leaders—for instance, the senior class president, student government president and perhaps two or three others—be allowed to attend the inaugural on January 21st.

"It would be a nice experience for them," the Governor-elect added.

"That's a fine idea," agreed President Sims conveniently, giving no indication that he suspected a rigged trip, if, in fact, he did. On schedule, a car of eager, chattering girls

from the Rock Hill school drew up at the capitol grounds
for the Governor's inauguration.

Again in February a group of Winthrop students descended on Columbia for an event of some kind, using the
opportunity to visit the Governor's office. In the crowd was
Jean Crouch.

"We're getting saturated with Winthrop these days, it
seems to me," observed an unenchanted employee in the
building.

Someone on the first floor of the Capitol just then
glimpsed W. Lowndes Daniel, Jr., the Governor's executive
secretary, and asked him over to meet the Winthrop delegation.

After the introductions, Colonel Daniel turned to Jean
Crouch and said smilingly, "I've heard of you before."
Whereupon the entire group of girls "closed in toward me
like in a football huddle," the aide said afterwards, and
they all chorused, "What have you heard?"

"Eh-oh-eh," he mumbled, extricating himself. "Well, I
hear she's a particularly fine girl." He remembered that those
words were the exact ones the Governor had recently used
in pointing out Miss Crouch in a group photograph.

Governor Thurmond, unusually expansive, considering
his customary businesslike, no-nonsense office manner, invited Miss Crouch that day to have lunch at the mansion
with his sister and himself. Accepting before any tactless
soul could undo her with a loud, "But Jean, you've just
eaten," she hastily excused herself from the others, departing
excitedly for her second lunch of the day. Feeling ready to
cope with anything on the menu, the young guest was horri-
fied to be challenged immediately by a raw oyster cocktail.
She despised oysters. Faced with them after a full meal was
a nightmarish predicament. Taking up her fork, she poked
uncertainly at first one then another oyster; finally she braced
herself and gulped each down as if it were a huge pill,
all the while silently praying for peace in the digestional

tract. A full course meal went on top of the oysters. All the way back to Rock Hill, the other girls teased her, but happy not to be suffering acute indigestion from two meals in quick succession, a blandly smiling Jean leaned back in her seat and said nothing.

In March the Governor invited his Winthrop acquaintance to the American Legion horse races in Columbia. "Bring along a friend, a girl friend," he carefully specified.

It was on this occasion that Governor Thurmond appointed Jean Crouch to serve as Miss South Carolina at Charleston's annual Azalea Festival later in the spring. Jean, who participated in the April festival as a representative of the State and not as a competitor for other titles, was placed in a prominent position near the newly-selected queen. Who was there to crown the Queen of the Azalea festival but the Governor? He gave her the usual kiss accompanying such honors, and for good measure he planted one on Miss South Carolina. Miss South Carolina beamed and made a mental note about governors crowning beauty queens. The note was tucked away in a pigeon-hole of her mind for future reference.

Strom Thurmond had decided by now that he would like to see Miss Crouch socially on a more frequent basis, but to do so required altering plans for her to work in his office. Upon the tactful advice of his aide, Lowndes Daniel, the Governor offered to place her in one of the numerous state agencies, emphasizing that a position in the Governor's office automatically excluded any but purely official relationships with office personnel.

"What are you hunting? A secretary or a playmate?" the girl asked quickly.

"Come on down, we'll expect you," said the Governor, ignoring her reply.

"Well, I'll have to think it over," she said.

In due course she announced acceptance of the secretarial vacancy on the Governor's staff. Her decision meant only one thing to Thurmond, indifference toward him. He was deflated, yet had to accept the situation.

In the meantime Winthrop College had invited the new Governor to be the main speaker at commencement exercises on June 1st. After the address, members of the class walked single file across the auditorium stage to receive their degrees. Each acknowledged Governor Thurmond's presence with a smile or nod in his direction as she passed before him. But when the class president, who was graduating cum laude, strode by, she looked neither to the right nor to the left, ignoring the State's chief executive as completely as if he were not there. That afternoon she compounded the mystery of her behavior by doing an about-face and consenting to ride to Elko in the Governor's automobile.

Jean reported to her new job at the capitol on the first of July. When the Governor began making plans to attend the National Governors conference in Salt Lake City in midsummer, he decided to have two stenographers go along in case they were needed to type speeches. The trip was offered first to senior personnel, none of whom showed particular interest; so the offer filtrated down to Wilma Smith who could attend and to Jean, rank newcomer.

In Salt Lake City Governor Thurmond covered the full schedule of events. Now it was Miss Crouch's turn to be roundly ignored, and the reversal of positions did not set too well. One night the Governor and Colonel Daniel, his bachelor aide, escorted to a rodeo the attractive daughters of California's Governor Earl Warren. The next day Governor Thurmond's new stenographer, who had sat in her room the previous night typing a speech for him, began to tease her boss about his date until it was obvious to Strom that the girl had been unnecessarily piqued. The thought crossed his mind that perhaps she was not as disinterested in him as her actions would indicate; so he sat and chatted with her for a good two hours that night.

After the South Carolina contingent's return home, the

Governor decided it was dangerous for Miss Crouch to walk
the three blocks from the capitol after work each day to
the second-story apartment she shared with two former classmates at 1604 Senate Street. He often arranged his own
schedule so he would be free to offer her a ride to her
door. The afternoon rides from the office had been going
on for some time when Jean said that her "boy friends" were
finding this sort of competition a little stiff. She might possibly lose them. Now, if the Governor really liked her, that
was one thing; if not, there could be no more rides home.
Taken by surprise, he was speechless for a moment. He
was accustomed to doing the talking, and now this girl,
barely of adult age, was turning the tables on him. Veteran
of rugged battles that he was, he still could not summon
the courage to make any kind of declaration at that moment.
Finally he mumbled a few words about their both knowing
soon what they should do, that really they had not been
seeing one another so long after all.

A definite, though informal, understanding between the
two that they would marry had been reached by September 9 when Jean sat down to apply her most persuasive
powers to a letter she wrote her parents pleading for their
approval. The letter read:

... Strom and I started to come down to Elko Sunday
night but couldn't get off in time. We will probably come
this Saturday afternoon or night. Don't make any plans
cause we wouldn't have time to stay very long. We just
want to talk to you all about a serious matter. I suppose
you all know we're really serious now. We've thought and
thought about it. We know what we want. He'll always
be so good and kind to me, so we're going to do what
will make us happy for always. Please don't think for a
minute that I'm swept off my feet 'cause I know what
I'm getting into. He's Governor now, but that will last only
3 years. Marriage will last a lifetime. I know too that
being his wife would mean an awful lot of adjusting on

Mansion—1947—Governor and Mrs. J. Strom Thurmond.

Senator and Mrs. Strom Thurmond ride horses in Aiken, South Carolina, October, 18, 1958.

my part and very hard at times, but I love him enough
to do these things and enjoy doing them. I realize the
difference in our ages and we've talked about it—but both
agree it will make very little difference.

He doesn't know I've written you all this—he just said
let's go down Saturday and talk to my folks. Above all
I want to do the things you all want me to do. I've always tried to do just that. It will mean everything in the
world to me for you all to approve. Please think hard and
realize that I'd always regret not marrying him cause he'll
always love me to death just as I do him. This is what
I want and will make me *completely* happy.

My Mama and Daddy mean more to me than anything
in the world and I want to please them. Everything will
work out, I'm sure, cause you all have always made me
happy and done so much for me . . .

Only the formalities now remained, and one of these
Governor Thurmond took care of in his characteristically or-
derly way. There had been no official proposal as such, so
the Chief Executive tidied up that detail. On Saturday morning, September 13, he instructed Miss Crouch to return to
the office after lunch for extra work. There he dictated a
long, businesslike letter of proposal that began:

You have proved to be a most efficient and capable
secretary, and the high caliber of your work has impressed
me very much. It is with a deep sense of regret that I
will have to inform you that your services will be dis-
continued as of the last day of this month.

There followed four paragraphs dealing with Miss
Crouch's future assignment and with the Governor's statements of devotion. He then added with a further touch of
dry humor:

Anticipating an early reply and hope that it shall be
forthcoming as quickly as possible as upon your answer
will depend my future happiness.

Again assuring you of my deep love and expressing the

hope that the time is not too distant when we can be joined as one and live happily forever.

(George McNabb, the Governor's press secretary, afterwards found the letter and saw in it good publicity possibilities. The document was made available to *Life* magazine, which included it in coverage of the Thurmond marriage.)

The other formality in connection with the Crouch-Thurmond romance was the scheduled conversation with Jean's parents late that Saturday afternoon.

It was a nervous couple that drove up to the Crouch home in the leisurely, sleepy village of Elko, a farm community that would have to scratch to locate as many as 100 citizens. (In Salt Lake City Jean had gazed open-mouthed at the great Mormon Tabernacle choir and blurted out in amazement, "Why, there're more people in that choir than live in Elko.") The village was unaware that a significant conversation was about to take place in the large house off the main highway. Just inside the front entrance of the house was a small informal living room where Jean and Strom met with Jean's mother and father. Hardly had they sat down when the Governor decided to go on a reconnoitering mission of the premises, peering into corners and behind doors, apparently searching out enemies and evil spirits. Satisfied that no one was lurking about, he finally sat, looking at the others as if to say, "Now, here we are, ready to talk."

Inez Crouch said afterward that only twice could she remember seeing Strom Thurmond nervous and not in control of the situation. The first time was that afternoon in Elko, and the second was the day he was married. Had Jean not been so crucially involved, she probably would have been amused; but then nothing was funny that afternoon, so she, too, sat fidgeting and shifting from one position to another.

Strom now proceeded to ask Mr. Crouch in the traditional, old-fashioned manner for permission to marry his daughter.

A short, white-haired, bespectacled figure, Horace Crouch was endowed with a jovial nature, a love of fun and a good memory for stories. He often strayed afield of a discussion if an appealing tale came to mind. Peering through his glasses, he would insert into the conversation an incident that might be particularly relevant or ridiculously irrelevant. This strategy was used on occasion to remove himself from an uncomfortable spot, or again it was employed just for fun. Observing the Governor's uneasiness on this hot September day, Jean's father, with the combined purpose of teasing and maneuvering, gestured toward the barnyard. "You know," he said to his prospective son-in-law, "I believe I'm going to have to get rid of that mule out there!"

On he talked in top form, describing at length the mule's shortcomings. Strom listened until his edgy nerves could hold out no longer. "I didn't come down here to talk about mules," he interrupted. "I came to ask for your daughter's hand."

"Oh well, I guess you'll have to talk to Jean about that," was the nonchalant answer. Mrs. Crouch was next and hoped to heaven she would manage the situation properly. The dark-haired petite mother of four had always been a quiet tower of spiritual faith, selflessness and just pure strength in the family. She was especially close to her youngest child and only a few months earlier had cautioned Jean on the subject of her possible romance to "watch this very carefully now." Inez Crouch was concerned over the age difference. She could not help wondering if her daughter had been swept off her feet by the attentions of an older man who, in addition to other distinguished accomplishments, was the State's eligible bachelor-Governor. Jean had at that time made a bargain with her mother, "Let's see what happens within the next six months, whether it warms or cools."

In the meantime college friends were sure that Jean was sincerely in love with Strom Thurmond. They said later that they had never seen her react to any other man the way she did to him. She had gone through two disappointing

high school and college romances, but otherwise seemed
unable to decide which of a number of suitors she liked best.
In fact, her friends used to accuse her of being fickle. But
they detected a major change in her attitude after Thurmond's arrival on the scene.

Still, here was the mother with the natural anxieties of
any mother in such a situation.

"How do you feel about the marriage?" Strom asked Mrs.
Crouch, turning in her direction.

She suggested that they wait a while and get to know
one another better, but Strom insisted they already knew
each other well enough. After a masterful performance in
evasion by Jean's mother, the Governor said finally, "Well,
as long as you haven't voiced any objections, I'll conclude
that at least you don't object."

Long afterwards Mrs. Crouch told her son-in-law that at
the time of the momentous conversation, she really did not
know much about him, though she had "guessed" he must
be a good man. It was a humbling experience for a governor
to be confronted with people so unimpressed by his position.
They appeared to him to be solely concerned with Jean's
welfare. Yet he admired the fact that they had stood up
to him.

Jean's resignation from the position in the Governor's office was not announced to the public until the end of September when it became effective. Amid open speculation in
the press, she departed for Elko on October 1st to begin
wedding preparations.

Official announcement of the engagement of Jean Crouch
to Strom Thurmond was made in the newspapers on October 13th, and was carefully planned for release on a week-
day so as to not rob other prospective brides of the Sunday
headlines. It confirmed what everybody had known for
weeks. The wedding, it stated, would take place in the Executive Mansion in Columbia at noon on Friday, November 7,
1947. Just the two immediate families would be there, and

following the ceremony, there would be only a wedding breakfast before the couple's departure on a trip.

Jean and Strom had decided to be married at the mansion because it seemed to offer the best solution to the age-old problem of where to draw the line in the guest list. The little church at Elko was not large enough to contain even reasonably close relatives on both sides, much less friends. To the engaged pair, having just the two families at an unpretentious service at the mansion was the answer, and on this basis plans were formulated. Some years later, however, Jean said that if she had it to do over, she would have selected her Elko church despite the handicaps.

Now that the whole thing was official, the newspapers had a field day dispatching reporters and photographers to Elko for feature stories on the bride-elect from every conceivable angle. Jean's youth and general attractiveness made her appealing copy to editors and by the day of the wedding, the public had Jean Crouch all but running out of its ears. They had seen pictures of her doing everything from bicycle-riding to posing with a hymn book in her church across the road. One picture showed her quietly sewing away on her trousseau as if needle and thread were well-loved, daily companions; actually, sewing exasperated her. From another photograph she beamed enthusiastically over a house dress and apron, as she prepared to pour waffle batter into an iron. She looked the embodiment of domesticity. In reality, her knowledge of cooking was minimal. She often said that her mother and sister did the cooking and sewing at home because it was easier than teaching her.

Reporters at the State House had taken a liking to the new girl in the Governor's office during the three months she had been there. They had enjoyed bantering with her and they kidded her relentlessly, pumping for something definite. She would answer with a mysterious smile and a twinkle in her eyes as she propped chin in hand over her typewriter, "You never can tell what a girl might do!" Now that the engagement was official they adopted a brotherly, protective air towards their girl from Elko; if the Governor had shown even the faintest signs of wavering, they were prepared to blast him off his feet. Far from backing out, Thurmond was exuberant over his forthcoming marriage. One thing still puzzled him, however. Why, he asked Jean, had she decided way back in the spring to take the secretarial position in his office after he had said clearly what such employment would mean?"

"Because I figured you'd get busy and forget about me if I were in some other office," she explained sweetly, "but I knew if you saw me every day you couldn't forget me."

"Well, then, why did you ignore me the way you did at the Winthrop commencement?"

"Because!" her tone wanting to know how he could ask such a silly question. Strom decided that a woman's mind was as fathomable to the average man as the depths of uncharted seas.

A few minutes after 11 o'clock on her wedding day, Jean Crouch finished a last whirlwind inspection of the Executive Mansion's large drawing room where the ceremony would take place in another hour, then trotted upstairs to the left front bedroom which had been especially furnished in white for her use. She was ready at 11:45, some ten minutes before the groom.

Wearing a traditional full-length gown of white satin and wedding veil, Jean, accompanied by her father, descended the stairway and entered the drawing room. An improvised altar at the north end was banked with floral arrangements and greenery. Awaiting the bride was her sister, her only attendant, attired in a blue satin gown. Before the altar was the officiating minister, the Reverend George M. Rogers, pastor of the Elko Baptist church, in white tie and tails. At the right stood the beaming bridegroom, and beside him his older brother, John William, the best man. The two groomsmen were another Thurmond brother, Allen George, and Robert Crouch, brother of the bride. Mrs. William Wise, a friend who had sung at the Governor's inauguration, was the soloist. In the background Dean Fred Howard Parker of the Columbia College music department played the wedding music on an electric organ. Twenty-six close relatives and a newspaper reporter witnessed the short service. At 12:11 the ceremony was over, and the Governor of South Carolina had a bride.

The doors were then opened to the full delegation of reporters and photographers who swarmed over the room, outnumbering and overwhelming the guests. While some cameramen stood on chairs, others tripped over each other, trying to place tripods in position; still others were crouching and kneeling and all were pleading with the bridal couple and members of the wedding party to pose over and over again. It was a noisy, hectic hour. The "breakfast," as a result, was not served until shortly after one o'clock.

It was 2:20 when the smiling couple rushed through the front entrance to their automobile for a wedding trip to Miami, Florida, and Havana, Cuba. The two families along the pathway merrily pelted the couple with a send-off of rice.

Overhead, the sky was darkly overcast as Governor and Mrs. Thurmond drove away in a sudden downpour of rain to begin life together. After a two-week wedding trip, Governor and Mrs. Strom Thurmond returned to South Carolina and set about establishing their home at the Executive Mansion. These were the days of settling down to routine living —as routine as the lives of the State's first family could be. The honeymoon was over, and coming to grips with reality meant the daily hurdling of multitudinous crises—hopefully one at a time.

The first major jolt was *Life* magazine's coverage of the wedding. Among the pictures featured in a three-page spread was a full-page shot taken the day before the ceremony showing Governor Thurmond in tennis shorts standing on his head. Jean was in the background, dressed in shorts and sweater, leaning on a bicycle. The picture with a straightforward caption might not have been damaging, but *Life* in its most withering style had held the Governor up to ridicule. The caption read, "VIRILE GOVERNOR demonstrates his prowess in the mansion yard day before wedding. He asked photographer to feel his muscles and observed, 'Why, I can stand on my head,' and promptly proved it. Then the Governor noticed his fiancée's sweater and commented, 'If I could look that good in a sweater, maybe I'd put one on!'"

The political repercussions of that picture and caption haunted Strom Thurmond for years. When every other fact about him escaped people, somehow they always remembered "the picture." Having served less than a year in office, the Governor was still somewhat naive in his dealings with the press. In his gay premarital mood, he had unthinkingly allowed himself to be maneuvered into antics that were detrimental to his public image.

Those who knew the Governor well were aware of his mania for physical fitness and "health foods" and fully understood how Thurmond could trap himself so neatly. As a boy in Edgefield, Strom saw his father walk the mile from home to law office each morning, walk home for lunch, walk back to the office, then walk home again at night. Moreover, the family table featured "good, wholesome, country food." Will Thurmond was an enthusiast on the subject of body fitness and proper eating. He daily stressed these virtues to his family, but none of his offspring responded with the vigor that Strom did. In fact, years later Strom attributed his own interest in physical culture primarily to his father's influence.

During student days at Clemson, Strom joined the track and cross-country teams, and his concern over keeping fit developed into a spartan determination to stay trim. Once, he and four companions from the cross-country team resolved to set a record for the twenty mile distance from Clemson to Anderson. The boys often had run five to ten miles and were convinced that with a little effort they could do the stretch of road between the two towns. Since regular spike-soled track shoes could not be used on the hard road surface, Thurmond had bought a new pair of tennis shoes for the undertaking. After running the first five or six miles, he realized that his new shoes were rubbing his feet badly, but he was not about to give up the race, and decided to suffer the remaining distance. The boys achieved their goal, but in the doing Strom's feet became so terribly bruised that he finally lost all of his toe nails. For days he limped around campus, hardly able to walk, and for weeks he received medical treatment.

"But if I'd stopped when my feet began to hurt, we couldn't have set a record," he explained to less stoic souls.

Strom's running caused something of a sensation in his home town during those college track days. While holding down a mill job in the summer, he made a point of exercising either in the early morning or at night. He would don his track suit and take to the roads on the outskirts of Edgefield. The only hitch was that not everybody knew who he was or what he was doing. An anxious citizen came to the Thurmond home one morning to burble excitedly, "Mr. Will, there's some crazy boy running down one of these roads in his shorts. Do you think we ought to get the sheriff to lock the nut up?"

"Oh," explained an amused Will Thurmond. "I know who that is. That's my boy, Strom, getting his exercise. He's on the track team at Clemson."

When Strom was four years old, his family moved from the downtown house where he had been born to a large, two-story white frame house on the edge of town, so that according to their father's desire for them, he and his older brother, John William, Jr., could "learn to work on a farm."

"I grew up used to hard work," Strom recalls. "I milked

from four to five cows morning and night until I went off to college."

He also learned how to ride every animal on the place —horses, goats, bulls and whatever else was strong enough to hold him. During Strom's service in the State Senate, he and a fellow senator once competed in a mule race with two members of the House of Representatives. Strom won, naturally. He knew how to pick his animal.

(He also got into his share of mischief, but when he did, was quick enough to escape the spankings that the other children received. "By the time I got a switch," his mother remembered, "Strom had found out what was up and had got away. He used to scramble out of the window and climb up on the ridge of the roof where I couldn't get him.")

After becoming Governor—and later United States Senator—Thurmond would urge his staff members to lead more healthful lives. He would suggest that a heavy smoker quit cigarettes, another stop eating rich desserts, and he would instruct a paleface to "get out for some exercise and sunshine—you need it!"

"Yes sir," all would chirp obediently, but their accomplishments did not always measure up to their promises.

It remained a constant frustration to Strom Thurmond that so few fellowmen shared his utopian vision of a world of healthy, hardworking people.

While others pursued their unhealthful ways, Thurmond adhered to his strenuous daily routine of fifty to sixty push-ups, morning and night—a habit from track days—and to what he considered the right foods. In addition he ran or walked to and from work when possible. He rode horses; he rode bicycles; he hunted (when time permitted). He played tennis, and he danced. All of these pastimes were good exercise, and all of them he did well.

"What Thurmond does, he does boldly," said an acquaintance. "When he's right, he looms over the horizon as a tall figure. On the other hand, when he makes a mistake, there's no hiding that either!"

The *Life* picture was a mistake, one the Governor heard about for years. It was a dear lesson learned the hard way but learned well, and it never had to be repeated.

Keenly feeling the backlash of criticism about her husband, Jean immediately became as conscious as he of his political and public image. She assumed in her own way a conscientious guardianship, training her instincts to weigh every move for public reaction. So sensitive did both Jean and Strom become on the matter of image that she remarked laughingly to a friend who mentioned the *Life* picture, "That subject is taboo in our house!"

In a later political campaign, the couple was greeted at an airport by an assemblage of local dignitaries, among them an Air Force general. Photographers kept asking the general to push his hat farther back so as not to shade his face.

"Why, of course, boys. I'll do anything you say," he offered magnanimously. "I'll even stand on my head if you want me to."

"You'd better not if you ever expect to enter politics," warned Thurmond with a grin as the crowd laughed knowingly.

In her new mood of watchfulness, Jean added a second taboo to the list of "don'ts" for the Governor, and this was the crowning of beauty queens—it had to stop.

"The people do not elect a governor to go around crowning beauty queens," she stated firmly.

The general public impression of Governor Thurmond was that of an intensely earnest man who looked upon government as serious business. In fact, his serious manner tended to belie the fact that he really did possess a sense of humor.

Before answering Strom's verbal proposal of marriage, Jean Crouch had examined all her doubts and misgivings. Life in many ways would be more difficult because of her position as First Lady of South Carolina. At twenty-one she would have responsibilities that most women would never face in a lifetime.

In the late summer of 1947 the tomboyish girl from Elko with her winsome blue eyes and friendly smile had enjoyed the daily hubbub of the capitol. Life there was a fascinating new experience to her, but the Governor's talk of marriage had a sobering effect. At night she lay awake mulling over the various facets of such a marriage. She had to resolve for all time whether or not she loved Strom Thurmond enough to make the sacrifices required of a politician's wife. At the end of a wakeful soul-searching by night and cold analysis by the clear light of day, the decision was yes.

It was in a spirit of unswerving, quiet determination that Jean Thurmond undertook her obligations as First Lady of South Carolina. After the pro and con reaction surrounding the Governor's choice of brides, she sensed that the marriage was a politically liability to Thurmond. It was up to her—and she was aware of every ounce of the burden—to change the marriage into an asset.

Thus, with many resolutions and emotions the youngest First Lady of the State since 1789 went through those early days. It was a far more complex, demanding role that the 21-year-old Jean was assuming than was the role—difficult as it was for the times—of the 18-year-old Mary Eleanor Laurens Pinckney, whom Governor Pinckney had married in 1788, seven months prior to taking office.

Hardly had the new Mrs. Thurmond unpacked when a full schedule of official functions caught her up in its whirlwind not to let go until January of 1951 when she became a private citizen for the first time in her adult life.

In mid-November Jean began plans for her first reception at the mansion. It was to be a gigantic affair from 3 to 6 p.m. on Sunday, November 30, when the public was invited to meet the Governor's bride. Meanwhile the bride was in a daily series of huddles with the housekeeper and staff of seven servants, trying to arrange for an unpredictable number of guests. As things turned out, the detailed plans were warranted. Over 5,000 people jammed their way into the house. At one time during the afternoon the line of guests curved out the gate and down the street for five blocks. After one and a half hours Governor and Mrs. Thurmond took a short break so the bride could massage some feeling back into her cramped right hand. It was her first encounter with handshaking on a massive scale. At last, the falling temperature and darkness drew the reception to a close forty minutes after the allotted time. It had been the largest in Columbia's history, and a real baptism by fire for the new First Lady. Wearing her wedding dress and clutching a bouquet in her left hand, Jean had stood in high heels beside Strom for almost four hours. They had smiled at everyone until their facial muscles had practically frozen that way. That one day turned the novice into a battle-tested reception hostess.

Newspaper coverage of the reception had shown pictures of a photogenic, poised First Lady and the public began to relent in its wait-and-see attitude. Invitations arrived by mail and telephone. Would the Governor's young bride help such and such a charity drive; could she spare time to pose for publicity shots for certain worthy local causes; would she be guest speaker at the next meeting of this or that civic group; would she and the Governor be special guests at a banquet of such and such an organization?

It was December and Jean had been First Lady barely a month, but now appeared to be the appropriate time for policy setting. Pressure was mounting to do too many things. There would have to be a declaration as to what she could and could not undertake.

Presenting awards with brief little talks was not overly difficult. Jean had just complied with such a request from the Charleston Symphony Orchestra at a concert in December. Posing for publicity on behalf of various civic and charitable drives created no problem either. Attendance at banquets was mandatory. There was, however, the matter of being guest speaker for innumerable groups. Though experi-

ence as a college class president had enabled Jean to culti-
vate a considerable degree of articulateness and certain ease
on her feet, she could not bear the thought of constant
speech-making.

"Strom can make all the speeches," she decided.

Another subject that came up was the question of
whether or not to serve cocktails at the Executive Mansion.
From the day of his inauguration, Governor Thurmond had
carried out a policy of not serving whiskey. His bride concurred with the previously established rule, and so the policy
continued. With them both, black was black, and white was
white; no grays of compromise existed in their personalities.
In fact, Jean never bent so much as to sip champagne on
special occasions. Making the rounds of official cocktail parties, she always asked for a soft drink. At one Columbia
party a gentleman offered to pour her cola drink into a
cocktail glass, but Jean decided that principle was at stake
and replied, "Oh, no thank you, I'll just stick with my Coke
bottle."

In later Washington years she adhered to a similar policy
despite the constant, elaborate social functions. Once she
and Strom were to entertain at their apartment the South
Carolina delegation to the national newspaper editors convention.

"Jean, what are you going to do about drinks?" another
Senate wife asked her. "These are newspaper people, you
know."

"If they want whiskey, they'll just have to get it before
they come to my apartment. They all know, or they should
know, I don't serve it," was the emphatic answer.

Those two policies laid down by Jean Thurmond that
December proved to be lifelong.

Jean's first post-marriage press interview was with a
woman reporter of *The Columbia Record.* It turned out,
though not intentionally, to be one of Jean's strongest. She
plunged headlong into the subject of education, a topic
always of keen interest to her.

"Parents," she felt, "leave too much of their children's education up to the teachers. A child's education should start in the home so that a better understanding of the subject can be attained."

Then she moved on to the question of federal aid to education. "I think aid should be given the rural school to help the youth of today to take better advantage of educational opportunities. It could help a lot in those situations, and I don't think it would necessarily socialize or federalize the education system."

Quoting a favorite expression on the subject, she added, "I say, 'Tax the wealth where it is and educate the children where they are.'"

Under the subsequent tutelage of her husband, Jean more and more saw the "error" of her viewpoint. Having come out of college with the theoretical ideals of a new graduate, she soon revamped her thinking as she became increasingly convinced that federal aid had to mean federal control.

It was at this time that the Governor, who at one point favored federal aid to education, too, was undergoing a fundamental re-evaluation of the merits of such a plan, and he was taking his young wife with him to a reversal of positions. By 1950 he would have his new stand on the matter firmed up to the extent that he would tell—prophetically so—the annual meeting of the South Carolina Education Association on March 31st of that year:

... Several years ago I publicly advocated federal aid for public education, provided that such aid be without federal control and the state public school system remain entirely under local control where it belongs.

With the growing centralization of power in the federal government, and the flagrant violation and disregard of the rights of states and local authorities by the present national administration, I have been forced to the firm conviction that we cannot accept federal aid for our public schools without ultimately losing control of them to the federal government.

I have also been forced to the conclusion that even if we should escape nationalization of our public school system in accepting federal aid, restrictions will soon be imposed which will prevent the states with the greatest educational need from receiving federal funds.

In spite of this initial venture into a politically sensitive issue followed by quiet retreat, Jean found dealing with the press interesting and actually fun. She became adept at circumventing touchy questions. On their part, reporters found her youth good for a story regardless of angle, circumstance or time of year.

Another facet to the role of Governor's wife was the less glamourous, yet essential, smooth daily operation of the mansion household. Running the establishment—despite and because of a large staff of servants—was like running an ordinary home magnified five times. Although Jean Thurmond was a greenhorn in the ways of home management, she dived in with enough zeal to compensate for many lacks. Taking over from the Governor's sister, Gertrude, who continued to live at the mansion in an unofficial capacity, Jean executed domestic responsibilities for the first few months both with and without a housekeeper. In March of 1948 Mrs. Ruby Sawyer, a widow from Ridge Spring, South Carolina, was persuaded by the Governor to accept the position of housekeeper and assistant hostess. She had told him first all her good reasons for not coming.

"I don't know anything about handling a governor's mansion. I haven't had any training for this kind of work, and I just plain don't want to come. I'm scared of the mansion."

"I'll expect you to report on March 1st," Governor Thurmond informed her. Having decided that Mrs. Sawyer, whom he had known for years, was the one for the job, he typically refused to accept no for an answer. "Miss Ruby,"

as she was called, moved into the Executive Mansion on
the appointed date. She stayed there for the remaining three
years of Thurmond's term and emerged as a staunch ad-
mirer of the State's first family.

The youthful Mrs. Thurmond and the older Miss Ruby
had, during that spring of 1948, a common bond of inexperi-
ence to start them off on a footing of congeniality.

"Neither one of us knew very much," said Mrs. Sawyer,
so the two pooled their meager knowledge and went from
there on sheer organizational ability and grit. They consulted with each other on arrangements for all functions at
the Governor's home. Most importantly they thought alike,
establishing a mutually supportive relationship. They soon
learned to take hectic schedules in stride.

At first Jean complied with formality even to the extent
of finger bowls at the more elaborate dinners. She went to
great pains to have the staff place camellia petals in the
bowls lest an unthinking guest get the wrong idea. Still,
the plan never worked with complete success and the First
Lady agonized for those erring souls who had obviously
never seen a finger bowl before.

The First Lady's innate love for simple, informal entertaining showed through the traditional stiffness of the mansion. She mastered the elusive art of achieving dignity while
maintaining a relaxed atmosphere.

At one formal dinner, however, things were informalized
a bit more than anticipated. Jean spied from her end of
the table a huge roach appearing from the old pantry and
making its lumbersome way across the dining room carpet.
With dismay she saw it creep ever closer toward the ele-
gantly attired guests at the long table. She debated whether
to ignore the insect a while longer or to sound a general
alarm. The former course of action prevailed as she quickly
stepped up the conversation. Suddenly the Governor spotted
the offending pest approaching his end of the table. In his
usual wide-open manner, Strom made no pretense of letting

the bug pass unchallenged. He leaped up and went into battle, pursuing the insect furiously around the room while every guest ceased eating to watch in restrained mirth. The whole affair now obviously beyond ignoring, Jean joined the general laughter. A victorious Governor glowing with satisfaction at last returned to his chair. Several days afterwards a shipment of insect spray arrived with the compliments of a dinner guest.

Receptions, too, could have their bad moments, Jean learned. The unpredictable element could never be removed even with the most careful planning.

The mansion had a policy of allowing civic, charitable and other well-known organizations to hold special receptions there. Depending on the nature of the event, Mrs. Thurmond and Mrs. Sawyer would decide whether expenses should be paid by the group or by the State, though in all cases, they and often the Governor were present at the function. In cases where the groups were furnishing refreshments, there was the constant worry over whether or not ample supplies had been provided. Once, the president of a woman's organization planning a mansion reception had been so limited by her members in funds that she had a total of $15 for refreshments. Thoroughly miffed, the president thought it would serve everybody right to let the food give out. The First Lady and her staff were horrified. Unfed guests would never realize that their own group was at fault instead of the Thurmonds. Regular household supplies were placed on a stand-by basis. When the panicky black face of Philip, the butler, peered around the kitchen door, motioning for help, Miss Ruby hastily departed to expand the "mansion punch" customarily used for receptions. Fortunately, "mansion punch" consisted of fruit, fruit juice and ginger ale, and the basic recipe for one hundred servings could easily be doubled or tripled. Emergency juice and cookies always had to be kept near at hand for receptions.

Daily life at the Executive Mansion was less grueling

than were the more lavish social functions, and every once
in a while there was time for relaxation.

The average day began at 7:30 or 8 a.m. The most wholesome, nutritious breakfasts known to man would be brought
to the Governor and First Lady in their room upstairs on
the southwestern corner of the house. There was an odd
thing about breakfast. If it did not consist of the most healthful cereals available, it went to the other extreme—a piping-
hot, fattening country breakfast of hominy, sausage or ham,
eggs, muffins and butter.

Mid-morning activities for the First Lady varied from
day to day, depending on the schedule of events. If there
were nothing on tap at home and no engagement elsewhere,
Jean usually checked plans for upcoming events with the
staff. She would putter around the greenhouse where she
kept an eye on special projects or she would wander about
the grounds. She nursed along several varieties of roses to
use as corsages for guests. Behind the scenes, the country-
bred girl went in for old-fashioned "dirt-farming," planting
in secluded areas beds of artichokes and other vegetables.
These home-grown vegetables which looked so simple in
their neat little rows were anything but simple from the
financing standpoint, however. All money spent on personal
things, the vegetable garden among them, came from the
Governor's personal bank account. Consequently, the office
staff nearly stood on its collective head at times trying to
figure out how to pay for a sack of fertilizer used on both
the State-owned flowers and the Thurmond-owned vegetables. To avoid any question, the entire cost more often than
not was paid from the Governor's own account. The fact
that the vegetables as well as the flowers found their way
to the table at official dinners did not alter the picture in
the eyes of the Thurmonds.

"You must always appear right as well as be right," the
Governor quoted his father to the staff time after time.

"There's no such thing as rounding corners where Strom

Thurmond is concerned," a long-time aide once said. "Corners are squared to the last inch."

On many free mornings Mrs. Thurmond would indulge in shopping sprees. The only damper was her dislike of wearing hat and gloves on such casual business in downtown Columbia. "People will think I'm putting on now just because I'm First Lady," she declared.

"You'd be criticized a lot more by the public for not wearing a hat and gloves down the street than you'd be for wearing them," cautioned her older sister Frances, who was still living and teaching school in Columbia. "The Governor's wife is expected to set a high standard of correct dress. Humility is fine if it is understood as that and not ignorance. In your position you can't risk people's placing the wrong interpretation on what you do."

Mrs. Thurmond, therefore, dressed to the last matching accessory for downtown store-hopping.

The thrifty First Lady adored bargains. It was almost a game. If she wanted a dress priced at more than she felt wise to spend just then, she would ask the clerk to call if and when it went on sale. A substantial part of her wardrobe was procured through sales. She dressed conservatively, preferring simple lines and solid tones. (As a matter of fact, she turned Strom into an increasingly conservative dresser. One of her main accomplishments was talking him out of always wearing a red tie. She convinced him that it was not necessary to wear a touch of red to symbolize a fighting spirit.) She bought quality rather than quantity and actually possessed a rather modest number of outfits, considering her prominent position.

After a morning downtown, the First Lady would return usually for a one o'clock lunch. Frequently the Governor would have called in the meantime to announce guests for luncheon. Guests could mean from one to six, so the staff automatically would go on "S.O.P." (standard operating procedure) and haul out the old stand-by, asparagus—fresh in season or otherwise canned—but asparagus, regardless. It was served without garnish—more healthful plain! A regular visitor at meal time might have been led to wonder if a whole region of South Carolina was paying its taxes in asparagus. Creamed tuna, salmon balls and apricot salad were other emergency items Jean liked to have for small crowds. It was the general practice at the mansion, though, to have beef, pork roast or chicken as the regular meat, providing a more easily expandable meal. For large meals turkey was a favorite. The State kept well supplied a tremendous freezer with three compartments—one for beef, another for pork and chicken and the third for storing ice cream and blocks of ice.

On free mornings or afternoons, Mrs. Thurmond often enjoyed a drive to Elko for a visit and would return by dinner time. She was like a horse turned homeward. The closer to the little village she drew, the heavier her foot rested on the gas pedal. Companions would hang on for their lives, faith in her driving ability rendering small comfort at high speed. Elko was a haven where there was no worry about dignity or decorum. She could be a girl again for a short while. On entering the door of the Crouch home, she would kick off both shoes. (Jean had developed a real knack for slinging a shoe across the room with one good flip of her ankle.) She then would patter around barefooted all afternoon so carefree she hardly recognized herself.

Despite her youth and an innate love for meeting people, Jean Thurmond found the pace of First Lady more than her health could stand at times. When the "banquet circuit," as it was called, became especially crowded, the Governor and his wife shuttled from one locality to another with hardly a break. Jean would become noticeably run-down but would rather collapse than admit fatigue. Strom, on the other hand, could go indefinitely, and friends often remarked that it was well after all that he had married a young girl because a woman his own age could never keep up with him.

II

A Rebel Comes to Life

In February of 1948—while life at South Carolina's Executive Mansion went on, unsuspectingly preoccupied with its day-to-day activities—the President of the United States, Harry S. Truman, sent a civil rights bill to Congress. The bill was the strongest ever and dismayed southern Congressmen and governors. Not only did it make a frontal attack on the institution of segregation, but it also proposed in concrete terms the establishment of a fair employment practices commission to prohibit racial discrimination in employment. Such comprehensive legislation was more than the South could digest in 1948, and it rose up in anger.

Immediately Governor Thurmond consulted with other southern governors. With the approval of the chief executives of North Carolina, Texas, Arkansas, and Maryland, he fired off a heated message to the National Democratic Party in that election year, informing officials that the South was no longer "in the bag" for the Democrats; so the party had

better beware of pushing civil rights for the purpose of ob-
taining northern Negro bloc votes.

Southern discontent smouldered all spring, finally erupt-
ing into the first small sparks of revolt with a meeting on
May 10th in Jackson, Mississippi, of states' rights supporters
among the various southern politicians. Three governors were
there—Fielding Wright of Mississippi, Ben Laney of Arkansas, and Thurmond of South Carolina. The main result of
the gathering was the agreement to meet again after the
National Democratic Convention. The second meeting would
be to plot a course of action should President Truman be
nominated on a platform hostile to the South.

Then, on May 19th, the South Carolina Democratic convention fell in behind Governor Thurmond as a favorite son
candidate for the presidential nomination. In any event, the
twenty delegates to the Philadelphia convention were to
withhold their votes from Harry Truman. The furious South
Carolinians further decided to withhold the State's eight electoral votes from Truman in the general election should he
be the Democratic nominee.

The Thurmonds arrived in Philadelphia on Saturday,
July 10th, for what was Jean's first national political convention. Prior to the opening session on Monday, July 12th,
the southern delegations caucused to fume over Truman,
but they failed to get one of their own number to serve
as an alternative candidate around whom they could rally.

As feared, the convention adopted what southerners regarded as a radical civil rights plank which, in effect, en-
dorsed President Truman's position. This particular plank
had originally been drafted by a minority group of the platform committee and was presented to the full convention
as a minority report. Under the aggressive leadership of
Hubert Humphrey, then mayor of Minneapolis, it was accepted by the gathering in a bitter, tumultuous floor fight.
The entire Mississippi delegation stalked out of the hall,
followed by about half of the Alabama delegation. Their

departure was accompanied by jeers and boos from northern delegates. The atmosphere in the building became taut as remaining southern delegations seethed in rage. Before the convention ended, southern spokesmen rose to defend their stand against the civil rights plank. Among them was Governor Thurmond, who spoke at the final session. Actually, in the light of platforms adopted by subsequent conventions, this one was almost mild, but for that time it was a real jolt to conservatives. As expected, Harry S. Truman emerged as the Democratic presidential nominee.

Plans for the tentatively arranged Birmingham meeting were pushed up and the gathering rescheduled for Saturday, July 17th. The Mississippians went directly there from Philadelphia and with each hour the meeting assumed increasingly the proportions of another convention. The Thurmonds returned to Columbia on Friday. Somewhat cool to the idea of the Birmingham meeting anyway since he thought there was too little time to organize properly for constructive accomplishments, Governor Thurmond had no plans to attend. Moreover, he was committed to be at Camp Stewart, Georgia, at 10 a.m. the next day for inspection of the 228th AAA Group, a South Carolina National Guard unit in training there.

"Governor Wright, Governor Laney, and other southern leaders contacted me upon my return to Columbia on that Friday," Strom Thurmond recalled. "They said it was important for me to be at the Birmingham meeting on Saturday and urged me to attend. I informed them of my engagement at Camp Stewart but promised to go on to Birmingham from there if this would not be too late for the meeting. A change in time from Camp Stewart to Birmingham was helpful, and I went on to Alabama after completing my engagement at Camp Stewart."

Jean was not inclined just then toward another trip, especially for a one-day meeting, so she happily remained in Columbia. The First Lady planned to drive up-state on Saturday to meet the Governor at the Anderson airport in time for him to fill a speaking engagement that night in the area.

It was afternoon when Thurmond entered the Birmingham meeting. Hardly had the Governor got his bearings when he was approached about accepting the States' Rights Democrats Convention's nomination for President of the United States. Governor Laney of Arkansas had just refused the honor. Delegates from Louisiana, Mississippi, and Alabama were the primary supporters of Thurmond's candidacy, and they gave him from thirty minutes to an hour to decide whether or not to take it.

Looking back on those fleeting minutes so heavy with uncertainties, his whole career at stake in what would be brazen defiance of the National Democratic Party, Strom Thurmond reminisced, "I knew that accepting the nomination would have future political repercussions, but I had little time to make up my mind, and I thought somebody ought to do something, so I finally decided to take the plunge. I didn't know then even if my own State would support me."

Governor Wright of Mississippi agreed to accept the vice-presidential nomination. In the bare twinkling of an eye, the Thurmond-Wright ticket was whipped through the convention which was eager to nominate a suitable slate. At 5:30 that afternoon, the two men were escorted to the podium to make their acceptance speeches. They strode down the aisle through the bedlam of over 7,000 yelling, waving, stamping States' Rights Democrats representing in small and large numbers the sixteen states of Texas, California, Louisiana, Mississippi, Alabama, North Carolina, South Carolina, Maryland, Arkansas, Tennessee, Florida, Oklahoma, Indiana, Georgia, Virginia and Kentucky. In the background a band blared forth "Dixie" which never fails to stir a southern audience to emotional heights.

The crowd had gathered originally for the purpose of planning a way to defeat President Truman. They were ending with the notion that they could do more; they even could elect a man of their own. As far as the States' Righters were concerned, the Democrats' Truman and the Republicans' Thomas Dewey were of one ilk, and they wanted nothing to do with either. They wanted to take from Truman enough electoral votes to throw the election into the House of Representatives. There the South, they reasoned, might elect its candidate or certainly would be in a good bargaining position. It was on these hopes that the campaign was based.

In their addresses, both Thurmond and Wright castigated Truman, the Democratic Party and the Democratic platform. Birmingham's crowded auditorium roared approval. The two southern governors planted themselves firmly atop an eight point anti-Truman, pro-state's rights platform drafted and adopted by their supporters that day. It disagreed strongly with the implementation of civil rights as contained in the National Democratic platform.

By now the States' Rights Democrats had gone beyond the point of no return. For better or for worse, they had taken a risky plunge with Thurmond and Wright. On the other hand, the two governors were taking an even riskier plunge with the States' Rights cause. For all anyone knew on that hot, steamy afternoon, these two men were taking their first steps toward political suicide. For Strom Thurmond, this date marked the first of many political rebellions that ultimately would characterize his career.

Conservative southern Democrats in times past had shown a measure of disenchantment with the New Dealish direction of the Party under President Franklin D. Roosevelt. In 1940, for instance, a small South Carolina group numbering less than 2,500 and calling themselves "Jefferson Democrats" had defected to cast their votes for Wendell Wilkie. Again in 1944, the same people, now tripled in number and bearing the name "Southern Democrats," refused to endorse FDR's quest for a third term and instead cast

their ballots for Senator Harry Byrd of Virginia. Other Democrats throughout the South had sought to thwart Roosevelt
by withholding votes from him, but these efforts were all
notably unsuccessful. The 1948 Birmingham meeting seemed
to be the first serious, meaningful effort standing any sort
of chance of frustrating the National Democratic Party. Even
this effort was taken lightly in most quarters.

Jean Thurmond left Columbia by car on the afternoon
of July 17th blissfully unaware that anything of significance
to her was happening in Alabama. She had already left
when a telephone call from Birmingham came through to
the mansion. Not until she arrived at the Anderson home
of Mr. and Mrs. Fred Pearman did she get the first excited
spurts of information about her husband's nomination for
President of the United States. She was dumbfounded. What
was all this? How did it happen?

"What has Strom gotten himself into?" she wondered.

Having missed his wife in Columbia, the Governor had
called to Anderson to cancel the speaking engagement. He
added a message to Jean that, by the way, he had been
nominated for President and circumstances in Birmingham
necessitated leaving there much later than planned. Would
she arrange to meet him at the Anderson airport later in
the night? As the plane taxied to a stop sometime afterwards,
an outwardly bubbling Jean and friends fell upon the new
presidential nominee. They all were talking at once and be-
sieging him with questions.

When the Thurmonds were alone for the first time, Jean's
excitement turned to anxiety. "What about the political repercussions? You're really sticking your neck out!"

The whole matter of the nomination had been handled
in a way contrary to her cautious nature. Had she been
involved in the decision, Jean would have sat down in a
quiet corner somewhere to explore all aspects of the nomination. There would have been meticulous analyses of foreseeable pitfalls, of likely public reactions, of all possible re-

percussions. Only after weighing in the balance all the pros and cons would she have arrived at a decision. Jean did not like to step into any situation without her eyes open and her heart willing to accept the consequences. Although pleased at the honor accorded Strom, she was far from happy over this particular situation. There were too many risks. Never would she have consented to only thirty or sixty minutes in which to think through the momentous question of running for the presidency. On the other hand, Strom tended to give matters what he considered a reasonable amount of thought and to make up his mind fairly rapidly—a result of military training, he always said. Once having made a decision, he was inclined to take a bold stand—right or wrong—and to fight to the end. His style often was at variance with Jean's instinctive desire to use the soft, diplomatic method, the way least likely to arouse antagonisms.

"You know, of course, what this means as far as you and the National Democratic Party are concerned," she told him. They both knew the answers to her questions. He had thought about these things, he replied, and he was willing to take the risk.

Only four days before in Philadelphia, Jean had celebrated her twenty-second birthday. She was still the youngest governor's wife in the country, and she had not yet been First Lady of South Carolina a year—nine months to be exact. Now suddenly, tonight, Jean Thurmond was the wife of a candidate for President of the United States.

"This will be the first political campaign of my life," she muttered, half to herself, half to Strom. "Who in the world would ever have imagined that my first campaign as a politician's wife would be for the presidency?"

Nevertheless, the die was cast and there could be no turning back.

"I'm sure everything will turn out all right in the end," she declared, using her favorite expression in times of crisis. "I'm not going to think about it any more right now."

The next day Governor and Mrs. Thurmond returned to the mansion and to a schedule more hectic than ever. Plans were being mapped to take them both campaigning through as many southern and border states as possible.

In the meantime, reactions began drifting into the Governor's office. State Democratic leadership in most of the sixteen states represented at Birmingham seemed to be giving second thought to the States' Rights movement and was showing obvious reluctance to bolt the safe folds of the regular Democratic Party. Too many office holders were beginning to show unwillingness to risk their careers.

It was against this developing background that Thurmond and other States' Rights leaders met for a strategy conference in Atlanta the following week. In an effort to secure the thirty-three electoral votes of Texas, planners decided to hold a rally in Houston's Coliseum on the night of August 11th. At that time Thurmond and Wright would make formal acceptances of the presidential and vice-presidential nominations. The Houston affair also would be the kick-off of the campaign speeches being arranged for key areas all over Dixie.

To some observers familiar with Thurmond's record in South Carolina, it looked as though he were being shoved into a paradoxical position. By southern standards, he was somewhat of a liberal; yet here he was, leading the conservative States' Rights movement. With no thought of integration, Governor Thurmond already had pressed for Negro advancement. One of his accomplishments was to be the establishment of industrial training schools for Negro girls. In addition, he was working for area trade schools for both races, for better public schools, for higher salaries for both white and colored teachers.

As Governor, he was raising education to the highest level in the State's history. He had begun his career in the field of education, and even during his days in the South Carolina General Assembly had taken special interest in pushing a variety of measures to advance education. He had authored the State's compulsory school attendance law (which was repealed in the 1950's), the nine months' school term, and the State's textbook law. In later years he established several educational and scholarship funds, to which he continued to contribute. Throughout his public career he also made numerous personal loans and gifts to young people for educational purposes. In line with his belief in doing as much as possible on the individual and local levels, Strom Thurmond often said, "I believe in changes that come from within the State, not from without by Federal or other outside dictation." For two years Thurmond had advocated repeal of South Carolina's dollar per year general election poll tax, although he opposed a federal anti-poll tax law. He had also urged a secret ballot law for South Carolina, the only state in the union then not having one. In addition, he had sought a new, streamlined constitution to replace the State's obsolete, amendment-laden document. Politicians had refused for years to bring it up for revision since at least some redistribution of power would be inevitable, but he had persuaded the 1948 legislature to pass a measure enabling a degree of state-government reorganization to eliminate waste and duplication. Somehow this record appeared inconsistent with Thurmond's current espousal of States' Rights philosophy. The Governor himself, though, saw no political contradiction.

"I believe in liberal, progressive government on the proper level," he would say over and over. "Those functions which should properly be handled on state and local levels I believe in having done on those levels. Only those functions specifically delegated in the Constitution to the Federal Government should be handled at the federal level."

He thought, actually, that his views tied in with States' Rights beliefs rather than being contrary to them. He never felt that he had been forced into a more conservative position because of his presidential candidacy.

Regardless of his own feeling about himself, the 1948 presidential race did mark an historic transition in Strom Thurmond's career and in his image. In the public eye, he changed overnight from a liberal to a conservative. As Governor he had advocated many progressive programs and, therefore, was described as a liberal. He voiced the same views—that is, progress on the proper level of government —as a figure on the national scene and promptly was labeled a conservative. What was liberal on the state level was not necessarily liberal on the federal level. Thurmond's elevation to national prominence automatically placed him in a new light. In later years he still would adhere to his original concepts of government, but as the times became steadily more liberal, he was more and more pictured as an ultra conservative.

As a matter of fact, Thurmond's views remained so unchanged that an address he made in April 1961 to the student body of the Massachusetts Institute of Technology on the purpose of government could well have been made in the autumn of 1948. He said, in part:

Government, as any other human institution, has various potentials, some for good, some for evil; similarly, government is by its very nature limited in its usefulness. The tests of a government lie in its capacity to be utilized to its maximum potential for good, its degree of incumbrance with safeguards against its potential for evil, and its confinement to those purposes for which it has the capacity for fulfillment. Since our government is designed to be operated by the people subject to its jurisdiction, its success is dependent on the ability of the public to distinguish between its potentials for good and for evil, and to appreciate the limits on the purposes to the accomplishment of which the instrument of government may be efficiently, safely, and adequately directed.

... The purpose originally conceived for our government was the creation of an instrument of society to provide the necessary protection from external sources and the essential order among internal forces to permit individual liberty to flourish and be exercised.

... The United States Government was clearly conceived as an umpire, not a participant, in the activities of society; it was conceived as an instrumentality to insure fair play and the absence of fraud, not as one to guarantee the economic or social success of individual or cooperative endeavor, nor as one to mitigate the burden created by the failure of such endeavor. This intention is apparent from the combination of the plenary nature of the powers actually delegated and the careful circumscription of the number of areas of fields of activity in which *any* power to act was granted.

... In recent years, we have increasingly confused the incidental benefits produced by the relatively unfettered efforts of free individuals possibly because our government was devoted to preservation of individual liberty, with the purpose and responsibility of the government itself. America under the Constitution has been blessed with unequaled material abundance. No nation has ever enjoyed a higher material standard of living. Not only have we had more goods, but a greater proportion of the people have enjoyed the products of their labor than in any historic or contemporary system. In other words, we have enjoyed both high production and broad distribution. This benefit is a product of individual liberty, however, and not a product attributable directly to government effort. Economic abundance, in and of itself, is not a prescribed goal of our governmental system.

Unquestionably, a government can undertake and accomplish the production of goods by direct participation in the activities conceived in our society to be functions of the individuals; but for government to do so imperils, and in most instances, dooms individual liberty ...

... The only equality which is consistent with individual liberty and a government devoted to it is that equality which by its very nature produces inequality—equal justice before the law. To dispense it requires an objective and non-participating umpire who enforces a previously codified set of rules impartially. Even this measure of equality—that of justice before the law—can be obtained only from a government which acts solely as objective judge and never as a participant. When this element of equality pertains, it means that the individual attainment is left to individual talent, imagination and initiative. Since these qualities vary within the broadest of ranges, inequality is assured.

... When the purpose of government is distorted and multiplied far beyond its potentialities, it becomes incapable of accomplishment of either protection or order.

Our system of government as designed is superior to any one yet conceived, including communism and socialism. We cannot convince the peoples of the world of its superiority, however, on the basis of its ability to excel in material abundance, nor on the basis of its ability to achieve equality, nor because it has a humanitarian character, nor yet as a dispenser of charity; for it is not, and is not designed for, any of these things. The heart of any deception is contradiction, and the contradiction of such a position is apparent.

The people of the world will accept the superiority of a system which provides the protection and order under which individual liberty may flourish, provided they are given an example which proves its operability. We cannot, however, sell something which we don't have. We must first return our own system to consistency with its original design by acknowledging its true purpose and re-accepting individually those responsibilities which are rightfully ours and which we have previously attempted to shift to government.

You must decide what is the proper purpose of your government. The separation of the wheat from the chaff is your job. The present indecision and ineptness of your government is but a reflection of the indecision of the public which, fortunately, still plots the government's course. Without a clear and unequivocal decision by you, our failure to meet the test of contemporary times is assured, for in the words of Disraeli, "The secret of success is constancy of purpose."

Meanwhile, in the election year of 1948, Strom Thurmond had yet to gain a reputation as a "constitutionalist" and consistent conservative.

While the men planned the campaign, Jean Thurmond helped with secretarial chores and made her own preparations for traveling since she would be accompanying her husband on his speaking tours. Now that he was running, she was ready to enter wholeheartedly into the effort as the candidate's wife. Jean knew that everywhere she and the Governor went, people would be scrutinizing her as much as him. They would be watching closely to see how this girl —only a year out of college—weathered the campaign trail.

Though the Governor had made an earlier speech in Cherryville, North Carolina, the Houston rally was the first major engagement on the agenda. As soon as Governor and Mrs. Thurmond arrived, the wife of the nominee was hustled over to a private nook for an interview that appeared on the front page of the August 11th edition of *The Houston Press*. An accompanying photograph showed her smiling over a bouquet of roses. Mrs. Thurmond's youth and the story-book romance were the focal points of the story. It followed in general the tone of a story in a Philadelphia newspaper upon her arrival for the National Democratic Convention back in July. These two encounters with the out-of-state press were the first in a number to be crowded into that summer and autumn. All in all, the wife of the States' Rights

Democrats presidential candidate would get almost equal billing with her husband on their joint trips. Mrs. Thurmond's appeal to the press seemed to be with her at every campaign stop.

The rally in Houston was for all practical purposes a repetition of Birmingham; only this one was about 3,000 people larger and that much noisier. The same sixteen states along with some others were represented, and the two candidates, Thurmond and Wright, reiterated in about the same terms their stands taken at the Alabama meeting. There were the same flag-waving, chanting demonstrations with "Dixie" resounding throughout the Coliseum. To Jean Thurmond, it was as if the whole Birmingham convention were being restaged just so she could be part of it. She had to admit there was a certain fascination about political conventions that seemed to draw one irresistibly into the spirit of the occasion. She could sense her quickened heartbeat as the evening was brought to a deafening climax of applause for the cause and the candidates.

On August 24th, the campaign went into high gear as Presidential Nominee J. Strom Thurmond and Mrs. Thurmond left Columbia by airplane for a two-day speaking foray into Tennessee and Arkansas. For young Mrs. Thurmond, it was the first political campaigning of her life, and with mixed feelings of anticipation, apprehension and determination, she boarded the aircraft for Memphis where she got an abrupt introduction into the rugged ways of campaigning on the road. Two days later she wrote her family this hurried account of the trip:

August 25—Newsmen wake us up 2:00 a.m. (to make arrangements for a later appointment). Breakfast—again with photographers! Officials from Marianna (Arkansas) came to hotel to drive us 60 miles to Marianna. The plane trip was perfectly safe compared to that 85 mile per hr. trip between two patrol cars to Marianna. Did not stop in town but were driven on out 7 miles on winding *dusty* road to the Bedco Creek Lake Hotel—on famous Crowley's Ridge. Newly completed building. Shake hands with each of the many persons waiting on the porch of hotel for us. On up to room. No coat hangers, no telephone, and nowhere to get things pressed. I pressed my own—sent Strom's to town. Strom was whisked away to press conference and to lunch with men. Mrs. John Daggett (wife of Marianna attorney who was member of States' Rights executive committee) came for me later for ladies luncheon at the Hotel Pavilion (sic). I had on my same dusty dress. At lunch photographers tried diligently, but in vain, to get Mrs. Daggett, Mrs. Gordon (wife of Arkansas's lieutenant-governor) and me to pose heads together with chicken legs in our mouths. Instead got picture of ladies peering into my purse. Later headed photo—"Unnecessary —but ladies pretty up." We ladies sat in on men's discussion after lunch. Men had another meeting, so I slept all p.m. . . .

Thus was Jean Thurmond initiated into the world of politics.

Newspaper interviews had already become second nature to the wife of the States' Rights nominee. The story pattern was largely the same: Mrs. Thurmond's youth; what she had planned to do as a career until her unusual marriage changed things; life at South Carolina's Executive Mansion; the fact that she had missed the Birmingham meeting where her husband had been nominated for President, the usual quote being, "We didn't expect anything to happen, but hereafter I'm going to keep up with him"; her talent for the piano, violin and saxophone; her love for swimming, tennis, bicycle riding; and lastly, her new knowledge of cooking on which she made a point of commenting—as if to compensate for all the years when she and the kitchen were strangers.

In the Dallas interview later printed in other newspapers, Jean branched out a bit. Her youthful seriousness impressed the reporter. She said for the record, "It's very possible that neither President Truman nor Governor Dewey will get a majority of the electoral votes. That would throw the election of the President into the House of Representatives. If so, I think my husband has a good chance."

Did Mrs. Thurmond ever give her husband advice?

"I always try to give helpful criticism," was the reply. "My husband welcomes suggestions."

She did often look over the Governor's notes and made recommendations as to what might be said more effectively— or not at all. She was one of his most trusted critics. One thing South Carolina newsmen would note amusedly in years to come was her influence on the length of Strom Thurmond's speeches. She would be seen time and again quietly tugging at his coattail when she thought he was talking too long. Customarily seated beside him, she could signal without a flicker of change in her smile. The message usually got through and he would hastily conclude his remarks.

In late October, Governor and Mrs. Thurmond made an appearance in Shreveport, Louisiana. Once again reporters drew the candidate's wife aside for an interview. This time she shed some light on her role as adviser.

"Yes," she answered. "I'm with my husband on all his speaking tours. Yes, I was his secretary. No, I don't make any speeches, but I still help him with his notes. I've got some to go over today," pointing to papers under one arm. "I let my husband do the speaking, but I help him in any way possible."

The homestretch of the campaign got underway with another swing into Tennessee and Arkansas on Friday, October 22nd, as the Governor and his wife arrived in Nashville. By now Mrs. Thurmond was also in the homestretch of her physical endurance. She was keeping up with her husband's torrid pace—but at a price. Dark circles of fatigue

were showing visibly beneath her eyes, and as the going
became overly strenuous, she was losing her appetite and
living on campaign excitement.

As a usual thing, there were four to five speeches every
day. The daytime ones varied in length from thirty to forty
minutes and were mainly "off the cuff"—or unwritten—
whereas the evening ones were major written expositions of
the States' Rights view and were from fifty to sixty minutes
long. As presidential nominee, Thurmond followed the platform set down for him by the Birmingham meeting. In brief
it was a stand against President Truman's civil rights proposals for federal action. It was the States' Rights Democrats
position, as opposed to that of the National Democratic Party,
that these were matters for the individual states to handle.
When he was not blasting away at the National Democratic
platform, Candidate Thurmond was tearing more particularly into both President Truman and Governor Dewey, who
held similar views, and into the Progressive Party's Henry
Wallace, whose view he regarded as even more liberal.

With the campaign nearing its frenzied end, Jean Thurmond was close to exhaustion. Even her youth could not
compensate entirely for what practice might have taught
her about conserving her strength. As soon as the couple
left one place, she would anticipate the next stop, girding
up to take the customary round of handshaking, the smiles
of acknowledgment, and the usual round with news reporters and photographers with poise, freshness and enthusiasm.
At night there would be an average of only five hours sleep.
The Governor could stretch across the back seat of an automobile or lean back in an airplane and go fast asleep, but
his wife would sit there, eyes wide open, her mind rapidly
ticking off things she needed to know for the next appearance. He would wake up refreshed and ready for a hearty
meal. She reached a point where vivacity was forced and
food was totally unappealing. What her husband did not
shove down her, she did not eat.

Upon landing in Nashville, Jean was obviously run down

and had a bad throat condition. The Governor decided it was time to put his foot down. Either his wife attended to her throat immediately and began eating properly, or back to Columbia she must go.

Maybe he had a point, Jean grudgingly admitted. Certainly Strom was enduring the grind remarkably well, and, after all, the major burden was on him. It would appear that his stress on proper nutrition was paying dividends. Anyway, like the idea or not, she must improve both her eating and her throat or she would be homeward bound. After going through most of the campaign, she just could not fold up in the last week.

"It's strenuous, but I don't want to miss anything," she declared. "Besides, these last few days will probably be the most exciting of all." She obediently secured medical attention for the throat and gave earnest thought to food, though it was the last thing in the world she wanted.

The Thurmonds spent October 25th and 26th in Arkansas, swept back into Tennessee to stop at Memphis, then dipped into Louisiana for a visit to Shreveport, and finished the campaign with an arduous, three-day, nine-county sweep through Texas, covering in particular the cities of Fort Worth, Austin and San Antonio. They returned to Columbia over the weekend so the Governor could prepare an election eve address for an extensive radio network hook-up Monday night.

On election day, November 2, 1948, Governor and Mrs. Thurmond drove up to Edgefield to vote. The young wife of the States' Rights presidential nominee was voting in a presidential election for the first time and her first vote for an American president was cast for her husband.

The results of the 1948 presidential election caught the United States by surprise. Harry S. Truman had been counted out long before November, and early on election night some of the metropolitan newspapers went so far as to proclaim victory for Governor Dewey of New York. The nation awoke the next morning to the astonishing fact that

President Truman had been re-elected. It was an accomplishment he owed largely to his own fighting spirit.

Governors Thurmond and Wright carried the four states
of Alabama, Louisiana, Mississippi and South Carolina, gar-
nering their total thirty-eight electoral votes plus one from
an independent-minded elector in Tennessee, making thirty-
nine in all. The election so far as the States' Rights candidates were concerned closely followed the prediction. For
some weeks it had been obvious that the state Democratic
leadership in other southern states would not bolt the national party, and without that support the newly-organized
States' Rights movement in those states could not hope for
success. By August 11th the state Democratic parties of
Alabama, Mississippi and South Carolina had pledged their
electoral vote to Thurmond and Wright. Louisiana Democrats followed suit on September 10th by substituting Thurmond and Wright in place of Truman and Barkley on the
ballot. What would have happened in these four states without support of the state party leadership remained a matter
of speculation, but it is highly doubtful that the hurriedly-
formed movement could have swung them otherwise. Even
so, the States' Rights movement came closer to its goal of
throwing the election into the House of Representatives
than most political observers thought possible.

Two "ifs" could have changed the situation drastically.
If North Carolina and Texas had joined the four bolting
states in giving their electoral votes to Thurmond and
Wright, the election would have gone to the House because
neither Truman nor Dewey would have received a majority.
The second "if" concerned Ohio and Illinois. Both states
had been expected to fall into the Republican column but
instead went Democratic by small margins. In Ohio, the
Democratic edge was a squeakingly close 7,102 popular
votes; in Illinois, the Republicans lost the State by 33,612
votes. In other words, a reversal of 21,000 votes in these
two states would have turned the trick. President Truman
would have been denied the necessary 266 electoral votes.

In this situation, too, the election would have gone to the House. Had such come to pass, the South conceivably might have elected its candidates, or at the minimum it would have achieved the powerful bargaining position it had dreamed of for so long.

As the dust of the election settled, and the nation sat down to figure out how Harry Truman had confounded the experts, the First Lady of South Carolina sat down also to ponder in her youthful way a few aspects of the election. To her this new world of politics was at the same time fascinating and puzzling. The primary puzzle was the South. She could not understand her own people. It was equally disappointing and exasperating to her way of thinking that the southern people had failed to unite and to vote as a region so their power could be felt. In this particular case, her husband's candidacy had afforded a means of effective protest against the allegedly unfair treatment the South received from the National Democratic Party—treatment that southerners had been screeching about in anguish ever since the Philadelphia convention. The matter, consequently, was of more personal concern to her than it would have been normally. If southerners really were as outraged as they had claimed to be, why hadn't they shown it by voting for her husband or even by going Republican? Instead, they had, except in the four bolting states, trotted meekly to the polls and voted the Democratic label as they had done all their lives. They were following the tradition of their fathers and grandfathers "even though" as the Thurmonds put it, "the Democratic Party had abandoned States' Rights and no longer stood for the constitutional principles upon which it was founded." The most oft-stated reason given at election time was "I'm a Democrat, and I've never voted anything but the Democratic ticket."

To Mrs. Thurmond, who had just voted in her first presidential election, the issues were clear. If one did not care for the Democratic candidates or for the party platform, then one voted for someone else. She belonged to the post-

World War II generation of Dixieland voter emerging on the scene, and her mind was not encumbered by the blind loyalties that were the self-imposed shackles of many in her region. With their stubborn, unthinking adherence to tradition, many southern voters more effectively chained themselves to their fate than any outside force could ever do. Though her father had been a Democratic office holder for years and her own natural instincts pulled her in that direction, she felt that it was high time people began to use their heads at voting time. Jean Thurmond was not the first and certainly will not be the last to analyze and to speculate vainly over the unique creature known as "the southern voter."

Not to be outdone in the realm of analyses, the electorate turned the tables and did some analyzing of its own. Especially was an assessment made by the people of Governor Thurmond's young wife after her first test in politics. A full year had passed now since her marriage. She had received at best a lukewarm reaction from the State. No only had this young girl been tested by the usual duties of First Lady, but she had been particularly challenged by her husband's race for the presidency of the United States. The States' Rights campaign began as a major trial for her; it ended as a kind of personal victory. In the public mind she had acquitted herself becomingly in what would have been a real test even to the most battle-proved, mature wife. Her presence on the many speaking tours had become an asset to her husband. She shone most noticeably in the area of public relations because she talked easily to the press and amiably greeted thousands of supporters. Behind the scenes she was a respected adviser. The States' Rights Democrats race had served as a superb basic training course in practical politicking for the girl. In a future year under conditions just as strange and unexpected as those of 1948, this training would bear the sweetly satisfying fruits of triumph.

The States' Rights movement within the Democratic

Party was concluded on election day except for a small drama to be played out during the Presidential Inauguration on Thursday, January 20, 1949, in Washington.

On that afternoon officials and parade march units of all the states passed the presidential reviewing stand to honor President Harry S. Truman and Vice President Alben W. Barkley. In return the two men acknowledged with the customary gestures the passing of each state. As the Governor and First Lady of South Carolina rode by, Vice President Barkley raised his hand to greet them. President Truman reached over, caught and held down the hand. At the same time he ignored the car and turned aside to whisper to the Vice President. Someone later claimed to have overheard the President say to Barkley, "Here comes that (uttering one of his famous descriptions) now!" in reference to Thurmond. The remark was not verified and so may or may not be true. The President's action in turning aside, however, was resented by South Carolinians, who regarded it as an insult to both Governor Thurmond and the State of South Carolina.

Though lacking certainly in graciousness and magnanimity, the impulsive action was human. Harry Truman had emerged the victor from a rough campaign after the whole country had repeatedly drummed into him that he did not stand a chance against Governor Dewey. In addition, the States' Rights Democrats and Governor Thurmond had harassed him at every turn. Today was Harry Truman's day, and he was having the last laugh. It was thus that the presidential candidate of the States' Rights Democrats received a final unmistakable snub from the American President he had sought diligently to turn out of office. For Mr. Truman, it must have been a highly satisfying finale. On this note, the 1948 bolt of Southern Democrats came officially to an end.

III

The People Render Judgment

AFTER the rigors of the States' Rights presidential campaign, Governor and Mrs. Thurmond settled down once more to live as the first family of South Carolina.

The staid aura of the governorship was a challenge to Jean's high-spirited youth. Early during her second year at the Executive Mansion Mrs. Thurmond one night decided to slide down the stair railing in the front hall. Wilma Smith of the Governor's staff was there that night waiting with the others for Governor Thurmond's late return to the city. Sitting in the library, she thought she heard a girlish "Whee-e-e!" and peered curiously into the hallway to investigate. Her astonished eyes beheld the First Lady astride the bannister and descending at breakneck speed. Landing feet first, Jean was the picture of self-satisfaction as she told the open-mouthed Miss Smith, "There! I won't do that again, but I just had to try it once."

The fact that state penitentiary trusties composed the

staff of servants at the Executive Mansion was responsible for many amusingly awkward moments. Visitors never failed to be shocked on learning that they had been in close association with convicted killers. The Governor often pointed out that it was better to have trusties who were serving life terms for killing rather than terms for stealing because they were "more trustworthy" with one's personal possessions. People seldom were relieved to hear this.

In February 1949, Cedric Foster, the well-known radio commentator of the Mutual Broadcasting System, was a house guest. He had met the Thurmonds during the presidential campaign and had become a friend. At the end of the visit, Foster sent his luggage down to the front entrance by one of the servants, tucked his briefcase under one arm and sauntered down the steps. Conversing with Mrs. Thurmond on the way down, he remarked, "I'd like to tip the servants."

"Oh, I don't believe that's necessary," his hostess replied graciously. "They're prisoners, you know, and we pay them regularly."

"They are? What are they in for?"

"For killing," she said as casually as if she were saying, "Oh, for overparking!"

"My God!" Foster's face went stark-white and his free hand gripped the stair railing. "You mean I've been sleeping here with prisoners, and I haven't been locking my door?"

"It sorta looks that way, doesn't it?" said the First Lady.

On another occasion Governor Thurmond's sister, Mrs. W. G. Bishop, and her family were to come from Greenwood, South Carolina, for a weekend at the mansion. Mrs. Bishop telephoned several days ahead to find out if she should bring along a nurse for her baby.

"No," assured her sister-in-law. "I have a trusty who can look after him."

"Well, eh-er—what is she in the penitentiary for?" came the anxious inquiry.

"For sticking out somebody's eyes with an ice pick." The gasp followed by prolonged silence at the other end of the line prompted the hostess to add comfortingly, "Don't worry about a thing. We'll be expecting you, hear now?"

Once the initial shock wore off, guests evidently adjusted reasonably well because they always returned and the Thurmonds' good friend, Cedric Foster, was given a key to the house.

"I'm sure I'm the only tenth generation New Englander who ever had a key to the South Carolina Governor's Mansion," he used to tell his host and hostess.

Foster often went hiking and horseback riding with them as well as to political gatherings and to dinners. Moreover, he occasionally joined them for Sunday service at the Baptist Church. The folksiness of the Southern Baptists always amazed him, and he would observe in fascination the ushers standing in the aisles and waving toward the door as they eagerly called, "Room for one more!"

In February, 1950, the famous Baptist evangelist, Billy Graham, stayed at the Executive Mansion during his three-weeks South Carolina crusade. The Columbia visit was a milestone in his career. In the autumn of 1949 Dr. Graham had conducted his first successful revival in a rented tent in Los Angeles, California. He drew less than 3,000 people to his final rally, but was given a helpful push by William Randolph Hearst, who ordered his newspapers to "puff Graham." Beginning the Columbia crusade in the last week of February, the Graham staff set up headquarters in a downtown hotel and held nightly services at the city's municipal township auditorium. Before the week was out, the evangelist was so besieged by the public that rest became impossible. Governor and Mrs. Thurmond invited him to stay at the mansion where he could be shielded to some extent. The change was made and Dr. Graham's visit proved a moving experience not only for his hosts, but also for the executive and household staffs. All succumbed to the magnetism of the Graham personality.

Thurmond, noting that the preacher always drank hot water before a speaking engagement, asked, "What in the world are you doing?"

"I'm loosening my vocal cords," replied Graham, adding that hot water helped his speaking voice. Thurmond adopted the practice—not that his voice needed strengthening—and maintained in after years that it "helps, very definitely helps."

On Sunday, March 12, Billy Graham closed the Columbia crusade with a rally that sponsors had hoped would attract a creditable showing. Attendance exceeded the wildest expectations as some 40,000 persons jammed into the University of South Carolina stadium which at that time had a capacity of only 36,000. It was the first large crowd that Billy Graham had ever drawn. The subsequent national publicity launched the fabulous career of the North Carolina evangelist.

In the fall of 1949 Governor and Mrs. Thurmond undertook a series of receptions before the University of South Carolina's football games. It was a challenge to process the large crowds past the Governor and First Lady, through the house, out again to a picnic lunch on the grounds and away in time for everyone to arrive at the stadium for the 2 p.m. kick-off.

One of the largest guest lists—2,500 to 3,000—was entertained on "Big Thursday" prior to the annual game with Clemson. Guests began arriving at 11 o'clock and were hustled through the mansion so quickly they hardly knew what had happened. About twenty local college girls had been recruited to stand at key points along the routes of entry and exit and to smile at lagging visitors, and to urge them politely to "Come this way, please." The entire crowd was "processed" in two hours.

Nothing matched the Saturday, though, when the mansion survived the onslaught of 6,000 Boy Scouts, who were to be special guests at a university football game. How 6,000 boys shook hands with Governor and Mrs. Thurmond, went through the house, ate an outdoor picnic lunch and got to

the stadium not only in their 6,000 individual pieces but
also in time for the game, no one knew. The grounds looked
as though a track meet had been held on the flower beds
and across the shrubbery. Extra help from the penitentiary,
plus weeks of tender, healing care were required to restore
the yard to order.

As the pleasant summer and autumn passed and the
winter of 1949–50 arrived in South Carolina's capital city,
the atmosphere was permeated with talk of the coming
Democratic primary in the summer of 1950. The major con-
tests would be the governorship and a seat in the United
States Senate.

Since the Governor of South Carolina by law cannot
succeed himself, the logical next step on the political ladder
is the Senate. Despite the odds—and they are usually great—
this race is one the Governor is compelled to make or else
risk political oblivion. At best he faces an uphill fight to
unseat an incumbent, and unless that incumbent has been
caught in major blunders or miscalculations, the task is
almost impossible. The decision to run against incumbent
United States Senator Olin D. Johnston was one Governor
Thurmond knew he had to make in the affirmative if he
expected to remain alive politically. Everyone else in the
State also knew he had to make the race, although customarily the official announcement would not be made until
spring. Yet, the matter of political survival was only one
point considered by the Governor in making his decision.
Of comparable importance to him was what he regarded
as a basic difference in viewpoint between Senator Johnston
and himself.

"In the 1950 election," Strom Thurmond recalled years
later, "the basic issues as I saw them turned around limited
government versus big government at the national level, a
willingness to put political principle above political party,
and an emphasis on integrity in government service. I placed
strong emphasis on my record of public service, particularly

my tenure as Governor, which proved that there is indeed such a thing as states' responsibilities as well as states' rights. I tried to show by my record that there can be and must be progress at the appropriate level of government if our country is to move forward and at the same time observe our constitutional system of government."

Against this background the question of running was resolved. The various political forces maneuvered for position, and social gatherings of state leaders became prime settings for the turning of wheels within wheels.

That winter Jean Thurmond was introduced to the rough and tumble of state political rivalries. Not even the presidential campaign had prepared her for the forthcoming party primary. Practically the entire state political machinery had gone along with the States' Rights movement and it had been handled rather politely so that there had not been the rugged in-fighting of a senatorial race.

The winter, therefore, was a new phase in the education of a politician's young wife. Conversations were not harmless pleasantries any more; they were loaded with political nuances and innuendoes. As Mrs. Thurmond went from one dinner or party to another, she carefully developed the art of sizing up people and of discerning what they really were saying. In due course she began to astonish the governor with her accuracy in analyzing and prophesying the actions of people. After what would appear to be a general "How-are-you? I'm-fine" exchange, she would predict privately that such and such an individual either could or could not be counted upon as a friend.

There was a human weakness that particularly angered her about politics, actually about all of public life. It was the flagrant insincerity that manifested itself constantly in so many ways.

"I can understand why people would be in favor of an opponent. I don't expect everybody to support my husband," she would say heatedly, "but why can't they be honest about it? Why do they have to say they're for Strom when all the time they're working for the other side? I can't respect people who do this."

There were times beyond number, prior to and during the senatorial campaign, when Jean faced such people. Knowing even while she chatted with them that, despite their volunteered pledges of support to Thurmond, they were in the "enemy camp," she mentally catalogued each name. She developed conversational discretion to a fine point, consciously—and sometimes frantically—searching for topics that while harmless were not boringly inane.

The necessity to maintain equilibrium in public and never to explode in a spontaneous outburst of irritation or hurt was one of the most difficult aspects of living in high political circles and a hard lesson for a spirited girl to absorb. In her childhood Jean had had a temper, but during her teens, she had learned to master it to such an extent that few people suspected it was one of her traits. Her quest for self-perfection went on until her death. It was a quest that friends attributed to her deeply religious nature. She worked consciously toward acquiring self-discipline, and it above all else was responsible for her ability to smile and hold her tongue even under great provocation. The inner struggle often was titanic.

In her efforts to rid herself of faults, Jean Thurmond sometimes gave the impression that she did not want people to know her intimately for fear they might uncover a defect for which they could criticize her.

"She is very sensitive to criticism, I believe," said an acquaintance once. "She enforces rigid standards on herself to avoid it."

There would come a time some years later when this wife's grasp of human nature and politics—in fact her total personhood, its character being shaped as it was—would play a decisive part in the most challenging political race of Strom Thurmond's life. In 1950 no one then could foretell the causes and effects of things yet to happen, but that year was playing a significant role in Jean Crouch Thurmond's life. In the meantime, it would bring a full share of disappointment to the Thurmonds.

The long-expected official announcement of Governor J. Strom Thurmond's candidacy for the Democratic nomination for junior United States Senator from South Carolina was made on April 29, 1950. The only other candidate for the office was incumbent Senator Olin D. Johnston, who had filed already for re-election to a second term. With battle lines drawn between these two veteran campaigners, the State braced for what it knew would be one of the most rugged political fights in recent history. Because of South Carolina's traditional one party system, the victor emerging from the primary election automatically would become senator. The November general election would be only a rubber-stamp formality.

In conjunction with the primary there was an exhausting county-by-county pre-election speaking tour of all state-wide candidates. The tour was an obsolete hangover from the past and totally needless in 1950, an era of good roads and modern communication, but South Carolina was loath to forego tradition, so the Party decided to schedule the usual speaking jaunts. The only change from previous years was a division of the candidates into two groups: those seeking federal office and those out for state and county offices. This arrangement was the one concession toward making each appearance shorter and less tiring to audiences.

The kick-off date for the two-a-day addresses in South Carolina's forty-six counties was May 23rd. Congressional candidates were to be in Lexington and Saluda that day, while candidates for state offices were making their opening speeches in Sumter and Camden.

The star attraction among four gubernatorial hopefuls was former United States Supreme Court Justice and Secretary of State James F. Byrnes, at long last making a bid for

the governorship of his native state. The poised, confident
elder statesman easily outdistanced his opponents to win
the office of Governor. There was a real fight, however, in
the senatorial contest. Governor Thurmond started the race
by attacking Senator Johnston's criminal-pardon record
when Johnston had been Governor years earlier. Thurmond
was to ride this issue over and over, accusing his opponent
of having pardoned or paroled 3,221 convicts. Johnston ignored the charges. Not until late in the campaign would
the Senator begin to reply, but when he did, he opened
up with ferocity. The two men were at each other's throats
from then until election day.

The two senatorial candidates were both old-school politicians in their style of oratory. Each could stomp across
the room, pound the table, flail the air dramatically with
one or both arms and shout home a point. Invariably during
the course of his talks, Thurmond would wave a finger dis-
approvingly at Johnston and remind him of the "twelve
convicted murderers" Thurmond said were released on
Johnston's last day as Governor. Meanwhile, Johnston sat
poker-faced, ignoring his opponent. As the campaign wore
on, charges and counter-charges filled the air, and each
tried to prove that he had opposed President Harry S. Truman more vigorously than the other. The Governor would
display a photograph of Johnston posing with a group including the President's cabinet appointee, Attorney-General
J. Howard McGrath, the man to enforce integration decrees
upon the South. Senator Johnston would counter by showing audiences the famous picture of Thurmond standing
on his head.

Inevitably, the race issue—with each man making charges
against the other—entered the campaign, but only about two
weeks prior to election. The unfortunate injection of the
subject into the Senate race probably threw both candidates
into more extreme positions on the issue than they really
held. Certainly, no one would have gathered by the tone

of the political oratory that Thurmond, during the first year of his governorship, had unhesitatingly put his full weight behind the arrest and prosecution of twenty-seven suspects in the Greenville Negro lynching case. The Governor could have kept hands off, but instead he sent state law officers to assist in the immediate apprehension of the suspects. (A local jury afterwards acquitted all of the accused.)

The race issue was responsible for the senatorial candidates nearly coming to blows at a joint appearance in Newberry on June 26th. Poking a finger at Olin Johnston, Strom Thurmond charged that his opponent had voiced no protest against the implementation of integration policies in the armed services. To the Governor's surprise, Johnston shouted, "Liar!" Taken back, Governor Thurmond angrily offered to meet him outside after their talks and proceeded to label the Senator "demagogue" and "hypocrite." Later, a Johnston aide intervened to prevent a fist fight as the candidates met on the steps of the courthouse.

During the homestretch the senatorial race became a verbal slugging match. The two men were toe to toe. Senator Johnston now was replying to the Governor's charges, and both were accusing each other of all kinds of political sins. Large crowds were flocking to the meetings to hear the two men blast away at each other, but audiences were befuddled by the counter-accusations and the fluttering of damning photographs.

Some newspapers in South Carolina were so concerned about the tone of the campaign that they lamented the absence of a third choice. They editorialized that the senatorial candidates were acting like bad little boys trying to bully each other. Both men were given editorial spankings. As for the candidates, it would take years to erase the bitterness between them.

It was into this kind of a political fray that Jean Crouch Thurmond was thrown as she sought to help her husband win a seat in the United States Senate. As the campaign became progressively more bitter, Mrs. Thurmond got her first taste of a no-holds-barred fight between two seasoned politicians. In comparison, the 1948 States' Rights Democrats presidential race seemed as refined as a ladies' afternoon tea.

As the weeks of stumping passed, the charges thrown by the Governor at Senator Johnston were so strong that Jean questioned the wisdom of employing such sledgehammer techniques. Actually, Governor Thurmond was running on his record, too, but his list of accomplishments was overshadowed by the impact of his attacks on Olin Johnston's alleged abuse of the pardoning power. The Governor usually led into his own record by waving his right arm at his audience as he declared "and I ended that abuse of the pardoning power by creating the State Probation, Parole and Pardon board." From there he would go on to cite what he considered the other most important achievements of his tenure as Governor: industrial development, "streamlined" state government, a new election law providing for the secret ballot in South Carolina, "the greatest advances in education in the State's history," revitalization of the State's financial rating, and the reduction to almost zero of the occurrence of labor disturbances. Still, these points lost the spotlight to his charges that Johnston abused the pardoning power. Thurmond never let up on the subject of Johnston's record, certain aspects of which he hoped voters would consider glaring weaknesses. Jean thought her husband was applying the sledge hammer too heavily and was afraid that such tactics would generate sympathy votes for the Senator.

"Why, I almost feel sorry for him myself!" she remarked. "I think it would be better to concentrate on your own record and qualifications."

The Governor's political advisers, Robert McC. Figg and Walter Brown, disagreed and urged him to continue his criticism—in other words, to take the fight to the Senator— which he did. Viewing the campaign in retrospect much later, Thurmond commented, "It is hard to tell who was right." By then it was evident that various interwoven factors had influenced the outcome.

No matter what she thought at the time, Jean went along with her husband's cause. Often, during May and June of 1950, she returned, weary in her very bones, to the Executive Mansion, but when advised to rest before taking to the hustings again, she would perk up and answer cheerily, "I've got to go out and get votes for my husband." And would be off again to rejoin the team.

The two joint appearances per day arranged for the senatorial candidates were in the county seats of South Carolina's forty-six counties—one town in the morning, one in the afternoon. In addition, each candidate branched out on his own for other talks or for handshaking missions at night.

The Thurmond entourage, starring both Governor and Mrs. Thurmond, usually arrived in each town well ahead of time to allow team members to spread out among the townspeople, distributing campaign literature and "talking up" their candidate. While the Governor went down one side of the main street, greeting people along the sidewalk and in stores, Jean Thurmond took the other side.

After the morning stint, the Thurmonds and staff members customarily took time for lunch before moving on to the next county.

Afternoon politicking followed in general the morning pattern of handshaking and speech-making. As the speeches became hotter and the campaign more acrimonious, the crowds grew from paltry handfuls at the early meetings to standing-room only, and audiences reveled in the fierce combat. After dinner each night the Governor and his wife prepared to meet the change of shifts at local mills. The Thurmonds, each accompanied by a staff member, would hold forth at separate entrances, handing out campaign leaflets, greeting workers and asking for their votes.

In upstate South Carolina, more commonly called the Piedmont, they found themselves in hostile country. This was evidenced by the number of Thurmond hecklers and the amount of pro-Johnston applause at the daytime gatherings. It was made even clearer as the couple stood at mill gates night after night, handing out literature. In most instances the workers either blankly accepted the leaflets or threw the pamphlets down and stepped on them with open antagonism. The Thurmonds pretended not to notice.

The pro-Johnston sentiment among the textile workers was no surprise. Olin Johnston had always derived the bulk of his political support from them. He emphasized his knowledge of and sympathy for the factory hand because in his youth he had worked in a cotton mill. The reiteration of Johnston's textile background worked like a charm. "Votin' for Olin" was as habitual to them as taking a shift at the mill. Johnston's tremendous strength in this heavily populated region had given him the State's governorship twice and had enabled him to beat out the elderly "Cotton Ed" Smith six years earlier for the latter's seat in the United States Senate.

Focus on the roughness of the Piedmont campaign was sharpened abruptly in the foothill town of Walhalla. Several overall-clad textile workers waited for the Governor at the bottom of one of the double stairways leading down from the courthouse. A member of the state constabulary sent word to the Governor to walk down the other stairway to avoid the workers. Looking about him, Strom Thurmond demanded angrily, "Where are they? Where are they?" When his eyes lighted on the men below, he strode down the steps, ready to fight. Before he could reach them, the state law enforcement officer bulled into the group and yanked away the workers who already had begun to leave when they saw that the Governor meant to accept their challenge.

There was also an unpleasant incident in Greenwood when a group of people tried unsuccessfully to batter their way into the Thurmonds' hotel room as they were preparing to leave for a campaign address at the local football field.

It was apparent that neither candidate was finding the senatorial race any picnic. Senator Johnston was having to endure the fierce verbal charges of the Governor, and the Governor, on his part, had to endure his share of charges from Johnston, plus appallingly rough harassment in the upcountry Johnston strongholds.

With the passing weeks the young Mrs. Thurmond grew in the art of politicking. Her easy manner with people made her especially adept at the personalized approach.

"Jean Thurmond complements her husband in this sense," observed an acquaintance. "He is a keen politician on the broad, over-all basis but lacks something of the warm, personal touch. Here, she fills in. She is unbeatable at person-to-person politicking. The girl has a knack for knowing how to approach people and knowing what to say."

Despite Mrs. Thurmond's value on campaign trips, the Governor said afterwards in recalling the 1950 senatorial battle, "If I had it to do over again, I believe I'd put Jean in the office at headquarters where she could devote more of her time to contacting people rather than to keeping me company on the road."

All the charm, all the handshaking, all the hammering away at Johnston's record from ancient times through the spring of 1950, all the discussion of issues, all the tiring footwork and speech-making of the entire Thurmond team was for naught in this race for the United States Senate. The incumbent Senator Olin Johnston was reelected—by only 24,534 votes, his closest scrape—but reelected, nevertheless.

A Washington reporter later asked Senator Johnston how he had managed to beat Thurmond.

"Well, the doggoned fellow had to go stand on his head, else he woulda whipped me!" the Senator is reported to have replied.

Such an estimate of the situation may have been correct to some extent, but it is more likely that Strom Thurmond's defeat resulted from a combination of factors. For one thing, the Governor ran completely out of campaign funds two weeks before election day. Secondly, the Korean conflict, which had just begun, tended to make voters reluctant to change office-holders in the middle of a crisis. Thirdly, the CIO labor union poured substantial money into the State to defeat Thurmond, or so it was reported. Fourthly, President Truman reportedly had worked covertly through labor and Negro leaders to beat him. In addition, there was Olin Johnston's long-standing strength in the Piedmont. One last factor was the lack of a current issue sufficiently moving to stir the electorate into ousting the incumbent.

The election results could not help but disappoint the Thurmonds. By nature both were accustomed to throwing themselves completely into what they were doing. Defeat after a hard-fought battle, therefore, was a hard pill to swallow. Still the day after the election the couple wore cheerful faces. They had to; so many disappointed, depressed friends were rehashing the election and wallowing in gloom that the two people most concerned felt compelled to help lift the funereal atmosphere.

With politics out of the picture—for awhile anyway—the Thurmonds turned their thoughts to a new life.

IV

A Team Battles the Odds

GOVERNOR and Mrs. J. Strom Thurmond left the Executive Mansion as South Carolina's first family on the morning of Tuesday, January 16, 1951. They joined the new occupants, Governor-elect and Mrs. James F. Byrnes, to drive to the Byrnes inauguration on the capitol steps in midtown Columbia.

After the Byrnes inaugural Jean Crouch Thurmond became a private citizen for the first time in her adult life. Her new feeling of freedom was strange, almost bewildering. For Strom, too, private life was strange. It was an experience he had not had in years and, of course, not at all as a married man.

The couple planned to settle in Aiken because new industry was making that properous little town a good place in which to practice law. It also happened to be halfway between Jean's parents in Elko and Strom's mother in Edgefield. The magnolia-lined sandhill town had been a fashionable winter resort for years, especially for horse lovers.

Life as private citizens in Aiken meant a number of new things. First was the opportunity to use their wedding gifts which had been in storage while the Thurmonds used state-owned furnishings in the Governor's mansion. Only the week before leaving, the couple had ordered an inventory of everything in the mansion to compare with a similar inventory taken when Strom Thurmond moved into the house. The only missing item, a silver butter knife, was replaced with a new one. Now a whole house had to be furnished. Friends were aware of the situation.

On Monday, the day before leaving the mansion, the Thurmonds were visited by supporters who gave the Governor a new Cadillac and handed the Governor's wife five one-hundred dollar bills to buy furnishings for their new Aiken home.

Three significant steps in the personal lives of the Thurmonds were taken shortly after arriving in Aiken. The first in early February was the announcement by Mr. Thurmond that he was dropping the James from his name and hereafter would be known simply as Strom Thurmond. The change was in response to the suggestion by newspaper columnist John Temple Graves, who complained that the name sounded cumbersome. The second development was the formation in mid-March of the law firm of Thurmond, Lybrand and Simons. The Thurmond partners were Dorcey K. Lybrand, state senator from Aiken County, and Charles E. Simons, Jr., another prominent local attorney. (Upon Strom Thurmond's recommendation, Mr. Simons was appointed in 1964 as a United States District Judge.) Third, was the letting of a contract for the construction of the couple's first home—a seven-room, brick veneer house, to be located on a slope beneath towering pines, on lovely Kalmia Hill, a western section of town.

It was midsummer (more like an eternity to Mrs. Thurmond, who had watched the placement of almost every brick and plank) when the former Governor and his wife moved into their comfortable spacious house. Outside, the ivory scratch brick and maroon shutters made a strikingly attractive contrast to the deep green and brown of the pines. The floor plan aimed at efficiency. At one end were two guest rooms and a bath; across the front were the living and dining rooms; at the back, a paneled den with floor to ceiling bookcases, a paneled kitchen and a screened-in porch. The rooms at the rear were built as a unit with the Thurmonds' bedroom and bath, which were also at the back. Such an arrangement made it possible to cut this living area off from the rest of the house unless guests were there.

Happily the couple set up housekeeping in their new house. Whether Jean needed it or not, she got plenty of advice from her husband, who was still a firm believer in military methods. It made great sense to him to alphabetize the canned goods so that various types of foods could be located easily. Jean thought the idea made such a good story to relate to friends that she willingly set about her task, but there were a few knotty problems to solve first; How should corned beef be classified so she would remember where to look, "C" for corned, "B" for beef or "M" for meats? Then came the matter of soups—by name or what? And what was the proper grouping for the Thurmonds' array of cereals and other breakfast foods. The kitchen shelves contained every kind known to the American market!

As for clothes arrangement, Mr. Thurmond wanted items placed in dresser drawers in prescribed military manner. He had been used to this method since college days.

"Why that's the funniest thing I've ever heard of. I don't see the need of it," Jean laughed as she looked through one casually filled dresser drawer after another to find something of her own. He sat and watched.

"It makes for more efficiency," he needled.

Gradually—and quietly—Mrs. Thurmond applied his system to her own clothes.

The Governor liked the same neatness applied to the

grounds. He would instruct the gardener to trim the hedge down to a low, neat height. On the other hand, Mrs. Thurmond liked a tall hedge. As soon as her husband would drive out of the yard, she would persuade the workman to compromise somewhere between high and low.

"It took me nine years to train Jean," Strom was heard to remark some years later in regard to proper operation of a household.

Rolling up her domestic sleeves, Mrs. Thurmond put her shoulder to the wheel of cooking. She and the Governor liked to alternate rich old-fashioned southern cooking with health foods. One of the Governor's favorite foods was turnip greens which Jean prepared for him but did not like herself. She could never bring herself to eat more than a token helping, although her husband, a great believer in the body-building qualities of greens, tried to tempt her by holding out spoonfuls of the vegetable as he recited its merits.

"It's loaded with vitamins," he would declare, as if to say, "How can you resist?"

"I'd rather take a vitamin pill," was her invarible reply.

On leaving the Executive Mansion Jean had expected a substantial reduction in entertaining, but the only difference turned out to be the number of guests rather than the number of occasions. Both Thurmonds enjoyed entertaining, and their circle of acquaintances was wide; so here, too, they were receiving friends constantly.

During the summer they often packed a lunch and drove for a midday swim at nearby Aiken Outing Club. They were avid swimmers and used to race each other across the lake. Jean would win the short, fast stretches; Strom, the long, tiring ones. The tall, blue-eyed girl eased in and out of the water as if it were her natural habitat. She liked to sun herself for hours, too, until she was as tanned as a tropical islander.

In other sports Mrs. Thurmond gave no quarter to the Governor. She kept pace with him at bowling, tennis, horseback-riding, bicycle-riding, or hiking. The lovely wooded trails surrounding Aiken were ideal for walking and horse-back-riding. It was an unwritten rule of the Thurmond house that all inhabitants, unless physically disabled, should participate in nightly walks around Kalmia Hill. House guests found themselves huffing and puffing up the hilly paths behind their energetic host and hostess before they knew what had happened. Staff members fell victim to the rule more often than anyone else, and they were not about to say no.

Quite often the Thurmonds drove up to Clemson College for football games. Mrs. Thurmond liked football so well that she often was more ready to battle traffic and inclement weather to get there than was her Clemson-graduate husband. One raw, rainy Saturday Jean insisted that they go to a game with some friends, as planned. She piled her companions, raincoats, umbrellas and blankets all into the back of the car and headed for the law office to pick up the governor.

"But this doesn't make sense," he protested. "This is crazy, going to a football game in this weather. It's pouring rain!"

"You're always giving me lectures on adjusting to life," answered Mrs. Thurmond from the driver's seat. "We had already planned to go, and Eloise has gotten a baby sitter and all. It's raining, so we're adjusting to the rain. I'm adjusting to life—just like you tell me to do. Your raincoat is in the car. We're going to Clemson."

They went to Clemson.

To passengers, the ride alone made those various trips memorable. Mrs. Thurmond took an impish delight in darting her car a block or two in the wrong direction on Aiken's double streets, waving gaily to people, while her companions came close to apoplexy. After she learned her way around Washington, D. C., a few years later, she used to make a frolic out of showing South Carolina visitors how she could

skid her car in the snow. Yet she had less than complete
confidence in her husband's driving.

Once, the couple left late for an event.

"Speed up, Jean," instructed the Governor.

"No, this is fast enough."

"Well, I'll drive!"

She stopped the car and moved to the rear seat.

"What are you doing?" he asked.

"Over there on the right side is the death seat, and I'm
not going to sit there with you driving."

An acquaintance visiting in the nation's capital once recalled that "riding in Washington traffic with Jean driving
and Strom advising is an experience never to be forgotten."

Four gay, wonderful years of living in sports-minded
Aiken were the only days of Strom and Jean Thurmond's
married life that were free of pressure and official responsibility.

While the former Governor concentrated on his law
practice and related fields of interest, Jean turned her attention to civic and charitable activities. She had the time
to give in those days and felt conscience-bound to work in
behalf of worthy causes. Her only major unfulfilled wish—
the wish for children—was never to come true, and it was
the one big disappointment Jean knew. She compensated
by giving her attention to other children in the family and
to community enterprises. In 1953 she served as chairman
of Aiken's Cotton Festival and made it her most significant
civic accomplishment. The local chamber of commerce afterwards chose her as the country's "Woman of the Year."

Thus the Aiken years of private life phased out for Strom
and Jean Thurmond. Destiny once again was at their side.
Soon it would decree that they come face to face with
momentous challenges.

Those challenges came with shocking unexpectedness.
United States Senator Burnet Rhett Maybank, senior senator
from South Carolina, died of a heart attack in his sleep

Wednesday morning, September 1, 1954 in the family summer home at Flat Rock, North Carolina. Funeral services
were scheduled for 11 a.m. Friday, September 3rd, at historic St. Michael's Episcopal Church in Charleston. Burial
would be in the city's Magnolia Cemetery.

A native of Charleston and a member of one of the city's
old, prominent families, the 55-year-old senator had been a
political wizard. He had ventured into politics as a city
alderman while still engaged in the cotton exporting business. From Charleston's city council, he had ascended to
the office of mayor at the age of thirty-two. In 1938 he became the first Charlestonian since the Civil War to charm
the State into electing him Governor of South Carolina. It
was Maybank's first try, and he won over seven opponents.
From the governorship he was elected to the United States
Senate in 1941 to fill James F. Byrnes' unexpired term upon
the latter's appointment to the United States Supreme Court.
Burnet Maybank eventually obtained membership on the
Senate's Banking and Appropriations committees. He had
never known defeat in his twenty-seven years of political
life, and in the summer of 1954 he had been renominated
without opposition by the state Democratic Party to another
six-year term in the Senate. No opposition had been planned
by the strife-torn Republican Party of South Carolina, so the
legislator's nomination was equivalent to election.

When the news of the Senator's death was flashed
throughout the State that Wednesday morning, the wheels
of power politics immediately went into motion. At stake
was the coveted jewel of a full Senate term. Before the day
was over, machinery had been well lubricated to assure
smooth transition of Senator Maybank's seat to another figure in South Carolina.

On Thursday rumors were traveling the rounds of the
news media to the effect that Governor Byrnes would seek
his old Senate seat (this rumor was discounted quickly by
the Governor) and that two other likely prospects were

former Governor Strom Thurmond and Donald Russell, president of the University of South Carolina. At the same time, State Democratic Party Chairman Neville Bennett of Clio scheduled a special meeting of the state Democratic executive committee for 3:30 p.m., Friday, September 3rd, to make plans concerning the Senate vacancy. By Friday morning still another rumor—the strongest of all—was headlined in the press that supporters of State Senator Edgar A. Brown of Barnwell County, the most powerful man in the General Assembly, were pushing him. They had polled the committee (composed of forty-six county representatives and several general party officers) on Thursday, rounding up sufficient votes to give the nod to their choice as Democratic nominee for the Maybank seat.

In Friday morning's edition, *The News and Courier* of Charleston already was sniffing the air for scents of political skullduggery. It carried that day a short, low-keyed editorial on page one, expressing hope that the committee would decide to hold a special primary election. Reporters and photographers swarmed around the entrances of St. Michael's as a Senate delegation and other national officials arrived from Washington. They were joined by current and past high state and local officeholders, including former Governor and Mrs. Strom Thurmond of Aiken. An estimated congregation of a thousand people crowded into the church; outside another thousand packed the sidewalks and leaned out of office windows on the four corners of the Meeting—Broad street intersection at St. Michael's.

Following the church service, the cortege formed for the slow funeral procession uptown to Magnolia Cemetery. Before the cortege reached Magnolia, however, Senator Edgar Brown's long Cadillac pulled out of line and sped to Columbia. In close pursuit was *The News and Courier*, which had sniffed the air once again, and pricked up its ears at what seemed to be a too-hasty departure. Like a hound on the scent of a fox, the Charleston press took off behind the Cadillac. That night the news came through that Senator Brown had been nominated by the Democratic executive committee to fill the entire six-year Senate term. *The News and Courier* then knew it had taken the right trail. Indignation spread like fire over the State within hours as Governor Byrnes and other officials maintained that the group should have called for a primary election rather than choosing on its own the new senator for the full term. A write-in movement on behalf of former Governor Thurmond was being launched that night by Mayor Francis F. Coleman of Mount Pleasant. By Saturday the pursuing *News and Courier* had been joined by *The Charleston Evening Post* and by every other daily newspaper in the State except Wilton Hall's two Anderson publications which were always staunch supporters of the Democratic organization. There was now a pack of hounds—substantial in number and in influence—all joined in full cry and nipping constantly at the heels of both nominee Brown and the committee. The chase, led by the press of Charleston, Greenville and Columbia, was not to end until the night of November 2nd.

There was nothing legally wrong with the committee's action; it had the right under law to do what it did. However, the action was regarded by many as morally wrong. In the opinions of the almost unanimous press and the majority of citizens, the committee had violated a moral obligation to the people to let them choose their senator when a way was open to do so.

The issue of the ensuing campaign was never Edgar Brown's competence and intellectual fitness for the Senate. In fact, there was no more able man in the General Assembly. He had done an outstanding job on state finances as chairman of the senate finance committee. Through seniority, force of personality and political acumen, he had made himself a tremendously powerful man, enjoying both the chairmanship of the finance committee and the position of senate president pro tempore. Yet, the Barnwell County Senator had never been elected to a state-wide office. In 1926 he ran unsuccessfully for the U. S. Senate against incumbent Senator Ellison D. (Cotton Ed) Smith; in 1938 he again entered the U. S. senatorial race against "Cotton Ed" Smith and against a third candidate, Olin D. Johnston, but withdrew before the first primary election. Ironically enough, it would appear that Edgar Brown's assets were at the same time his liabilities where his public image was concerned. Many apparently considered him already too powerful and too good a politician; hence the U. S. Senate had always been a little beyond his reach. Now, at last, the prize was his by action of the Democratic executive committee.

The issue here was the method by which Edgar Brown became the nominee, and it was upon this issue that a protest write-in movement began.

Prior to Friday night's deadline for filing candidates with the South Carolina secretary of state, a group of Republicans presented the name of William A. Kimbel of Murrells Inlet, but it was rejected because the name had not come from the officially certified State Republican Party. Mr. Kimbel had served in 1952 as chairman of the Citizens for Eisenhower organization. On learning that his name had been given to the secretary of state, he promptly withdrew it, saying the action had been taken without his knowledge. With Governor Brynes out of the picture and with Donald Russell and Congressman W. J. Bryan Dorn of Greenwood still feeling around the water's edge, another political veteran dived in. That man was former Governor Strom Thurmond.

Since Friday night, telephone calls, telegrams and letters had poured into the Thurmond home and law office. From various sections of South Carolina came requests for him to run as a write-in candidate in the November general election—as a protest if nothing more, they added. A stinging protest seemed to be about the most a write-in movement could hope for, since the state party organization was back-ing Edgar Brown. Election to any major state or national office had never been achieved that way. Such a feat was a practical impossibility and any practical politician would say without hesitation that it could not and would not happen. There was little reason to think it could happen now, even with the overwhelming sentiment of the people and of the press behind a write-in candidate. Just the me-chanics of writing in a name at the polls, instead of marking one already printed, made victory seem impossible.

With this cheerless prospect before him, Strom Thurmond spent the weekend thinking over the question of whether or not to run. Pressure was mounting by the hour.

"Like in 1948, it seemed to me that somebody ought to do something," he said.

A significant element in favor of Thurmond's making the effort was the fact that only four years earlier he had made a strong showing in the senatorial race against Olin Johnston. Moreover, he was the immediate past-Governor, a well-known personality and a vigorous campaigner, and to many voters he seemed a logical choice for "man of the hour." He was not holding just then any public office that could be jeopardized, but he did stand to give up his flour-ishing law practice if elected. Too, if he were to run and lose, this loss coupled with the one to Senator Johnston in 1950 could ruin him politically for years—maybe for all time.

Yet, Thurmond later reflected, "If I had not had confi-dence in the people of South Carolina, that they wanted to have the right thing done, I would never have entered the race. The disfranchisement of the people would be the strongest possible assault on a democracy that we intend to preserve. It was a challenge to me. That's the way I felt about it. We didn't have an organization, and we didn't have any money, but I was sure the people of the State would not accept their disfranchisement if the situation were prop-erly presented. So—when telegrams, letters, phone calls and committees asked me to enter the race, I consented. For me it was really a matter of democratic principles rather than politics, and I was willing to make the race, regardless of outcome."

After thorough discussion of the situation with advisers, the closest of whom was his wife, Strom Thurmond made his decision. He telephoned Bryan Dorn to ask if Dorn planned to run. If so, he himself would not consider the matter any longer, Thurmond said. Congressman Dorn still was unable to decide. Thurmond made the same telephone inquiry of Donald Russell. Despite strong urging by his friend, Governor Byrnes, Russell did not intend at that point to become a candidate. The field now seemed to be left to the man from Aiken.

That man announced late Tuesday afternoon, September 7th, at a Columbia news conference that he would be a write-in candidate in the November general election for the U. S. Senate seat of the late Burnet R. Maybank. On September 18th, Marcus A. Stone, a Florence and Dillon lumberman and a frequent candidate for public office, was to announce his write-in candidacy, but he was not regarded as a serious contender. On the 31st, Congressman Dorn definitely stepped out of the running, leaving the race to Brown and Thurmond. The pro-write-in press—that is, the 14 of 16 dailies and 73 of 86 non-dailies in the State—threw its support to Strom Thurmond. He symbolized the write-in campaign, and hopeless-looking rebellion against the state Democratic organization.

Once again, old foes were contesting each other. Memories recalled the 1946 gubernatorial race when Mr. Thurmond made the "Barnwell Ring" an issue. No love had been lost between the two men since that time.

The fight for the Senate would be waged on two issues. Edgar Brown placed his appeal to the voters on the basis of party loyalty. "The only real issue is whether people want a regular Democrat or an independent," he said.

Strom Thurmond pitched his campaign on the method by which Edgar Brown's nomination had been obtained. He worked out a general keynote sentence stating the issue as he saw it: "Whether thirty-one men shall choose the United States Senator or whether the people shall choose him." Thurmond also carefully emphasized that he was running as a South Carolina Democrat and if elected would vote with the Democrats in organizing the Senate.

That fateful September weekend of discussion, analysis and decision-making in the Thurmond home passed entirely too quickly for the principals involved and upon whom the consequences would fall. As in 1948 and 1950, there would be no turning back. Reflecting upon the Thurmond write-in candidacy, Jean remarked to an Aiken friend that she had come to love the leisurely way of life in the small town after the responsibilities of the Governor's Mansion.

"I don't have any desire to leave here. I have too much of Elko in me," Mrs. Thurmond continued, "but Strom wants to go to Washington, and I'm going to do all I can to help him get there. Beyond that I have no aspirations."

The "all" that Jean Thurmond planned to "do" on behalf of her husband's candidacy for the Senate was of more substantial proportions and more importance than probably even she realized.

She had always been more than just Strom Thurmond's wife; she had been his active partner in political campaigns. Her role had always been more than that of the smiling lady accompanying her candidate husband. She had been his trusted adviser and critic. She seldom had to volunteer advice because her husband usually sought it first. More and more in their life together, he had come to value her uncanny insight into the workings of the public mind. She could analyze people's motives and predict their reactions with a sagacity that few politicians in South Carolina could surpass. In a word, therefore, Jean Thurmond's winsome personality combined with her political sixth sense, her as-

tuteness, made her a real asset in any campaign. Furthermore, Strom Thurmond had never faced a more uphill battle
for public office in South Carolina than the one to which he
had just committed himself. If ever he needed a perceptive,
hard-working organization, he needed it now. With Edgar
Brown's name the only one printed on the ballot, Brown's
opposition would have to do a staggering amount of work
to counter-balance that advantage. Fully aware that her husband was attempting something never before accomplished
in American history—almost heartbreakingly conscious of the
small chance of success—Jean remained true to form in meeting the challenge with everything she had. In fact, the situation looked so impossible that its daring aspects appealed
to her sporting blood. So it was that the girl with "too much
of Elko" in her to want Washington, but with too much spirit
in her to turn from a fight, entered fully into the write-in
campaign for the United States Senate.

Everything Jean Thurmond had learned in three and a
half years of public life as South Carolina's First Lady, everything experienced as a presidential candidate's wife in the
1948 general election, all the hard lessons absorbed in the
U. S. Senatorial race of 1950, as well as those years of
working with people in Aiken's various community efforts—
in short, all the knowledge of politics and people gained in
seven years of adulthood was brought to bear on her husband's race against Edgar Brown for the Senate. Those
seven years had instilled a sureness of touch, a self-confi-
dence that enabled Mrs. Thurmond to proceed in her work
with speed and decisiveness.

On the next Tuesday, the Thurmonds left Aiken to set
up campaign and living quarters at the Hotel Columbia in
Columbia. Shortly afterwards, N. Heyward Clarkson, Jr., a
prominent Columbia attorney, became Strom Thurmond's
campaign manager. Mrs. Strom Thurmond became the unofficial co-manager. She devoted much of her attention to
special contacts and to matters of overall strategy.

In the 1954 senatorial campaign, Jean Thurmond's range of friendships was such that she knew in all sections of the State whom to contact not only for their support but also for their influence in lining up other local supporters. These attributes were of considerable advantage to her in conversation at headquarters and by telephone. Her characteristic and persuasive "Hear, now!" at the end of a chat did no harm at all. Co-workers were impressed by her knack for keeping ward heelers enthusiastic when they asked for money with which to push local Thurmond campaigns and there was no money to give. She would flash a smile and promise to "see if we can do something about that real soon."

Another plus factor was her ability to remember names. Upon entering public life seven years earlier, she had recognized the need for a ready knowledge of names and put her memory to work. Consequently, receiving lines and other forms of introductions were much less arduous. At state Democratic conventions she could greet politicians by name without a slip. Members of the General Assembly often were observed banked in a semi-circle around her, waiting to have a word. She would greet each as if he were nothing less than Speaker of the House of Representatives and would ask about his family. In return, every man would beam his pleasure.

During his years in public office, Governor Thurmond had acquired a remarkable knowledge of South Carolina family connections and family trees. He gradually passed the information on to his apt pupil, Jean. Her keen memory took over from there and she became a walking, talking reference service. Whenever her husband's memory failed to click, he automatically turned to her for help. On one such occasion, the Governor spied a familiar face in a crowd. "Hey, I know that man!" he exclaimed. "Why, I know him well. I've known him for years. He's a good friend. In fact, he's one of my best friends. What's his name, Jean?" Amid peals of laughter, the name was supplied. This gift proved an asset at Thurmond headquarters for the write-in campaign.

"Never has Jean Thurmond been more beneficial than right now," a pleased Thurmond worker commented. "There are people who don't know Strom or else don't have any special feeling one way or the other about this election, but they do know and like her. A good many of these have said they'll vote for him because of her. Now, there are also those who say they hate his insides but that they like her. I wouldn't predict which way these'll go."

Meanwhile, the wheels of politics were turning. Governor James F. Byrnes still frowned on the state Democratic executive committee's nomination of his old friend, Edgar Brown. Only three days after the group's action, the Governor had accomplished in one move his dual purpose of slapping the committee's wrists and at the same time honoring an outstanding citizen of the State. He did so by appointing Charles E. Daniel, 59-year-old Greenville industrialist, to finish out the year as U. S. Senator in the late Burnet Maybank's place. Senator Daniel's selection, of course, was a direct slap at the Democratic committee since it ignored that group's choice, Edgar Brown.

Then on September 14th, Governor Byrnes once again asked the committee to rescind the Brown nomination and to call a primary "to do away with bad feeling." There was not a complying peep from either the committee or nominee Brown. In fact, a few days later an Associated Press poll of committee members revealed still the original 31 to 18 line-up against a primary. The organization seemed bent on compounding one blunder into a series by underestimating the public wrath.

The second refusal to hold a primary was made to look even worse by a major strategic move of the Thurmond forces. After a lengthy discussion with his advisers, Strom Thurmond released a news statement on September 18th (three days before the AP poll results were announced) stating that if elected he would resign soon enough in the spring of 1956 to place the position in that year's primary, the first one scheduled after 1954's general election "in order to preserve inviolate the principle of allowing the people to choose a senator." The winner of the primary would serve, of course, the remainder of the term, something over four years. He was making this promise as an act "of faith in the people," he said. "The people would then have a choice in naming the man for the last four years."

In the decision-making stage, Jean Thurmond strongly opposed this idea, as did most of the people around the former Governor.

"She felt it would almost be a miracle for anyone to win on a write-in basis," reminisced Strom Thurmond afterwards, "and that if I won under such difficult circumstances, the people would expect me to serve the full six-year term. Furthermore, Jean felt that justice demanded that I serve the full term out of consideration for the loyal, faithful supporters who would be called upon again in less than two years to wage another campaign."

"Governor Byrnes originally suggested the idea, and some others favored it," Mr. Thurmond recalled. "I listened to the proponents and to the opponents of the novel idea, and, being sympathetic to the proposal, I made the decision forthwith to do it."

Candidate Thurmond claimed the promise to resign would prove further that his race was one of principle. His own instincts led him to feel that such a promise would be right. His reluctant wife, like any other team member, fell in line behind it. As events were to show, the offer to resign after serving fifteen months and to enter the primary election was a smart psychological move—an important one for the Thurmond forces. With the play given by the press, the resignation promise served further to crystallize the issues and to widen the so-called "good guy–bad guy" contrast between the candidates. The Thurmond campaign thereupon gained momentum. In this instance, Jean Thurmond's usually keen insight into the public mind was clouded by another trait of hers—caution. Her husband obviously made the right decision.

About mid-October, the Thurmond camp began to sense a turning of the tide in its favor. Just how much of a ground swell was rising, though, no one was willing to estimate in more than a hopeful guess. The overwhelming support of the press was known to be contributing to the increasing pro-write-in sentiment, but still the overall picture remained hazy. Then Strom Thurmond was striken with food poisoning on October 14th. He was out of action for about ten days, while his organization nervously bit its nails. Mrs. Thurmond left the office long enough to substitute for the candidate at a speaking engagement in Orangeburg on October 19th. She gave there a talk centered around the keynote theme and then hustled back to Columbia to resume regular duties. Though Thurmond supporters did not think so at the time, those anxious ten days actually proved a boon. That slack period followed by the last week's mad flurry of activity brought the write-in campaign to peak on election day.

All the while, the bulk of the State's press was carrying on the fight with daily editorials. On the one hand, they were blasting the state Democratic organization and Edgar Brown; on the other hand, they were exhorting the populace to give the committee its comeuppance by voting for Strom Thurmond. Every few days they featured illustrations on the mechanics of casting a write-in vote on machines and on paper ballots. The press was not sure of its effectiveness until late September when various powers of the South Carolina Democratic organization started lashing out at "the Republican-minded" newspapers—particularly the morning newspapers of Charleston, Greenville and Columbia.

On October 23 Governor Byrnes announced his endorsement of Strom Thurmond. In a lengthy statement the Gov-

ernor discussed the background of the situation and gave
the reasons for his opposition to the Democratic committee's
action. Strangely enough, Edgar Brown had been a friend
in past years, while Thurmond had never been particularly
close. But the present race was drawing Byrnes and Thurmond together. What James Byrnes said in part was:

> ... As Governor, on many occasions I have had to read
> the files as to transactions during Strom Thurmond's term
> as Governor. From the records of this office I know that
> as Governor he was honest, forthright, capable and cou-
> rageous.
>
> Strom Thurmond is clean in his personal life as well as
> in his public life.
>
> No one of us is perfect. Certainly Strom Thurmond
> made mistakes. But there never has been even the breath
> of scandal as to his service either in the state senate, on
> the bench or in the office of Governor. There has never
> been even the slightest suspicion of Strom Thurmond
> ever using public office for personal gain. ...

The Byrnes' prestige added strength to Thurmond's campaign in central, eastern and southern South Carolina, but
hurt among certain labor segments in the Piedmont among
whom the Governor was not popular.

Shortly afterwards, straw polls began to show substantially more sentiment for Thurmond than for Brown, but
the big question in everyone's mind still was just how well
sentiment could be translated into votes—especially write-in
votes. Another worry was whether or not the integrity of
the poll managers, all Democratic regulars, could be trusted.

Edgar Brown was having his worries, too. Well-meaning
friends kept saying the wrong things—at least within earshot
of newsmen.

In an October 4th interview in Washington, U. S. Senator
Olin D. Johnston, who later in the month publicly announced

his support of Edgar Brown, was quoted as saying, "On voting day I don't expect there will be a big turnout. And besides, one out of three people that go to the polls that day will not even know Edgar Brown and Strom Thurmond are running. They will just mark the straight Democratic Party ticket."

The next day at the National Press Club, National Democratic Chairman Stephen Mitchell was asked about the South Carolina senatorial race and Edgar Brown's chances. "They may have a different level of education down there," he answered, "but in Illinois if a man had his name printed on a ballot and if the people had a choice of marking 'X' by his name or writing in the name of J. Strom Thurmond, the man with the printed name would win."

The Johnston and Mitchell statements were pounced on with glee by Thurmond workers and were construed to mean that Olin Johnston had said South Carolinians cannot read and Stephen Mitchell that they cannot write. Write-in supporters had a field day playing up these alleged insults.

Mr. Brown's happiness did not increase with the publication of a telephone interview October 15th with ex-President Harry S. Truman's one-time military aide, Major-General Harry H. Vaughan, at his home in Alexandria, Virginia. Recalling that Strom Thurmond had run for President in 1948, Major-General Vaughan was quoted as commenting that Harry Truman "can forgive small things like rape and murder but he can't forgive a guy that goes back on his party." The former Truman aide went on to add that he joined the ex-President in supporting Edgar Brown. In view of anti-Truman feeling still existent in South Carolina, public endorsement from Truman quarters was considered by State Senator Brown not to be in his best interests. He promptly claimed that the State's newspapers were playing the Vaughan interview in such a way as to prejudice voters.

The final political mistake of the Brown campaign was a

speech to a meeting of the Columbia Junior Chamber of Commerce on October 13th. In the speech he accused Strom Thurmond of "desertion" of the Democratic Party in 1952 by the latter's public support of General Dwight Eisenhower for President. To elect Thurmond, he said, would be to give aid and comfort to the Republicans.

Soon after this address, a flicker of recollection stirred in Jean Thurmond's mind as she worked at write-in headquarters. It seemed to her that at some point in the not-too-distant past, Edgar Brown had made a statement saying he regarded Strom Thurmond and Fielding Wright as the only Democrats to run in 1948's presidential election and had indicated his support of Thurmond in that election.

"If this statement can be traced down, it may give us a chance to corner Edgar on this very thing of party loyalty he's emphasizing so much right now," she said hopefully.

Telephoning her friend William D. Workman, Columbia correspondent of the Charleston *News and Courier,* she asked if he remembered such a remark by the Barnwell legislator. Could there be anything on it in the voluminous Workman files? He did have a similar recollection and forthwith dug into his records. Bill Workman then fed the information to Mrs. Thurmond, who assumed the story was from *The News and Courier.* She passed the material on to her husband to use in a speech at Laurens on October 26th.

Former Governor Thurmond told his Laurens audience that if Senator Brown considered him a deserter from the Democratic Party for supporting General Eisenhower in 1952, then Edgar Brown himself was guilty of the same disloyalty to the National Democratic Party in 1948 by supporting the Thurmond-Wright States' Rights Democratic presidential ticket. Giving as his source *The News and Courier* of October 17, 1952, Thurmond quoted Senator Brown as saying, "We voted for Thurmond and Wright four years ago because they were the candidates of the Democratic

Party of South Carolina and because they were the best Democrats in the race." His opponent's code of loyalty had changed with the years, charged the former Governor.

Immediately Edgar Brown released a statement saying he had just read *The News and Courier* of October 17, 1952 from cover to cover in a vain effort to find the story to which Mr. Thurmond had referred. The Thurmond statement, he declared was "malicious" and "utterly untrue . . . a tissue of lies." Senator Brown added that he personally had never voted for Thurmond "at any time for anything."

Jean Thurmond hastily checked back with W. D. Workman (himself a Republican candidate for the U. S. Senate eight years later against the same Democratic organization). The information came, he told her, from a story in the October 10, 1952 edition of the Columbia *State,* not *The News and Courier.* The newspaper contained the complete text of a radio talk Edgar Brown had made at that time from his Barnwell office on behalf of Adlai Stevenson's candidacy for the presidency. Both Mr. Workman's file copy and the printed version of the speech had been released by Democratic headquarters in 1952 and contained the reference to Thurmond and Wright.

Write-in headquarters rushed out photostatic copies of the story as it had appeared in *The State* two years earlier. On Wednesday, October 27th, a news conference was held by the former Governor at headquarters, and he produced the photostats. The incorrect source of the story, he said, was "due to a clerical mistake" in his office.

Issuance of the photostats quickly pushed Senator Brown back into the corner from which he thought he had extricated himself. On October 29th Brown made a further effort to maneuver out of his uncomfortable spot by asserting that his opponent was "misrepresenting the truth." He had not been speaking "personally" in 1952 but "as chairman of the Democratic Party of South Carolina."

Senator Brown in his prepared statement went on to say

that the preliminary text of his 1952 speech had contained the reference to Thurmond and Wright as "the best Democrats in the race" but that the reference had been deleted in actual delivery. He demanded that newspapers which had carried the "incorrect version" of the speech "be decent enough to print in the same place . . . the exact language which I did use."

No sooner did the Brown release get to various editorial desks throughout the State than Jack O'Dowd, executive editor of the *Florence Morning News*, started going through his files. He wrote for his own publication an answering story which was picked up by the Associated Press and circulated for release on Sunday, October 31st. Mr. O'Dowd maintained that Senator Brown really had not deleted in his radio talk, as claimed, the reference to Thurmond and Wright as "the best Democrats in the (1948) race." The writer said he had followed the talk with the prepared speech in hand, crossing out deletions as they had occurred during delivery. The phrase in question, therefore, had not been omitted, Mr. O'Dowd asserted.

Once again, and as a sort of climax to the whole peculiar senatorial campaign in which Edgar Brown had been plagued by blunders, he found himself slammed hard into the party loyalty corner. The day was October 31st, and he would remain against the wall through election day. There was too little time for further maneuvering. A kind of poetic irony hovered over the situation, somehow, in that Senator Brown was being trapped by the very issue he had made the basis of his appeal to the voters.

Back at write-in headquarters, her fellow workers were commending Jean Thurmond for this last significant contribution to her husband's bid for the Senate. The encounter which she had engineered seemed now to be an important tactical move in this fight against difficult odds.

As election day dawned, November 2nd, the tension at Thurmond headquarters was almost overbearing. There were

so many imponderables in this election that no prediction on
the outcome could be made without qualifying "ifs." In mid-
October, W. D. Workman went out on a limb to forecast a
Thurmond victory, but practically everyone else was giving
the former Governor at best only a "fair" or maybe even a
"good" chance. Most people felt that the write-in movement
had come a long way from its inception in early September,
but still this kind of thing had never been done before in
the quest for a major office. What magic combination of
factors could possibly work now to bring success? Thurmond
workers were fretting more than ever on election morning.

"We may have a lot of feeling going for us," they said,
"but will people be able to master the mechanics of voting?"

To help their supporters do just that, Thurmond headquarters had come up with an idea that strategists figured
could make a difference between success and failure of the
campaign. Thousands of small pencils with "Write in Strom
Thurmond" printed on the sides were purchased along with
an equal quantity of sample ballots. Both items were dis-
tributed at polls throughout the State by Thurmond people.
It was pointedly suggested that citizens take their "write-in"
pencils and sample ballots into the voting booths so they
could see on the pencils how to spell Strom Thurmond and
could see on the sample ballot where to write in the name.
Whether or not the idea would pay off remained to be seen.
Never had pencils and a knowledge of spelling been so
crucial to the outcome of an important race.

An unexpected sidelight was the almost complete absence of the secret ballot at polls where voting machines
were used. For one thing, onlookers could see below the
curtains and note the stance of each voter, particularly in
the case of women. If the voter had her feet firmly planted
on the floor, she was voting for Edgar Brown. If she were
on tiptoe or on a stool, she obviously was writing a name—
most likely that of Strom Thurmond—in the write-in slot high
on the face of the machine. The most telltale indication of

all was the loud click—or absence of same—of the shutter over the write-in slot. Voters emerging from the theoretical seclusion of the booth were greeted by choruses of "We know how you voted!" from those waiting in line. Citizens became indignant, but there seemed to be nothing anybody could do to remedy the situation. In the background, Thurmond poll watchers counted clickers, while Brown watchers counted non-clickers.

The Thurmond organization's strangest ally—and one never remotely envisioned—was plain, simple human curiosity, the kind that motivates people to reach behind "wet paint" signs to touch the paint. Having heard so much about write-in voting, a surprising number of Brown supporters lifted the shutter of the write-in slot "just to see what was there," not to write anything. They found to their consternation that lifting the shutter automatically locked the machine and prevented them from pressing the Brown lever. Incensed, they did the next best thing—wrote the name of Edgar Brown in the slot. The votes still did not count because it was illegal to count write-in votes for a candidate whose name was already printed on the machine. These little quirks of nature and machine were the last straws, the final thwarting twist of fate to State Senator Brown, who supposedly had all the voting mechanics on his side.

While Thurmond headquarters stewed over the possible outcome of the election, Mr. and Mrs. Thurmond left Columbia for the two-fold purpose of voting in Aiken and of working at the polls until closing time. It was during their return trip to Columbia that evening that they heard the first election returns over the radio.

By the time they reached the Hotel Columbia at nightfall, the early returns were trickling over the wire and the write-in forces could hardly believe what they were seeing. The lead continued to grow until ultimately with all the returns in, Strom Thurmond, carrying thirty-seven counties, had a fantastic 143,444 votes to Edgar Brown's nine counties

and 83,525 votes. The final margin of victory was amazing
to veteran political observers who shook their heads in wonder that a write-in candidate in South Carolina could not
only seriously challenge the official Democratic nominee but
could go on to defeat him and to defeat him decisively.
Edgar Brown had possessed all the advantages the state
party machinery could place on his side. This was an array
that had not been beaten since Reconstruction; yet it was
going down on this momentous night. The thirty-one men
who had pushed Brown's nomination through the executive
committee and Senator Brown himself had grossly miscalcu-
lated both the anger of the voters and their ability to reflect
their anger at the polls.

The realization began to sink in at Thurmond headquarters with each passing hour after closing of the polls that
the write-in movement was pulling off a miracle in American
politics. The historical significance of the election's outcome
dawned more and more clearly on everyone. Soon, well-
wishers were swarming into the noisy, joyous Hotel Columbia to congratulate the new junior United States Senator
from South Carolina.

To no one was the significance of this night more pro-
foundly moving than to the 28-year-old wife of the victorious
candidate. She was exhausted from two grueling months of
political campaigning and from the accompanying mixture
of worry, hope and pure nervous tension. When it became
obvious with the mounting returns and building excitement
that former Governor Strom Thurmond was, indeed, the
victor, Jean Thurmond's pent-up emotions could not hold
up any longer. She slipped upstairs to the Thurmonds' personal suite, where her mother was sitting with two members
of the campaign staff. The new senator's wife fell into her
mother's lap, put her head on Mrs. Crouch's shoulder and
sobbed. The impossible had just been done. Strom Thurmond had become this night the first man in history to be
elected by write-in vote to either house of Congress. He

had become the first to win any major state or national
office by the write-in method. These facts alone assured him
a special niche in history. The battle had been fought, the
victory won, and this slim, youthful woman weeping on her
mother's shoulder here had been a big factor in winning it.

However, Jean soon dried her tears and rejoined her
husband to shake hands with throngs of supporters. The
new Senator made a talk to the crowd, publicly acknowledging the "dynamic role" Jean had played in the election.
This was the moment that established Jean Thurmond firmly
and permanently as a tremendous asset to her husband's
career. It was also the moment that established Strom and
Jean Thurmond in the public eye as a successful team because it was as a team that they had wrought this victory.

The write-in victory surprised the whole country, and it
was, without question, the most spectacular achievement in
the lives of Strom and Jean Thurmond. They had come
quite a distance since the troubling weekend in early September when they decided to make the fight. The Thurmonds were now very much back on the political scene.

Meanwhile, the outcome of the senatorial race was being
attributed by Edgar Brown to the people's having been
"misled" by the press.

"I feel that the more than 100,000 others who voted,"
he said after thanking his own supporters, "were misled
and didn't vote against me but voted for a symbol, which
had been manufactured for them by the Republican press
of the State." Earlier in the evening he had issued a statement saying only, "It appears from the returns that I have
received that Mr. Thurmond will be South Carolina's next
junior Senator."

This historic election of a write-in candidate to the Senate
drew front page headlines and editorial comment all over
the nation. It was agreed generally that the election had
been a real demonstration of the power of the press. Edgar
Brown in his own way said as much. When the write-in

movement began in early fall, people knew that if it were
to make a respectable showing, even as a protest, the movement would need the support of most of the State's press,
and the support would have to be more than tacit. It would
have to be crusading. It was.

The morning after the election, the pro-write-in newspapers, especially the leading influences of Charleston,
Greenville and Columbia, were exhausted but exuberant.
The Charleston *News and Courier*, which received a jour-
nalistic award for its part in the campaign, was somewhat
dazed by the feat it had helped accomplish. Long a militant
champion of lost causes, the publication hardly knew how
to act in its unaccustomed position on the winning side.
With surprising restraint, the newspaper confined its pride
to reasonably modest bows.

Personalities aside and judging the write-in election on
issues, it could be considered one of the most healthful,
wholesome political events ever to take place in South Carolina. It was a protest movement of the people that got
somewhere—got somewhere through unity of support and
action. One unhappy aspect of southern history in the past
had been the temperamental extremes of the people. Citizens
either dissipated their strength through such hotheaded
stubborn independence that they wrangled among themselves and took off in a dozen directions at once; or they
just as stubbornly remained glued to a tradition of genera-
tions and got nowhere because they were unwilling to
change old habits. Election day, November 2, 1954, therefore, was deeply meaningful to the people of South Carolina.

V

The Political Phenomena
Go to Washington

WITH the ringing acclaims
of victory still resounding in their ears and yet with the
prospects of a chilly Democratic welcome before them,
Senator-elect and Mrs. Strom Thurmond left Aiken by automobile for Washington after church on Sunday morning,
January 2, 1955.

The couple had packed only the clothes they would
need during the few days prior to locating and settling into
an apartment. After a final round of farewells, they were
on their way "with Jean driving and Strom advising."

Just south of Richmond, Virginia, the next day, the Thurmonds pulled off the highway to fill up on gasoline. Instead
of retaking his seat in the automobile as Jean prepared to
drive away, the Senator told her to go on ahead a mile or
so and to wait for him while he limbered up with a little
sprint along the side of the road. He thereupon shed his
coat and took off at a jogging run toward Richmond. In due
course, a laughing Mrs. Thurmond got him back into the

car and sped on to Washington. Her greeting to the office staff was, "Well, I want you to know that the new junior Senator from South Carolina ran part of the way to Washington!"

Despite car weariness and the fact that both had been to Washington many times, the Thurmonds still were somewhat awed by the lovely city, the aura of glamour in the atmosphere and the thought that now they were part of the exciting official life.

They were awed even more—"shocked" would be a better word—by the high rental costs. Washington was indeed a different world from drowsy little Aiken. The Thurmonds found a two-room and kitchen apartment in The Woodner, a well-known, luxurious hotel overlooking Rock Creek Park. After another move, they settled permanently in 1957 at the Potomac Plaza, a new apartment building on Virginia Avenue in Washington's Foggy Bottom section about three miles from the Capitol.

Strom Thurmond and thirty-three other newly-elected senators of the 84th Congress were sworn in by Vice President Richard Nixon and attended their first joint session of Congress on Wednesday, January 5th. Beside his wife looking down on proceedings from the gallery, were the Senator's sister, Gertrude, a sister-in-law, Mrs. J. W. Thurmond, and her children, Betsy, Ellen, and Billy. They were joined by a number of other South Carolinians, all close friends of the Thurmonds. Afterwards, Senator and Mrs. Thurmond entertained some twenty special guests, Senator Olin Johnston among them, at a luncheon in the old Supreme Court room of the Capitol.

Ever since election day the Thurmonds had wondered along with everyone else, just how much of a welcome they would receive from the Democratic hierarchy of Congress. True, the Senator had stated at the beginning of his write-in campaign that he was running as a "South Carolina Democrat" and that if elected he would vote with the Democratic

Party in Congress, but the memory of the 1948 States' Rights movement still was uncomfortably vivid in people's minds. The South Carolinian's defiance of the national party had not endeared him to the party faithful. Just recently there had been grim mutterings from some quarters that he would be shown only the barest courtesies; that he deserved nothing. People would be watching, it was pointed out, and he had better behave himself. In short, for the first two years, he should attend to the business of learning how to be a senator, indulge in no flamboyancies, and above all, keep quiet.

A hard fact of life to the Democrats, though, was proving to be a point in the new senator's favor, and this fact was not lost on the Democratic leadership. The fact was that the Democrats needed Senator Thurmond's vote to enable them to organize as the majority party of the Senate. The November election had resulted in a count of forty-eight Democrats (including Thurmond), forty-seven Republicans and one independent, Senator Wayne Morse of Oregon, who had renounced his Republican ties. Senator Morse decided to join the Democrats, making forty-nine. If the new South Carolina Senator were to be frozen out by the Democrats because of his 1948 presidential race, then there would be a split of 48–47 in the Senate. If Thurmond were forced to join the Republicans there would be an even split of 48–48 in which case Republican Vice President Nixon, of course, would vote with the Republicans and break the tie in their favor. This situation left the South Carolina Senator in a strategic position.

Senate Majority Leader Lyndon B. Johnson of Texas took the lead in being friendly to the Carolinian. He went out of his way to appear cordial to his freshman colleague. This one instance was an example of the astute Texan's ability to use the "right" approach on fellow legislators. Other southern senators in key positions also "looked out" for Thurmond in seeing that he was not exiled to complete

oblivion. The Senate leadership's "sunshine" treatment resulted in Thurmond's drawing three committee assignments:
Public Works, Government Operations, and Interstate and
Foreign Commerce. These were certainly par for a freshman
and compared favorably with the assignments of other new
senators.

Having been accepted by the Senate, the Thurmonds
found the "sunshine" treatment in effect socially as well.
Their engagement book was packed with functions that
they made a point of attending for several reasons. First,
they went to everything to which they were invited to meet
people. Secondly, as newcomers, they were expected to go
to most functions. Not until later does the courage—and
the physical necessity—develop to weed out the activities
that mean the least to one's particular interests.

On her part, Jean went to women's affairs because she
felt strongly that in this way she was helping to re-establish
her husband in the Democratic Party's good graces. It was
essential, she felt, that Senator and Mrs. Thurmond convey
images of conventionality. For this last reason especially,
she went to more events than she ordinarily would have
been inclined to attend. She was an extrovert by nature but
stretched her pace to exhausting lengths for the sake of
getting Senator Thurmond's Washington career off to a good
start. Teas, receptions, luncheons, and dinners became so
numerous that at one point she wrote to her family in South
Carolina, "I'm about lunched out, but I'm on my way to
another one in just a few minutes. I must run now and put
on my Sunday manners for the luncheon—I'm getting tired
of all this foolishness—wish I could just run around barefooted for a while." The shoes stayed on, though, and very
much on the go.

Thurmond's unique political history, which was the
source of certain apprehension about his Washington reception, was at the same time the thing that made him stand
out among new legislators at the Capitol. That political

uniqueness coupled with the Senator's storybook marriage
to a young, personable woman also made the Thurmonds
as a couple stand out socially among newcomers. People
were intrigued by the tale of the mature governor who had
married his 21-year-old secretary. They were intrigued by
the story of both the 1948 presidential race and the 1954
senatorial write-in campaign that had brought this pair to
the nation's capital. Moreover, Senator Thurmond just recently had been made a brigadier-general in the Army Reserve and was currently the national president of the Reserve Officers Association. Such an extraordinary couple
aroused more than common interest in the city, and therefore invitations were readily forthcoming. Two invitations
of particular note were one to address the Washington
Board of Trade and another to speak to the Southern Society
in New York City. Both were regarded as high honors.

Otherwise, Senator Thurmond worked at learning his
way around Capitol Hill and at getting his office into full
operation. Just as he had "trained" his wife—to the extent
that she would accept the instruction—in the military manner of operating a household for maximum efficiency, Strom
Thurmond used the same approach in organizing his new
Washington office (located at first in the Old Senate Office
Building, then changed several years later to the new building).

With great pride he composed what finally amounted
to a booklet of standard operating procedures and duties
for each staff member. In later years he delighted in passing
along copies, upon request, to other senators who admired
his system.

Friends could not resist smiling at this typical Thurmond
procedure. Fellow officers from World War II remembered
that during the Allied invasion of Europe, or for that matter
almost any time on active duty—Thurmond worked harder
and later than others around him. The light in his tent
burned late every night as he kept a string of subordinate

officers shuttling back and forth on assignments. Not only
did he work hard, but he worked thoroughly and according
to the manual. He was strictly the spit-and-polish military
man who did things according to prescribed procedures.
He put up with little foolishness. Thurmond always regarded
military methods as tremendously efficient; therefore, it was
inevitable that his office should reflect this feeling. Even
today he automatically falls back on S.O.P. for any situation
that occurs.

The Senator had, too, a military passion for visual aids.
Nothing impressed him more than a vast array of charts,
diagrams, pictures and such material. If these could be covered, then revealed dramatically at the right psychological
moment, so much the better.

The Senator's private office was described once as "a
reservoir of All That Has Been Good." It contains items
ranging from books on democracy and the Constitution to
barbells and food supplements. When moving in, he placed
behind his desk the American and Confederate flags. On
the walls he put neat row upon neat row of award plaques,
framed photographs, degrees, certificates and magazine cov-
ers picturing him at different points in his career. Through
the years more of the same have been added, along with a
large number of both favorable and unfavorable political
cartoons. Now, a mere glance about the room picks up a
synopsis of the Strom Thurmond story. While the Senator
was setting up his office, Mrs. Thurmond was working at
her job. Like every other Congressional wife entering Washington's official life, Jean Thurmond felt lost. Like the others
she had heard of formal city life, of the exclusiveness of
the Senate and had wondered if and how one met all these
people. She, too, had known the newcomer's nervousness
over whether or not she was doing things correctly, but
having had experience as a governor's wife, she probably
was less confused than some. Also she had the saving grace

of youthful enthusiasm and a certain gay irreverence that could relegate trivia to its appropriate level.

"Do you suppose they really leave all those calling cards with the corners turned down just so?" she asked with a grin and a twinkle in her blue eyes after boning up on Washington etiquette. "I think I'll do just as I have always done—do what seems right—and wait and see."

There are few things in Washington more nerve-racking to a new Senate wife than calling on the "proper people." The "proper people," according to tradition, are the First Lady, the Vice President's family, the Senate majority leader's home, the homes of one's husband's fellow committee members, and finally the homes of the state Congressional delegation. However, a brave generation of new wives in recent years has ignored to a surprising extent this prescribed etiquette, traditional though some still may consider it. History reveals that even at the turn of the century wives were irked by the system, and some dared occasionally to buck it.

One of the first items of business every two years as a new Congress convenes is the Congressional Club's practice of telling new wives what to do about the whole ghastly procedure of calls and calling cards. The Congressional Club, which has its own building in downtown Washington, is composed of the wives of all members of Congress, the wives of the Supreme Court Justices and wives of the Cabinet members. Its activities are among the more important ones for official wives in the city. Possibly one of its most helpful functions is acquainting newcomers with Capitol etiquette.

Jean Thurmond's bubbling youth and humor took much of the terror out of social calls and receptions during those cold, mid-winter weeks of 1955. At the same time the national press was attracted to the tall, slim Southern girl. Inadvertently dropping conversational "r's" all over the place and flashing a disarming, unsophisticated smile, she found during her first month in Washington that hardly a day was passing without a request from the news media for an interview. The colorful, independent-minded Senator was having a similar experience, of course. On some occasions, the couple were interviewed together.

Shortly after getting to Washington in January 1955, the new senators of the 84th Congress and their wives appeared together for a special program at one of the city's television stations. This coverage was part of the usual attention given by the news media to new faces on the national scene. There was nothing special about the telecast except that a lasting by-product of the occasion was the introduction of Mrs. Thurmond to a colleague who would become not only her closest friend in Washington but also one of the closest of all friends. The colleague, just as new and confused as Jean, was brunette, dark-eyed Welda Allott, wife of recently-elected Senator Gordon Allott of Colorado.

The casual meeting of the two women at a television studio resulted in one of the unlikeliest yet obviously one of the most congenial friendships Jean Thurmond enjoyed in her entire adult life. The basis for it could not have been less conducive to friendship, so the fact that the two were drawn to each other would have to be considered one of the unexplainable, remarkable facets of human nature. Jean Thurmond was twenty-eight, and the southern wife of a notably conservative Democratic senator from South Carolina. Welda Allott was twenty years older than Jean and the western wife of a liberal Republican senator from Colorado. These two backgrounds could hardly have had less in common.

People in the Capitol came to look upon Jean Thurmond's vivacious gaiety and sense of humor as the perfect balance wheel to her more serious husband. These were the same qualities that the Allotts of Lamar, Colorado, enjoyed in her as the two couples often ate at one another's apartments.

The matter of eating invariably reminded Senator Thurmond of his health foods, and as night follows the day, he could not resist dispensing bits of wisdom about good eating habits to the western couple. Witnesses recall seeing him guide Mrs. Allott around huge tables of delicacies at elaborate Washington affairs as he pointed out in his best fatherly tone the healthful foods good for her and the unwholesome ones she ought not to touch. Mrs. Thurmond would observe in unsubdued amusement. Whatever success the Senator had in teaching Mrs. Allott about the merits of other dishes, he made no progress at all on the subject of his beloved, southern turnip greens. She steadfastly refused to appreciate their virtues.

When her free time was not applied to shopping, swimming, or horseback riding, Jean often drove up to Frederick, Maryland, to visit the family of her brother, Dr. Robert Crouch, who soon established his medical practice there. Most of her spare time, however, was spent in the Senate gallery or on special reading for her husband. The net result was that she became recognized as one of the best informed women in Washington.

The reading was not of the pleasure variety. Mrs. Thurmond's hours were consumed mainly in going through the many newspapers and periodicals which came to them. The Senator simply did not have the time to cover all, so she read and marked the articles, editorials or paragraphs she thought he should see—"my husband's parallel reading" she called it.

Greatly treasured were the occasional nights that both Senator and Mrs. Thurmond were free and could relax before the television set or over their stacks of periodicals. Like most Senate couples, they found that attending "must" events filled their social docket. On those rare nights at home, after dinner the Senator still had to attend to at least some Senate business. A great deal of his time was applied to the study of pending legislation. "I study harder now than I ever have in my life," he often remarked, "just to keep abreast of bills coming before the Senate and of other matters on which I must be informed."

The traditions of the United States Senate, frequently termed "the world's most exclusive club," dominate and color the official lives of both the members and their wives. Membership in the club is limited, of course, since only the vice president and the senators of the fifty states belong. Only 101 people can be eligible at one time. This highly restricted group is as proud as any to be found on earth.

The "Ladies of the Senate," as the wives are called, likewise number only a few. They attempt to carry out in their own sphere the spirit and traditions of the U. S. Senate, which gives them reason for official existence.

Into this special world of the Senate came Strom and Jean Thurmond. One of the first things they learned, however, was that the spirit of reconciliation and cordiality shown by the Senate leadership did not seem to affect the relationship between the new junior Senator and his old political rival, Olin D. Johnston, senior Senator from South Carolina. Newsmen noted that at the swearing-in ceremony the two men entered the chamber by different doors. Moreover, they did not exchange greetings of any sort until Senator Johnston escorted Senator Thurmond forward. The faces of both were passive, indicating neither friendliness nor animosity. On a daily basis the lack of communication between the two senatorial offices was a well-known fact during those early years. It was obvious that the rough, all-out battle between the two men for the Senate back in 1950 had left deep, bitter feelings. Time eventually would do something toward assuagement, but that time had not yet arrived in January 1955.

This coolness between South Carolina's senators in those first years chilled the atmosphere until it also affected the relationship between the wives. It always had been the custom among Senate wives for the wife of the senior senator of a state to take under her wing the wife of the new junior senator and to introduce her to activities of the women. The lack of rapport between the Johnston and Thurmond offices resulted in a departure from that custom. Mrs. Johnston made no apparent move to help orient Mrs. Thurmond to her new world. Jean Thurmond, in effect, was left on her own to sink or to swim.

"Well," said one established personage in official circles, "here in Washington I've seen many things, but this beats all."

The grapevine of the nation's capital being equipped with keen eyes and ears and a ready voice, word of the situation soon reached Mrs. Richard Nixon, who, as wife of the vice president, was president of the Senate Ladies. Pat Nixon came to Jean Thurmond's rescue and saw to it that the newcomer at least started off at a swim. That initial push was all Jean needed. From then on, she swam—and quite well.

Pat Nixon's graciousness toward the young Senate wife from South Carolina earned Jean Thurmond's everlasting friendship. Through the years, Jean's gratitude to Mrs. Nixon turned to increasing admiration and devotion. One characteristic that especially impressed her was Mrs. Nixon's ability to give people unhurried, undivided attention in spite of her busy schedule. On her part, the vice president's wife treasured the friendship of the southern girl, to whom she referred in after years as "a sincere and enchanting friend."

Of special note to associates in 1955 was the fact that Mrs. Strom Thurmond was the youngest Senate wife participating in women's activities. Most of the others were forty and over; a few still lay claim to their thirties. Jean Thurmond, at twenty-eight, was actually the second youngest Senate wife, but Mrs. John F. Kennedy, wife of the junior Senator from Massachusetts, the youngest at twenty-five, was then with her ill husband in Florida. Jean, there-

fore, represented the youth of this circle in Washington. In
fact, Mrs. Thurmond looked so young, people often mistook
her for a Capitol Hill employee. Fellow students in a law
course Jean took to help her in helping Strom thought she
was merely an eager-beaver secretary. A cab driver once
said to her, "Say, Sis, which one of them old fuddy-duddies
up there do you work for?"

While Senator Thurmond filled his official calendar with
legislative business, speaking engagements and with organizations like the Reserve Officers Association, with which he
was particularly concerned, Mrs. Thurmond filled her official
calendar with women's activities.

For a Senate wife, the Senate Ladies group (meeting
weekly to make Red Cross supplies) and the Congressional
Club were practically "musts." Other organizations which
Jean Thurmond chose for reasons of interest were: the 84th
Congress Club (composed of wives whose husbands were
new in that Congress); the 85th Congress Club (after the
1956 elections); the Democratic Congressional Wives forum
(which held regular discussions on current issues in the
home states of members); and the International Neighbors
Club (composed of some forty or fifty women representing
"residential" Washington, the Cabinet, other executive offices, the diplomatic corps and Congress. The group's purpose was to offer informative political and cultural programs
on areas represented by the membership). Mrs. Thurmond
at various times held secretarial positions or important committee chairmanships in almost all of the organizations.

Hardly had Senator and Mrs. Thurmond settled into
Washington life when it was time for Thurmond to make
good on his pledge to resign and stand for reelection to
the remaining four years of the Maybank term.

"The time has come for me to fulfill my promise to the
people of South Carolina," the Senator said in a news statement on March 3, 1956. "Today I have delivered my letter
of resignation to Governor Timmerman. The text of the
letter states:

"In keeping with the pledge which I made to the people of South Carolina during the 1954 campaign, and in order that the State Democratic Convention can place the office in this summer's primary, I hereby resign as United States Senator effective on and as of April 4, 1956, and I respectfully request that you accept this resignation effective on that date."

"I shall be a candidate for nomination in the primary to succeed myself in the Senate," the junior Senator added. "My resignation will guarantee a free and open primary election for South Carolina Democrats. I believe the course I have taken in resigning, and in making this announcement a month before the effective date, fulfills to the utmost the pledge I made to the people in 1954."

The 1956 primary did not worry the Thurmonds but Jean took on the assignment as coordinator of campaign material. She carefully assembled the usual vast array of documents, position papers and other relevant matter. As expected, no opposition developed by April 5th, the deadline for filing. In the meantime, Governor George Bell Timmerman, Jr., used the Thurmond resignation as an opportunity to make an interim appointment of a friend to the Senate. He named Greenville attorney, Thomas A. Wofford, to the position. Some people wondered why the Governor did not appoint Senator Thurmond for his own vacancy since he had no opposition, but it was the Governor's prerogative to make an appointment of his choice, and he did just that. The cost to the State and to Strom Thurmond was a little seniority, but no lasting harm resulted. When the 85th Congress convened in January 1957, Senator Thurmond was back in his old seat. The following January he realized one of his chief ambitions, membership on the Senate Armed Services Committee.

The 1956 elections also made an impact on Mrs. Thurmond's world. Now firmly established in Washington, she found herself called upon more than ever by the various wives' organizations. Often she was engaged simultaneously in three or four undertakings.

One of the most important assignments Jean Thurmond drew in 1957 was Mrs. Richard Nixon's request that she serve as chairman of the Senate Ladies' annual luncheon for the First Lady. The chairmanship of this luncheon was regarded as a special honor, one not usually bestowed upon a young wife or upon one so new among the Senate Ladies. The only strictly social affair that the group stages each year, the luncheon includes as special guests wives of the Cabinet and of the secretaries of the Army, Navy and Air Force. It is, therefore, fraught with the intricacies of protocol and etiquette—to say nothing of ulcers in the event of slip-ups.

Jean called on her friend Welda Allott to serve as co-chairman, and the two then appointed nine committees to attend to different phases of the May 7th luncheon scheduled to be held in the Senate Caucus room. The chairmen and their committees made innumerable telephone calls and trips through the labyrinth of Capitol Hill in the interest of their big day.

At the appointed hour, Jean and her co-chairman, Mrs. Gordon Allott, met and escorted the First Lady to the door of the Old Supreme Court chamber, where they were to pose briefly for photographers. Suddenly, shouts echoed through the corridor. "Stand aside, stand aside, the Senate is coming through," commanded serious-faced Capitol Police leading a herd of chattering senators. They bore down relentlessly upon Mrs. Dwight Eisenhower, her secretary, and the two Senate Ladies. The men were returning from a joint session of Congress called to hear an address by President Diem of Vietnam.

"Oh yes, of course!" said Mrs. Eisenhower as she and her secretary squeezed against the wall in undisguised retreat.

Mrs. Thurmond and Mrs. Allott, dressed in their Red Cross uniforms, customary attire for meetings of the Senate

Ladies, took flight and threw themselves against the wall a few feet away. At the last minute, courtly Senator Theodore F. Green of Rhode Island, 89-year-old bachelor, took in the situation from the head of the group.

"Let's wait for the ladies," he told his colleagues, motioning them to halt. "We defer to you," he added with a gallant bow. Senators began banking up in confusion at the rear, noisily oblivious to the presence of the First Lady. Quickly a photographer snapped pictures of Mrs. Eisenhower receiving a basket of spring flowers from Mrs. Thurmond as Mrs. Allott watched. The ladies then disappeared into the room for their festivities, and Senator Green again allowed the Senate to move through the hallway.

After the luncheon Mrs. Thurmond escorted the First Lady back to her automobile and betook herself home for a needed nap.

Though she appeared at all the important social functions of her set in Washington, Jean Thurmond seemed to be on Capitol Hill for all the important happenings there, too. Her time and energy were divided almost equally between social and political interests.

"Jean wasn't tied down by family responsibility," an older Senate wife observed, "so she was able to go to the Capitol as much as she did. I'm convinced, though, that she would have gone there a good bit anyway. She was just that interested in legislation."

The remark is almost a paraphrase of one Jean herself made once when she admitted, "I love to follow a piece of legislation through. I find it interesting."

"Youth made a difference, too. She had the energy to do so much going," her colleague added.

Mrs. Strom Thurmond became not only part of the scenery in the family section of the Senate gallery but a special pet to the Senate, where her youth and magnetism won a unique place in the hearts of members and employees alike. She was at the Capitol on the average of two to three days each week, and at times every day in the week—more than any other Senate wife of her time. For that matter, she was in the gallery considerably more often than some of the legislators were on the floor. She became a familiar figure there to local society columnists who often described her attire—characteristically conservative styles with an occasional venture into red. Among reporters she was probably the best known of all the wives. Senators at their desks in the chamber below also noticed her. The men used to acknowledge with a smile or a wave the slender girl sitting so regularly amid the red upholstery of the gallery and looking toward Senator Thurmond on the back row of the Democratic side. She and Majority Leader Lyndon Johnson struck up a folksy friendship. He nearly always looked up at the gallery and greeted her with a wave.

"She made a point of attending the Senate sessions frequently and it was very customary to look up and see her following the debate intently," the Texan and future President of the United States recalled.

On a number of occasions, Mrs. Thurmond sat with Mrs. Allott, Mrs. Herman Talmadge of Georgia, Mrs. Spessard Holland of Florida, or with other Senate wives who happened to be there. At times none of the others were there, and she sat alone.

Whenever an opportunity arose, Jean Thurmond launched into a discussion of legislation with the various senators she came to know during her visits to the Hill. It might be in the Senate restaurant, in an office, a corridor or at an after-hour dinner or reception, but wherever it was she attained a reputation for being able to hold her own and for having definite ideas.

Often she brought up the same issues with other Senate wives, adding, "I imagine your husband discusses this with you." One wife replied, "Why no, he never talks with me about these things." It was clear that Jean was taken in on plans to an unusual extent by Senator Thurmond. She explained that in home discussions, "I often take the other side of an argument to help Strom clarify his thinking on an issue." He talked politics with her not so much because she was his wife, but because of her natural political instincts—her ability to grasp situations and to make helpful suggestions. On her part, she always worried over the possible aftermath of everything the Senator did, especially before the 1956 elections.

Aware of Mrs. Thurmond's anxiety, an acquaintance who wanted her husband to take firmer public stands used to needle her by saying, "When are you going to quit making the Senator be a politician and let him become a statesman? I thought you wanted him to be a statesman."

"Well I do," she would answer, "but let's get through the election of 1956, then let him become a statesman."

Because she was at the Capitol so often and because she was such an active participant in her husband's career, Jean Thurmond found friendly ties with the Senator's office staff a natural part of her life. Too, she was near the age of most staff members, and youth made a congenial bond. The office force came to look upon "Mrs. T.," as the girls called her, as a member of the staff family.

If a controversial issue were pending, Jean Thurmond would draw up a chair and discuss it with administrative assistant Alex McCullough or with Harry Dent, who assumed that position after Alex left to enter private business. Or she would discuss it with the staff legislative research specialist. She and Alex or she and Harry would exchange opinions on what the Senator should or should not do. Around and around they would go, not hesitating to disagree with one another. Yet, when the Senator and his advisers arrived at the final decision, everyone—including Jean —fell in line behind it. The relationship between the staff and the Senator's wife was such that their discussions were always on a friendly, family basis. Mrs. Thurmond often was the staff's best friend. Frequently, when office advisers were getting nowhere with the Senator on a matter, they would present their case to her, asking for help. The next day, the Senator would allow that he had "thought about things overnight" and had changed his mind. His discreet wife never gave the staff away.

The Thurmond office force had a reputation for working like trojans to keep up with the Senator, who worked himself just as hard, if not harder. "I want everything done yesterday," he would say.

Strom Thurmond was a perfectionist. An exceptionally capable personal secretary who worked for him over a period of years saw this aspect of his character brought out vividly one day. As a rule, she was errorless on 95 per cent of her work, but one day the boss caught a typing error in a letter.

"I'm just too busy to have to read for mistakes," he said, displeased. "I want you to get one of the men here on the staff to check these letters before they come to me so I won't have to worry about errors."

The crestfallen girl looked at him blankly.

"Now, mind you, I'm not finding fault," he said hastily, "You're a good secretary, probably the best I've ever had."

"Yessir, I know, Senator," answered his employee with a sigh, "good, but not good enough."

"But, young lady, don't you want to be a perfect secretary?" asked Senator Thurmond earnestly. "You can't blame me for trying," he added brightly.

"Yessir," came the weak reply.

The Senator's efforts to perfect staff members also extended to their physical welfare. Thurmond kept a fatherly eye on everybody's health. He became noticeably disturbed whenever he had reason to think his employees were not eating their vegetables. At times he sent his administrative assistant to oversee everyone's luncheon menu. The reluctant assistant then would try to explain that his presence at lunch, however well meant, would not be appreciated.

Often the Thurmonds had staff bicycle rides and picnics in Rock Creek park. With paternal declarations from the Senator that all needed sun and exercise, the staff would cycle forth manfully on these occasions. By the time everyone neared the agreed-upon destination, the cyclers inevitably were in two groups—the vigorous senatorial couple in the lead and a panting, disheveled pack of office workers bringing up the rear. Those rides in Rock Creek park were not unusual for the Thurmonds. The couple had a set of English bikes with gears and made riding through the park a Sunday afternoon habit. Consequently, they were more accustomed than their staff to strenuous exercise.

In later years Thurmond developed the habit of passing around a memo prior to each weekend he was in the city so office personnel could sign up for Sunday afternoon bike rides. Newcomers generally thought the idea was most democratic—imagine, bicycling with a U. S. Senator! Veteran staffers were considerably less enthusiastic. Nevertheless, if anyone had not been lately, he had better sign up because the Senator had a knack for remembering who had been and who had not been on recent excursions.

"What's the matter with that boy?" asked a puzzled Thurmond one day, noting the absence of a young fellow who had skipped out lately and whom he considered in real need of exercise. "Doesn't he know this is good for him? Tell him to put his name down here." The truant staff member did so without further delay.

The South Carolina legislator has advocated (in vain so far) that bicycle paths be provided alongside interstate highways and in the District of Columbia.

As far as his own health habits are concerned, Senator Thurmond maintains in Washington the same strenuous ones he has observed most of his life. Each morning he goes through calisthenics consisting of push-ups, knee bends, high kicks and a few other muscle-toning exercises. Then he has prune or orange juice, sugarless cereal and fruit with skim milk and wheat germ. At his office, Thurmond's personal secretary takes from a special storage cabinet beside the Senator's desk various food supplements for the Senator's daily pre-lunch consumption. She sets them up on the wide window ledge in the back corridor connecting the inner offices. One item is a bottle of mineral water. With that Thurmond washes down protein-rich, plain gelatin capsules (for energy pick-up) and a combination iron-vitamin B capsule. He avoids fatty foods, cigarettes and alcohol. Occasionally he succumbs to a country breakfast of ham and hominy. The most frequent luncheon choice in the Senate restaurant is chopped sirloin steak on toast (he carefully discards the toast) and leafy green vegetables. About once a week, however, he allows himself a dessert—either pecan pie or cheesecake.

Declares the Senator on the subject of food, "I subscribe whole-heartedly to the theory that 'you are what you eat.' Without question I owe a major part of my vigor to my diet."

"Exercise and high-protein food—they keep you fit," he once told a reporter, adding, "The secret of strength and health is proper eating, proper exercise and reasonable sleep."

The Senator contends that "when you take exercise and feel strong physically, it helps you make decisions. When you make decisions, that relieves tensions. I think tension, to a certain extent, comes from indecisiveness. I'll fight as hard as anyone to accomplish an objective, but if I don't attain the particular objective, I don't worry but look to the future. Although I think it's better to spend an hour a day exercising, I believe anyone could spend twenty minutes a day and keep himself in good physical condition. It's really a matter of whether one is going to merely live or live a full life."

In addition to early morning exercises, the Senator lifts several times daily the barbell he keeps behind his desk.

Moreover, he walks everywhere on Capitol Hill, scorning escalators, elevators and subway trains except when in a rush. He tries in vain to get staff members to do the same. Time and again he urges assistant, J. Fred Buzhardt, Jr., to take the stairway from Thurmond's fourth floor office in the New Senate Office Building. "It'll do you good," he maintains. The usual reply is, "Good for you, maybe, but not for me. I'll see you downstairs." With that, the aide boards the nearest elevator while the Senator takes the stairs at almost a run.

A few years ago, Senator Thurmond and his administrative assistant, Harry Dent, served their active duty stint for the Army Reserves on a trip abroad with other Congressional members of the Reserves. Included in the trip was a side jaunt to some of the pyramids near Cairo, Egypt. Thurmond leaped out of the sightseeing bus and led some of the energetic, younger Congressional assistants at a bound up the narrow, tortuous stairway of one structure to the chamber containing the body of an ancient Egyptian king. Others in the group began to lose interest in the site and one Congressman, trying to make the climb, fell by the way. Harry Dent went to his assistance and helped him back to the bus.

"By that time, of course, it was too late to rejoin the others going up the pyramid," Dent explained unconvincingly.

"You just aren't in condition, Harry," said the exasperated Senator Thurmond upon returning. "How could you miss seeing the king's tomb, anything as historic as that? Besides, going up there was good exercise. You're just not in condition, that's all."

At regular intervals throughout the remainder of the trip, Dent heard about his poor conditioning.

"Boy, you've had it!" remarked an amused fellow Congressional aide to the Thurmond staffman.

Senator Thurmond had a bad moment himself on that

trip when the group visited the national military academy in Turkey. As a major-general, the South Carolina Senator reviewed the corps of cadets. He made an impressive figure —tall (five feet, eleven inches), erect, shoulders back, very much the polished soldier. Shorter Turkish officers trotted to keep up as Thurmond walked with long, quick, military strides. Things having gone well so far, the Senator warmed to the occasion. He rejoined the others for a social gathering on the sun deck of one of the buildings. Toasts seeming to be in order, Thurmond decided to make one. He delivered first an elaborate speech about the brave Turks, their fine record in Korea, what excellent fighters the Turkish soldiers had been. He then proposed a toast to the "good people of Turkey and their friendship with America." He brought to his lips a glass of what he expected to be (and what usually is—for him) apple juice and began downing the contents in one gulp. When he got halfway down the glass, his mouth full, his face suddenly turned red and he choked. Strom Thurmond was struggling with pure Scotch whiskey. There had been a slip-up in liaison. Finally the Senator resolved the dilemma by spitting his mouthful of Scotch back into the glass. Nearby Turks went into a flutter of concern, wondering what awful thing had happened; members of the Congressional party went into ill-concealed snickers.

"Er-ah, I thought this was apple juice," said Senator Thurmond in innocent seriousness.

During the Thurmonds' first years in Washington, Jean had a restraining hand on her independent-minded husband. She was looking ahead to the 1956 elections, of course, but there was another reason prompting her to influence the Senator to stay quietly within the Democratic Party now that he had been more or less forgiven for 1948. It was the womanly need for security, the need to belong somewhere to something. Especially in Washington almost everyone feels the necessity to be part of a group, either Democratic or Republican. Jean Thurmond did not want to be on the outside. It takes a rebel to carve out a place alone, and she was not such a creature. The natural thing to her was to live within the fabric of the Democratic Party. If the issue at stake were important enough, however, Strom Thurmond followed his own judgment regardless of counsel from others and regardless of the consequences.

The first such issue arose in 1956. It concerned the United States Supreme Court's historic 1954 school desegregation ruling.

For some time the freshman Senator from South Carolina had felt that there ought to be some kind of statement or declaration of the southern position on that far-reaching court decision. He finally began in early 1956 approaching other southern senators with this idea of issuing a joint document. A powerful supporter of the idea soon emerged in the person of Virginia's Senator Harry F. Byrd.

Other southern senators were taken aback by the boldness of Strom Thurmond, a second-year senator, in seizing the initiative on a matter of this importance. Why, the fellow was a mere fledgling in the Senate, and he had the nerve to carry the ball on a proposal that should have come from his senior colleagues, leaders of the Senate's "inner circle"! True to form, Thurmond cared not at all what others thought and plunged ahead. When he won Senator Byrd over, other southerners were stunned. That a newcomer would dare come forward with such a proposal was surprising enough, but that he would get away with it—as he seemed assured now of doing—was amazing.

(The Senate soon learned that Strom Thurmond was just as likely to act unexpectedly and boldly in other directions. He belonged to a prayer breakfast group of thirty or more senators. The group met each Wednesday morning at the Capitol, and one of the members customarily gave a talk and led the others in prayer. No one thought it odd that Thurmond should give a talk on Robert E. Lee, but the day he gave a well-thought-out, very moving one on Abraham Lincoln entitled "The Long Road to Faith," fellow legislators were floored. A few years later he broke precedent to bring in a taped speech by a Southern Baptist clergyman against federal aid to church-related institutions and activities. Senatorial eyebrows rose in disapproval as Thurmond set up his tape recorder. The speech however, was so well received that it was followed by one of the best discussions the group had ever had.)

After expressions of doubt and reluctance by some who considered the manifesto useless in the fight against the court decision, almost all the members of the southern bloc in both houses of Congress eventually joined in the official issuance of this declaration, more commonly called the Southern Manifesto.

The manifesto, in essence, said that the Supreme Court's desegregation ruling would be resisted by all legal means. Thurmond prepared the first draft which contained his thoughts on the subject. He then reworked this into a second draft which went before a meeting of southern senators that Byrd and Thurmond, both, had obtained in the face of opposition. When it became apparent that the two men would proceed on their own, if necessary, others agreed to a meeting. Another factor prompting agreement to the sessions was that Senator Walter George of Georgia was up for reelection that year and could use, so it was felt, the political benefits of such a gathering. (As it happened the elderly Senator George retired later that year and did not seek reelection after all.) Senator George, as the Senate's senior southerner, therefore assumed leadership in the undertaking and called a meeting for February 8, 1956, in his office, but by this time Thurmond, rather than George, already had reaped the main publicity as originator of the proposal.

At the meeting, Walter George appointed a drafting committee of Richard Russell (D., Ga.), chairman, John Stennis (D., Miss.) and Sam Ervin (D., N.C.). Thurmond's draft was turned over to the group, and other suggestions were requested. More foot-dragging followed, so upon the prodding of Thurmond and Byrd, another meeting took place. At this time Senators Spessard Holland (D., Fla.), Price Daniel (D., Tex.) and William Fulbright (D., Ark.) offered a draft, a milder one than either Thurmond's or the committee's. The southerners then decided to name a new drafting committee. Chaired again by Russell, the new group included Stennis, Thurmond, Fulbright and Daniel. The committee was authorized to prepare a final draft and to obtain signatures to it, then to turn the document over to Senator George, who would present it to the Senate.

Various southerners in the House showed interest in issuing a similar statement, so a copy of the Russell committee's draft was given to Congressman Howard Smith (D., Va.) for circulation there.

Officially entitled "Declaration of Constitutional Principles," the Southern Manifesto as finally presented on March 12, 1956, carried the names of nineteen senators and eighty-one representatives—nearly 20 per cent of the Congressional membership. The document drew national headlines and much national editorial comment. It was the first expression of opposition to the court decision by any group of such major importance, and it carried the signatures of some of the most prominent members of Congress, including a number of committee chairmen. The paper, consequently, could not be too lightly dismissed.

The after-effects were interesting. The fact that he signed the manifesto was considered a contributing factor in Fulbright's failure to be selected Secretary of State in the Kennedy administration. In general, southerners who failed to sign had trouble getting reelected, and for some years afterward, voters noted the names of signers and of non-signers. Issuance of the declaration also inspired various southern states to "take new heart," as one person described the development, and to pass resolutions vowing resistance by all legal means. Particularly interesting was the conspicuous silence of a number of manifesto signers when debate got underway the next year on a civil rights bill.

It was this 1957 civil rights bill that also became the next Senate issue over which the independent Strom Thurmond exercised his own judgment regardless of opinions and repercussions.

After taking his Senate seat in 1955, Thurmond made a habit of asking himself three questions about new legislation before Congress:

1. Is it constitutional? (The Senator interpreted the Constitution strictly, so there were many proposals that automatically flunked this question. In years to come, Thurmond would acquire a widespread reputation for his strict constitutional views.)

2. Is it wise?

3. Can we afford it?

When a federal civil rights bill came up for debate in the summer of 1957, Strom Thurmond subjected it to his test. The bill failed the first and second questions, in the Senator's opinion, so he did not bother with the third which was not applicable anyway. He thereupon made his opposition known.

The Senate leadership had reached an agreement in mid-August on a compromise civil rights bill with sufficient support to pass the Senate. At the final caucus of the southern senators in Senator Richard Russell's office on Saturday, August 24, 1957, with Senator Thurmond present, it was generally agreed that organized extended debate would not be held. However, it also was agreed that each senator would be on his own to speak as long as he might deem necessary and to oppose the bill as he saw fit.

At the beginning, Thurmond had decided that he would oppose the bill vigorously, so he began that weekend to assemble material for a long speech. When debate resumed on the bill at the first of the week, he found that no long speeches were being made. The junior South Carolina Senator became disturbed that the compromise jury trial provision was not getting the attention of the American public. He was concerned about many provisions of the bill, but he was especially perturbed over the changes which the House had just made in the Senate's jury trial provision.

The southern senators had based the best part of their case against the bill on the question of the right of trial by jury in criminal contempt court cases arising under the legislation. The original legislation had made no provision for jury trial in such cases. In the Senate, however, long and eloquent arguments by the southerners had succeeded in getting into the bill what they considered a good jury trial provision. When the bill went back to the House, opponents of a jury trial provision were successful in compromising this section to provide for what Thurmond called a "split-level" jury trial provision. Under the compromise, a person charged with violating a judge's order could be tried by the same judge and sentenced to confinement for up to forty-five days or fined $300 without having the right to a jury trial. However, if the judge decided to impose a sentence of more than forty-five days or $300 in fine, the case then could be tried before a jury. This part of the bill, according to Thurmond, his southern colleagues and others, was a violation of the right of trial by jury as guaranteed to every citizen in Article III, Section 2, of the Constitution of the United States and also in the Sixth Amendment to the Constitution.

Believing that these points were not being put across to the American public and feeling once again that "somebody ought to do something," the Senator came to the conclusion that he indeed should make a very strong and long speech against the bill. Furthermore, he decided that since the Congress already was approximately one month overdue on adjournment, the southerners ought to give further consideration to the question of organized extended debate against the legislation. When he arrived at these conclusions, he sought out Senator Russell, chairman of the southern group. He met with Senator Russell early Wednesday afternoon, August 28th, in Russell's office. Thurmond informed the southern leader that he would make a long talk against the bill when next called on to speak. He also suggested that Russell call the southern senators into session again to consider the advisability of an organized effort. Senator Russell said that if a majority of the southern senators requested him to do so, he would call them back for another caucus, but that in lieu of such requests, he would not call another caucus because of the previous understanding on Saturday that each senator would follow his own course.

Thurmond was notified shortly thereafter that he was scheduled to speak that evening at approximately nine o'clock. Evidently the Senate leadership was concerned that Thurmond might speak at length, so the 9:00 p.m. spot was assigned to him that he might be closed out by midnight and that he would be talking at a time when few, including newsmen, would be present.

When Thurmond prepared for his one-man task, as he expressed it, of "informing the public on the many bad features of the legislation and especially to dramatize the jury trial compromise to the country," he did not set out to establish a new Senate filibuster record. Such, however, was the ultimate result, and his feat did receive top news treatment throughout the land.

Once plans had been determined, the Thurmond staff hustled around, gathering pertinent material with which to prepare the talk while the Senator prepared himself physically for the long speech. He left to take a steam bath "to dry myself out," he explained, and he followed that up with an afternoon nap. In the meantime, a staff member telephoned Mrs. Thurmond, informed her of arrangements and asked her to prepare a dry, but nourishing, supper for the Senator and to bring it to his office.

Jean Thurmond came to the office with deep misgivings about the wisdom of the proposed speech. She pointed out to her husband possible repercussions of this go-it-alone move. He could expect to lose the good will of any number of fellow senators, including southerners who would regard the speech as merely a one-man show. Moreover, Thurmond enemies in South Carolina could benefit through unfavorable publicity that surely would follow. Actually, he stood to lose all the way around. He was running the risk of hurting himself not only in Washington, but he was risking the loss of support in South Carolina as well.

Nevertheless, Senator Thurmond held to his decision "to educate the country" by means of a comprehensive speech on the subject of the civil rights bill. He took the Senate floor shortly after 8:54 p.m. amid stacks of material supplied by his staff. There with him were administrative assistants Alex McCullough and Harry Dent. Both men were to remain at the Senator's beck and call throughout that speech and were to emerge at the end more weary than he. In the chamber were some fifteen senators. In the gallery were about two hundred spectators; conspicuous among them was Jean Thurmond, dressed simply in a navy knit suit. During the civilized hours of the night, she had with her in the family section at various times, her brother, Dr. Robert Crouch, who had driven down from Frederick, Maryland, to keep her company, Representative John McMillan of South Carolina, other South Carolinians and friends who came to watch the proceedings.

Senator Thurmond launched into his marathon talk with a low, barely audible recitation of the election laws of the states—in alphabetical order. On and on he droned for hours. About 1:30 Thursday morning, Senator Barry Goldwater of Arizona gave him a break by taking the floor temporarily to read a lengthy report on military manpower policy. Afterwards, the South Carolinian was again on his own.

As the wee, pre-dawn hours came on, the Senate chamber presented a curious sight. The gallery was empty except for two people—the strangest combination imaginable. Mrs. Thurmond, a lonely frail figure in blue, still sat in the family section. Not far away in another section was Clarence Mitchell of the National Association for the Advancement of Colored People. Down below, the light picked up Senator Joseph Clark of Pennsylvania, the presiding officer, as he leaned back in the Senate President's tall, leather chair. A handkerchief was over his face, and he obviously was asleep. Directly in front, teams of stenographers took turns scribbling away for the Congressional Record and posterity every monotoned word from the southern senator at the rear of the chamber.

Not everyone's attention was focused on the slowly speaking Senator Thurmond. A news correspondent for South Carolina newspapers made this observation:

It was the balding senator who babbled through the night on the floor, but it was his bride of a decade, whose gaily sparkling eyes and flashing smile belied her normally demure pose, who caught the eyes of all present as she cheered him on from the galleries.

Mrs. Jean Thurmond joined Clarence Mitchell of the NAACP in looking down on the brightly lit floor where her husband battled manfully but apparently in futility for the southern way of life.

At intervals, Mrs. Thurmond left the gallery to join the racially mixed coffee party in a nearby ladies lounge; occasionally she became wrapped up in a hefty and obviously intoxicated doorkeeper who at one point roared gleefully for all to hear, "Honey, at last we're all alone." Mrs. Thurmond at that point fled the gallery in the direction of the mixed group quaffing coffee.

The cheerful Mrs. Thurmond had other burdens during the night—newsmen, Senate staff members, members of her husband's own staff, and even a senator, swarmed around her as bees to a flower.

As soon as the Senate cafeteria opened Thursday morning, Mrs. Thurmond again left the gallery—long enough this time to add a bowl of cereal to those cups of coffee. Her husband still was discussing the civil rights bill point by point between long interspersements of what he considered other pertinent material. He had gone progressively from election laws to recitation of the criminal contempt decisions of Chief Justice William Howard Taft and was due to go on to the history of the Anglo-Saxon jury system and to more on the American Constitution.

About 7:00 a.m., when the South Carolina senator should have been utterly exhausted, and his entourage thought everyone soon would be heading home to sleep, Senator William F. Knowland of California, Senate Republican leader, came into the chamber. Immediately the Californian started needling the apparently weary Thurmond about his purposes in filibustering. Rather than finishing off the southerner, Senator Knowland merely reinspired him. The stubborn Carolinian caught second wind and actually seemed to become stronger as he continued to drone on steadily.

However, staffmen McCullough and Dent were becoming increasingly fearful that the filibuster had reached the point of diminishing returns and begged him to stop by nine o'clock. They were unsuccessful. About the only comments from the Senator were periodic instructions to tell Jean, whom he could observe still in the gallery, to go somewhere to sleep. She responded by remaining obstinately in her seat. While well-rested senators and spectators began filing into the chamber, sleepy, red-eyed staff members shuttled back and forth between the filibustering husband and the listening wife.

The staff presently sought Mrs. Thurmond's aid in stopping the Senator. She said, "He must know what he is doing. He seems to have an extra sense about such things. I've seen him do things before on instinct. Maybe we better not push him."

Taking a mid-morning break from her exhausting vigil, Jean Thurmond went into the corridor to eat a chicken sandwich and to chat with reporters.

"I'm not really tired," she pretended, "but my eyes do burn a bit. I wish I'd brought some eyewash. Have I got any dark circles yet?" She was getting dark circles, but otherwise seemed to be bearing up surprisingly well.

While his wife talked with newsmen outside, Senator Thurmond on the floor was in his discussion of the Anglo-Saxon jury system. He was making the compromise provision on jury trials in the civil rights bill his chief target. The provision would provide jury trials in the right-to-vote measure only in cases involving stiff sentences. The bill would allow a judge to give an unlimited series of minor sentences to a defendant. A string of short-term imprisonments would amount to the same thing eventually as one long imprisonment, so actually the compromise jury provision did not give much protection after all. This point formed the crux of the Senator's argument.

Senator Paul Douglas of Illinois strode into the chamber shortly before noon and placed a pitcher of orange juice on the South Carolinian's desk. After allowing the Senator a few sips, Harry Dent hid the tempting pitcher on the floor and handed the legislator malted milk tablets instead. Before the marathon address ended, the orange juice was consumed, too.

A short break came at one o'clock to allow the swearing-in of Senator William Proxmire of Wisconsin, newly-elected to fill the deceased Senator Joseph McCarthy's unexpired term. Other breathers came during the course of the day when several colleagues engaged in prolonged questioning— "just to give the fellow a break," said one of them, Senator

William Langer of North Dakota, who actually favored the bill.

The galleries having refilled during the day, Senator Thurmond took on new vigor. On the other hand, senatorial tempers wore thinner and thinner as the hours wore on to twilight. Much side chatter was taking place. When cornered by the press about the bill's timetable, Majority Leader Johnson said in midafternoon, "No other speeches of unusual length are scheduled, but the one being delivered now was not scheduled either."

At nightfall, Mrs. Thurmond went down to the Senate floor momentarily to ask the two staff members whether or not her husband was all right physically. "And how much longer does he plan to talk?" she wanted to know. To that question no one knew the answer, not even Strom Thurmond.

Don White of the *New York Herald Tribune* described the Senator at this stage thusly: "The tall, gaunt Democrat dressed in Confederate Gray was teetering on weary legs and his voice had the dry rasp of a harvester in a drought-parched cotton field as he droned past the old mark of 22 hours, 26 minutes held by Sen. Wayne Morse, D. Ore."

South Carolina's junior Senator at last gave up the floor at 9:13 p.m. Thursday. He could have gone on longer, but Dr. George W. Calver, Senate physician, entered the chamber between eight and nine o'clock. He told Thurmond staffmen the Senator would injure his health if he continued and to get him off the floor. If the staff could not stop the legislator, "I'll take him off the floor myself," Dr. Calver stated firmly.

Before concluding, the South Carolina Senator entertained the now packed galleries with some dry humor.

"Mr. President," he addressed the chair, "a few years ago, when I was a young state senator, I made a commencement address in another county, about forty miles from my home. The commencement was held in a long school build-

ing in which the acoustics were very bad. People in the
rear could not hear, and looked as if they were going to
sleep—and maybe they were. So I raised my voice, and
said, 'Ladies and gentlemen, I want you to know that I am
speaking for the future citizens of South Carolina.' By raising
my voice, I woke up the people in the rear of the room;
and one fellow rose up, shook his head, and said 'Well,
brother, if you speak much longer, they will be here, too."

In superb understatement, Senator Thurmond added, "I
feel so good that I believe I could speak quite a long time.
Mr. President, I felt it my duty to make sure that I had not
failed to exert every effort to emphasize the dangers of this
bill." Then, as if it were an afterthought, he said almost
casually, "I expect to vote against the bill." The over-flowing
galleries burst into a final round of laughter and in another
minute the speaker sat. There was still a mass of people
waiting to get in to hear the South Carolinian's long speech.
In fact, the line extended through the corridors outside the
galleries, out of the building, across Capitol Plaza and down
Constitution Avenue.

Strom Thurmond set a new filibuster record of 24 hours,
18 minutes and in doing so, of course, irritated scores of
people at the Capitol. At the same time they admired his
stamina. People also marveled at the physical endurance
and loyalty of his wife who stayed there throughout the
speech with the exception of short breaks for food. Remarked one soul exposed to Thurmond oratory, "Well, one
thing for sure, his wife loves him, or else she's stone deaf.
Imagine hearing that voice for twenty-four hours straight.
He's no Dirksen, you know."

The Thurmonds together greeted a crowd of reporters
and cameramen outside the Senate chamber. Mrs. Thurmond admitted, "I am a little tired." The Senator, on the
other hand, was so keyed up that he could not stop talking.
"How long did you say I talked?" he groggily asked staff
members over and over. Was he going home now, the press

inquired. Why no, was the reply. He would wait around to vote against the bill before going home. Some hours later the bill passed by a 60–15 vote. It was the first civil rights bill in eighty-two years to clear the United States Senate.

At the Thurmond apartment, the telephone rang far into the night as friends called to chat. Finally the couple retired for some rest only to be re-awakened at a pre-dawn hour by another caller. Jean answered while the Senator remained in a deep sleep. After the conversation, she lay wide awake the rest of the night.

As if nothing unusual had taken place, the Thurmonds arose and dressed early Friday morning to arrive in time for a special appearance on the National Broadcasting Company's "Today" television program, which begins at 7:00 a.m. Afterwards, the Senator went to his office and put in a full day's schedule, despite pleas from the staff that he go home to rest. By the night of August 30th, Capitol Hill knew it had witnessed the most amazing display of physical strength to take place there in many a year.

Now the Thurmonds prepared to face the aftermath. Alex McCullough and Jean Thurmond warned the Senator that he probably was not popular in Washington just then and not to be surprised at whatever treatment he might encounter—at least for a while. As expected, Senator Thurmond did hurt himself in the Capitol and among opponents elsewhere. The mass of voters in South Carolina, however, backed him enthusiastically. For that matter, the mass of voters in other southern states not only supported the speech but criticized their own senators for not helping him. The filibuster additionally served to make him better known as a national figure, though with dubious distinction in liberal circles. The country was actually just beginning to hear from Strom Thurmond.

VI

Death Comes to a Senate Lady

THE Senate lady from Elko, South Carolina seemed to have a special ability to strike up acquaintance with unimportant people. Perhaps it was the irrepressible country friendliness she never lost. Sophisticates called it "good politicking," as, in truth, it was. Yet, the quality had to be more than that; for she employed it in places and among people whose votes or good will did not have the slightest influence on Thurmond political fortunes.

There was no political reason for her to bother with the elevator operators and the page boys at the Senate, yet she knew them by name and always chatted with them. When entertaining constituents she introduced them to the page boys and elevator operators "as if those eager, collegiate-looking boys were the most important people in the building, and the boys just loved it," commented a South Carolinian. "She seemed to know some special fact about each one, and, of course, the boys responded by knocking themselves out to do things for her."

The same treatment was accorded the Capitol Police.

She knew all the policemen connected with the Senate and made a point of asking about their families. She discussed the things that interested them. In return, the men went out of their way to give royal attention to young Mrs. Thurmond.

Jean Thurmond's life in Washington, of course, was geared to the benefit of Strom Thurmond's career as United States Senator. Yet, sharing equal position and overlapping with that concern was another responsibility that she never allowed herself to forget. It was the sense of obligation toward South Carolina. It took many forms. It called for her to participate in the conventional activities of Washington. It called for her to be multifaceted, to be everything to everybody and to be several places at the same time.

No aspect of this Senate wife's responsibility was more demanding than entertaining constituents in the capital city. Hardly more than two or three consecutive days passed without Mrs. Thurmond's taking visiting Carolinians in hand.

Her "best" tour was interesting—and exhausting. Jean's deluxe treatment included meeting visitors at the air or train terminal, then whisking them to every point of interest allowed by time. At the Capitol she led them through miles of corridor, into the great rotunda, into the Senate and House chambers and into reception rooms, accompanying the tour with bright descriptive narrations.

One friend from Aiken noting her hostess's enthusiasm concluded that Jean obviously had not been about the place very much. "All these things must be kind of new to you, too, you seem so impressed," commented the Aikenite. "How many times have you been here?"

"This is the thirty-second time, I believe," she answered, pointing out South Carolina's John C. Calhoun glaring down at passers-by from a statue here, a bust somewhere else and a portrait still another place. When she was not praising Calhoun, she was usually enthusing over another native South Carolinian, Andrew Jackson, whom she worked into the conversation at every opportunity.

After lunch in the Senate restaurant, where Mrs. Thurmond seemed to be one of the prize customers, she sped her visitors to nearby buildings.

South Carolina school groups, historical organizations and civic associations were constantly in and out of the city. Mrs. Thurmond took on all of them. Lunch at the Capitol was out of the question for large groups, so the Thurmonds often had simple receptions at their apartment. Girls from the office came to the rescue by helping with refreshments. School contingents were so large and numerous that for them a tour and probably a picture with the Senator on the Capitol steps had to do.

It was in this particularly tiring aspect of her life that Jean Thurmond's illness first became apparent in 1959. To visiting Carolinians that spring and summer, she was noticeably paler and thinner than when they had seen her last. People felt that something more than fatigue was the trouble, but no one dreamed of the serious nature of her condition.

The Thurmonds had entertained the Dean of the University of South Carolina Law School, Robert McC. Figg, and Mrs. Figg, that spring. Later, Mrs. Figg said, "I remember Jean's bravery the last time I saw her in May 1959. She came for us to have lunch with them at the Senate dining room. She laughingly told me that Strom had said to her that morning that she looked as pale as a ghost. We talked about her lack of appetite and I told her that she needed food as fuel for all her energetic rushing about. She was not giving in to feeling unwell and was not going to burden others. She suggested that I go back with her to the apartment but in the face of her evident ill health I said that I'd do it later. It was not more than a few weeks after this that she became too ill to pretend anymore."

Despite indications of sickness, Jean Thurmond continued her usual arduous, daily pace into Washington's hot, humid summer. She was seen almost daily at the Capitol on one mission or another, usually with touring constituents.

"When Mrs. Thurmond first became ill—even before she

knew she was ill—she came into the office one day and complained how completely exhausted she was," recalled Barbara Jennings of the Thurmond office staff. "She said she
just felt bad and all she wanted to do was go home, climb
into bed and just relax. I asked her why she didn't do just
that, and she replied that she was escorting some constituents
on a tour of the Capitol and they would be disappointed
if she asked to be excused."

As long as her strength lasted, Jean continued to visit
the Capitol three days or so a week, and to accompany constituents through the historic building. It was an environ-
ment as known to her as it was to the senators and representatives who officially belonged there. Both the place and
the coming and going were parts of a familiar pattern to
Jean. It was a pattern soon to be broken permanently.

The last normal day of Jean Thurmond's life was spent
as she would have wanted to spend it—at the Capitol, helping her husband in his work.

That last day was in early August of 1959. Senator and
Mrs. Strom Thurmond entertained a visiting constituent with
the customary lunch at the Senate restaurant. Afterwards,
Mrs. Thurmond drove the constituent to the airport and then
returned to her apartment on Virginia Avenue.

There she went about household tasks as usual, and at
6:45 p.m. sat down to watch the news on television. The
Senate was in night session, so supper would be late. Suddenly, she felt as if she were being pulled to the floor and
forthwith passed out in a collapsed heap. This fainting spell
was the first real sign of the illness that would take the 33-
year-old woman's life in a period of months. Earlier in the
summer there had been two isolated instances that in themselves did not seem significant. In July she had represented
the Senator at the annual Watermelon Festival in Hampton,
South Carolina, and after a day in the broiling sun returned
home with "the worst headache I've ever had in my life."
On another occasion she was driving from Washington up

to Frederick, Maryland, to visit her brother's family and
ran lightly into the back of a truck. Despite her fast driving,
she had never had accidents. This one puzzled her because
she could not remember how it happened. In a few weeks
from the fateful August night when she collapsed at home,
all the pieces would fit together. The early summer accident
in Maryland, it would be conjectured, had been due probably to a momentary blackout. The severe Hampton headache would be explained. Her whole pale, thin, run-down
condition that people had noticed recently would make
tragic sense.

At the moment, however, the unsuspecting girl managed
to pull herself up from the carpeted floor of her Potomac
Plaza apartment and to make her way somehow into the
bedroom. How she got there, she had no idea. Gradually
her alertness returned as she struggled vainly to overcome
the weak, sick feeling gripping her. Realizing that she
needed help, Mrs. Thurmond telephoned her husband's office and asked for him. Harry Dent was the one to answer.
He attempted to carry on the lighthearted, joking conversation that the two often had with one another. She failed
to respond and he knew something was wrong. Quickly he
assured her that Senator Thurmond was on his way home.

The Senator arrived about 7:30. Getting no answer to
his repeated rapping on the door, he concluded Jean was
either away or was teasing him as she was prone to do.
He was about to use his own key when the door opened,
and his tottering wife greeted him.

"I'm not feeling well," she said. "Come on back to the
bedroom."

Falling on the bed again, she told him, "Don't talk to
me for a while; just let me rest."

Strom immediately called a doctor and secured the suggested medicine to carry his wife through the night. Within
hours she was feeling better. The next morning following
her husband's departure for his office, Jean had another black-

out. In a few minutes she was able to telephone the Senator, who then got down to serious business. He asked Mrs. Gordon Allott to stay with Jean until the physician could get there. This was the prelude to her death. On came the rapidly progressing, devastating illness that would take the life of a remarkable young woman.

A day or so later, there was another seizure. Within a week the weakness and partial paralysis that had begun on the left side of the victim's face spread down to the left side and left foot which dragged when she attempted to walk. Her doctor had prescribed medication after the first seizure to prevent other attacks, but the medication had to be increased.

In the meantime, Mrs. Thurmond's physician told the Senator and his wife that the National Institutes of Health was the best-equipped hospital to handle this type of case. He said that he was taking steps to have her admitted. His efforts were successful, and Jean Thurmond was placed under the care of the Institutes, some twelve miles out from the city and across the road from Bethesda Naval hospital. There, the eminent staff surgeon, Dr. Maitland Baldwin, became her chief surgeon. He was to be assisted in the case by associate neurosurgeons, Dr. Edward J. Laskowski, Dr. D. Maccubbin and Dr. J. Adamkiewicz.

Jean entered N.I.H. on September 11 for an operation to remove a brain tumor, referred to beforehand as an intracranial cyst. Her entrance as a patient was preceded by weeks of examination, consultations and diagnostic studies. Welda Allott helped the Senator by chauffeuring Jean back and forth to the hospital for the many examinations and by running a variety of other errands. Girls from the office staff alternated spending the daytime hours with her "only for the reason of my drunkenness from the pills," she explained, in her first letter home about her sickness. The pills were intended to stop the seizures. Not until this letter of September 1 did Jean breathe a word of the illness to her parents. By then a "council of war," she wrote, had been held, and it was decided to operate. Her brother, Dr. Robert Crouch, and the Senator's brother, Dr. William Thurmond, already were in on developments.

"Strom nor I either one are upset or down about this," she cheerily told her mother and father. "Naturally, it isn't the nicest thing you'd like to have happen to you, but there's no point in worrying or fretting about it. It will all work out fine in the end. So, please don't you all worry about it —I'm sure it did a lot of good for me to make that statement —but really try not to, cause I'm not and I'm sleeping like a log every night." What Jean did not reveal was that she herself had fretted for days over what and how to tell her family.

Then, too, she and the Senator were playing a kind of "let's pretend" game with each other. Neither would let the other know how gravely concerned each was. Only with Mrs. Allott or with the visiting office girls—notably Jean Quarles, Marian Holley Ham and Barbara Jennings—did Jean Thurmond break under the strain occasionally. Her first worry was the care and grief she would be to her husband if she were to become badly paralyzed or incapacitated. When she was not worrying about him, she was worrying about her parents.

Jean pretty well concluded, upon the decision to operate, that she was fatally ill, in spite of her optimistic statements to other people. She knew she had to bear up for the benefit of those around her, and putting up that front was one of the hardest things she had ever attempted to do.

The wire services within a few days picked up news of the forthcoming surgery. Mrs. Thurmond's youth and prominence in the capital added a special newsworthy angle to the story. Distressed friends promptly went into action.

"Everyone up here is being so good to me—coming by to see me, cards, flowers, etc.," she wrote home on September 5. "I had *four* Senate wives come by yesterday, so you see, I don't have time to be bored. In fact, Strom accuses me of liking all this attention I'm getting! I do, too!! My apartment is beginning to look like a florist's shop. Wish you could see all the flowers." Then she added gaily, "Strom teased me the other night by saying he married me so I could take care of him in his old age and now he's having to take care of me in my 'young' age!"

During those long, anxious days prior to entering the hospital, however, a multitude of serious thoughts came to her mind. The Senate seemed to be going on everlastingly in day and night sessions, holding Senator Thurmond closely to the Capitol. Staff girls or friends were staying at the apartment with Mrs. Thurmond each day until he arrived. Nightmarish worries were haunting her. One was the dread of having her head shaved for surgery. Though she managed to joke about the prospect of a bare head, it really made her shudder in distaste. To relieve some of her anxiety, Mrs. Allott went shopping, as did Jean Quarles, for turban hats to be worn during convalescence.

Another, and by far the most horrifying concern of all to Jean, was the fear that the operation might impair her mental processes. That possibility to her was worse than death. She pleaded with the surgeon not to touch anything after going inside if he found that removing the cyst would damage her mental faculties.

"I can't live without my mind!" she told him.

Yet, Jean Thurmond was known to break into tears under the pressure only twice. One time was after a telephone conversation with her mother, to whom she still was very close. The other was on the day she entered the hospital.

"The day Mrs. Thurmond was to go to the hospital," related Barbara Jennings, "I was at the apartment helping her get everything ready. She appeared to be in a cheerful mood in spite of what lay ahead of her and had even been writing a few notes to friends who had sent her gifts, but right before she was to dress to go, she gave in to a human emotion and broke down and cried, but she was ashamed to show even a few tears. She begged me not to tell the

Senator because she said he was so worried about her that if he knew she was upset, it would only add to his anxiety, and she didn't want that."

Rigidly self-disciplined by years of effort and practice in public life, Jean had the idea that anything less than full composure on her part was humoring a personal whim or giving in to weakness. Failure was failure, and this woman hated to fail at anything.

On September 12th, the day after Jean was admitted to the hospital, she wrote a breezy letter to her parents, whom she had asked not to come for the operation. "I thought maybe they'd let me go back home for the weekend since the operation won't be till Thursday," she said, "but they keep on about this 'getting to know each other.' I told them I was real easy to get to know—let's get on with the sawing. They said I could go out anytime for a drive or for a meal but they believe they'd rather have me stay here otherwise. They really are quite nice here!"

People outside the hospital also were being "nice" to the Senate wife. Flowers and other forms of thoughtfulness were heaped upon her by those in official position, as might have been expected. The attention that came from unexpected quarters, however, touched her most deeply. She was over-whelmed at the sight of flowers one day from the Capitol Police. She had remembered them in her many appearances at the Senate. Now, they were remembering her. At this writing, the presentation of flowers to Jean Thurmond remains the one and only time that the Capitol Police have made such a gesture to an outsider. Flowers came, too, from the elevator boys at the Capitol. They, too, had long memories. One day a basket of fruit arrived from the corner grocer with whom she traded; another day he sent her flowers. The man's small grocery store, some three blocks from Potomac Plaza, had always appealed to the "country" in Mrs. Thurmond.

The surgery took place on September 17th, and a tumor

with no indication of malignancy was removed. The patient's brother, Dr. Robert Crouch, was a witness. Jean's other brother, Colonel Horace Crouch, Jr., of Fort Bragg, North Carolina, and his wife were at the hospital to lend family support.

The post-operative period revealed the same partial paralysis on her left side all the way down and Jean's slanted script, usually bold and even, now showed up some weakness even in her right hand. Her handwriting ran shakily down the right side of the stationery, and the letters ran into each other somewhat illegibly. Her alertness was slowed, too, but otherwise her mental processes were completely normal and remained so until her second and last operation the following January.

Convalescence went well enough for Jean to be taken to the Crouch home at Elko on October 11th. Her mother could care for her there with help from Jean's sister, Frances, who lived in Williston, a few miles away. Senator Thurmond, then a brigadier-general in the Army Reserve, left a few days later for two weeks active duty at Fort Leavenworth, Kansas. He went only after talking with the doctors who told him his wife was doing as well as could be expected.

Time, even in Elko, wrought no miracles. Jean did not improve except for regaining some strength, but at least she was not losing ground alarmingly. She busied herself at sending thank-you notes to the many people who continued to lavish her with attention. Not able to write, she asked either relatives or staff members to take dictation, and only signed her name.

Here, too, visitors came and went, all interested in her condition but, unfortunately, some not so tactful as others. One such was a clergyman whom Mrs. Thurmond did not know well. He strode into the Crouch home with a companion, pointed out a picture of Jean and remarked within earshot of the girl, "She was pretty when she had hair!" Jean showed no reaction until the man left that his comment had struck a sensitive nerve. She then observed, "He may have a large pulpit, but he's got a lot to learn."

In late October Jean went back to Washington for a post-operative checkup and further treatment at the hospital. There had been no dramatic improvement in her health. Writing from Fort Leavenworth to his wife upon her arrival in the city, the worried Senator offered to make what would be to him the ultimate sacrifice short of death if that sacrifice would help his wife get well. He wrote, "If it is your desire that I resign from the Senate, if this will facilitate your recovery, I shall carry out your wishes. You mean everything to me and I shall follow the course that is best for you. You may wish to talk this over with Dr. Baldwin." Her husband's resignation from the U. S. Senate was not even considered as Jean returned to the National Institutes of Health.

Senator Thurmond arrived in Washington in time to spend November 7th with his wife. That day was their twelfth wedding anniversary. They celebrated by dining at a restaurant near the hospital. The one other wish Jean had that day was to chat with her friend, Mrs. Gordon Allott, who was in Lamar, Colorado. The wish was granted by a telephone call to the Colorado Senator's wife. Jean said the conversation was her "anniversary present."

Many of the November days at N.I.H. were lonely for the Senate wife, whose colleagues had gone home after the final adjournment of Congress. However, other friends came to see her. One visitor during this time was Mrs. Robert LeBaron of "residential" Washington. Jean had become friends with her through mutual membership in the International Neighbors Club and often had gone swimming with her at the Sheraton-Park Hotel, where Mrs. LeBaron lived.

"When I went to see Jean," Mrs. LeBaron commented later, "her hair was completely shaved off because of her operation. Her balance was unsteady, and she walked with a cane. The Senate was not in session; very few people in

Washington knew she was ill and in the hospital. I doubt if she had very many visitors at that time. However, nothing perturbed her optimism, her good spirits or her hope for the future. One thing that did bother her was getting up in the night. As I said before, keeping her balance was extremely difficult. When I started to leave, she said she wanted me to see how much worse off everyone in her section of the hospital was than she. In her section there were hand rails along the corridors, so out of bed she got, using her cane and holding onto the rail. We looked in upon six or eight patients' rooms along the corridor. She told me the case story of each and compared the patient with her own good fortune. The whole experience was enough to tear your heart out."

As the days passed it became increasingly obvious that Jean Thurmond would not recover. The fact that time was running out began to creep more and more into her own conversation. She appeared to feel the necessity of convincing people that she was reconciled to her fate and was unafraid. She anticipated the grief of those close to her and tried to ease it by emphasizing the full life she had led rather than the things she would never live to do. The struggle within herself had been waged before her operation. She was ready now to accept death at thirty-three without self-pity or remorse.

"She was childish in her faith, naive enough to practice what she believed, yet mature," said the Reverend Austin Roberts, Jean's Aiken pastor, who visited her frequently at Elko during those painful last weeks of the girl's life. One day, when Dr. Roberts concluded his stay with the customary prayer ending, "Thy will be done," Jean turned to her mother nearby, her eyes pleading for understanding and acceptance, and said, "Thy will be done. That is my theology, not that I must get well."

She said several other times to members of the family and to friends, "If I die, I will have had a good life. I've had everything a girl could want. I've experienced more in thirty-three years than most people experience in a lifetime twice as long as mine."

The Thurmonds' good friend, Cedric Foster, was a visitor during her November stay at the National Institutes of Health. "She called me on the telephone in her last illness," he recalled, "and told me, 'you're the only one I'm calling, but if you can, won't you come out to say hello.' That afternoon I drove out to the hospital and had difficulty keeping back the tears. Her hair had been cut short as a boy's for the operation. She moved slowly and with not too great ease . . . She smiled in a quizzical way and spoke softly and slowly. She told me, 'I am ready, Cedric, for whatever is God's will. I am quite prepared for anything that may happen. I just want to thank you for driving out in all that traffic on Wisconsin Avenue to see me.' She was really concerned that I had made a tiring drive in rush-hour traffic. She told me goodbye and said, 'Take care of Strom, won't you. You are both busy men and I know you won't see each other too often, but don't forget him.' "

"I never saw her again," added Cedric Foster.

On Thanksgiving Day, N.I.H permitted Senator Thurmond to take Jean back to Elko. They stayed at the large, two-story Crouch home, and the Senator commuted each day to his Aiken office.

Jean's lethargic condition and unsteady gait became worse each week. About the middle of December, her state of health began an accelerated decline. She now spent most of the time sleeping. Dr. Baldwin had advised that she walk every day, so Senator Thurmond regularly helped her to take a few steps. When attempting to walk, she frequently fell from loss of balance or collapsed into unconsciousness. Severe headaches accompanied by vomiting came on daily. Yet, during conscious moments, Jean saw to it that gifts and letters from constituents were acknowledged. With tremendous effort she dictated the replies and wrote her signature.

Strom and Jean went to Greenwood on Christmas Day for a family dinner at the home of Dr. and Mrs. W. G. Bishop, the Senator's brother-in-law and sister. The decline in Jean's health was shocking. She could not eat more than a few mouthfuls. Even on this trip, she had to be taken to Dr. Bishop's office for special treatment. Slowly, haltingly walking up the steps to the office, she still was anxious to show her improvement. Others watched, barely restraining their grief.

People throughout the State sensed during the Christmas holidays that their junior Senator's wife had only a short time to live, and they showered her with attention—from cards to engraved silver. One of the gifts most pleasing to her was a round silver tray brought to her one day from the Senator's Aiken office by six staff members. Engraved on the tray was "To Jean C. Thurmond and her husband from Senator Thurmond's office staff—Christmas 1959." This was one of the last gifts she was able to acknowledge.

Not long afterwards, the Senator tried to help Jean to stand one morning, and she fainted in his arms. As he laid her on the bed, the U. S. Senate's hard-driving, battling, tough guy stood there in helpless anguish. Tears rolled down his face. Here before him lay the soft side of his life in the dying person of the girl he loved. Jean Thurmond's illness was one obstacle his fighting spirit could not overcome; the struggle to live was one that Jean's magnetism and versatility could not win. The prolongation of her life was the most important campaign the couple had ever waged together, the only one over which they had no control, and their most tragic defeat.

By Sunday, January 3rd, Jean was in such critical condition that doctors recommended she be returned to N.I.H. immediately. An Air Force hospital plane, which happened to be at Charleston, carried her and the Senator in an emergency flight that afternoon from the Barnwell airport to Andrews Air Force Base, Maryland. From there the couple went by ambulance to N.I.H., where they were joined by Dr. Robert Crouch. Jean's mother had said always that only an emergency would compel her to fly. Not wanting to alarm Jean any more than was necessary over the urgency of the situation, her parents, therefore, left by automobile on a lonely night drive from Elko to Washington.

Dr. Maitland Baldwin gave Mrs. Thurmond a day to recover from the flight. On Tuesday he operated to remove pressure from the patient's brain. He found a "rapidly progressing malignant tumor." Agonizing observers during the surgery were Dr. Allen George Thurmond and once again Dr. Robert Crouch, whose unhappy fortune it was to witness both terrible operations on the sister to whom he had been especially close since childhood. After surgery Jean lapsed into a coma. Dr. Baldwin told the waiting Senator and Mr. and Mrs. Horace Crouch that she probably would not last out the night.

"But this can't be. You can't mean that," insisted the Senator, who knew his wife was seriously ill but who could not accept the fact that death was imminent. In fact, all through the autumn Strom Thurmond had been unable to accept the awful reality that Jean was fatally ill. His heart refused to take in what his eyes saw, and each phase of her decline was a fresh shock to him. This latest report from the chief surgeon was no exception. Jean was the only woman ever to capture his heart, and Thurmond was utterly devoted to her. She had brought, among her other qualities, gaiety and gentleness to his existence. The prospect of life without her was unthinkable, and this strong man wept in grief.

The two families spent the saddest night of their lives in a waiting room at the National Institutes of Health. At the Senator's office, Harry Dent and J. Fred Buzhardt, Jr. kept an all-night vigil of their own. They answered an avalanche of telephone inquiries from the news media, Washington friends and South Carolinians.

Jean Crouch Thurmond never emerged from the coma. She died at 8:35 a.m., Wednesday, January 6, 1960.

"This can't be true! I can't believe it!" the sleepless, bearded, tired, grieving Senator replied to Dr. Baldwin's announcement of death.

"Senator," the surgeon repeated, "your wife is dead!"

The twelve-year idyll of Jean and Strom Thurmond was at an end.

The second session of the 86th Congress convened at noon on Wednesday, January 6th, only three and a half hours after Jean Thurmond's death. A familiar figure was missing from the galleries, and that absence received official notice.

The girl from Elko, South Carolina, had seen vast changes since the day of her marriage to the Governor of South Carolina twelve years before. She had become the First Lady of an apprehensive, critical State that was convinced this young girl would be a political millstone around the Governor's neck. That day was the beginning of Jean Thurmond's efforts to make herself an asset to her husband and to South Carolina. A universal feeling that she had succeeded poured forth in eulogies from members of the Senate as soon as the session was gaveled to order.

Funeral services took place in Aiken, South Carolina, on Friday, January 8, 1960. Notable among officials attending were Senator and Mrs. Lyndon Johnson, both of whom had been friendly to the Thurmonds during their Washington years. Others in the Washington contingent were Senator and Mrs. John McClellan of Arkansas, Senator and Mrs. Herman Talmadge of Georgia, Senator Richard Russell of Georgia, Senators John Stennis and James Eastland of Mississippi, Senator Ralph Yarborough of Texas and Mrs. Gordon Allott of Colorado. Senator and Mrs. Olin D. Johnston led the entire South Carolina Congressional delegation. With them came Governor and Mrs. Ernest F. Hollings, former Governor and Mrs. George Bell Timmerman, Jr., and a host of high state office holders, including the members of the General Assembly.

"No funeral has drawn such a list of dignitaries to this resort town since Nicholas Longworth, former Speaker of the U. S. House, died here nearly thirty years ago," wrote *The Columbia Record* that day.

Jean Thurmond was laid to rest on a wooded hillock overlooking the lovely small town of Aiken where she had known her only carefree years of adulthood. In the place of duty, there was now peace.

VII

A Senator Crusades for Victory

As people must, after great personal tragedy, Strom Thurmond began in January 1960, to pick up the pieces of his existence.

Though he had always been a hard worker, the Senator now completely submerged himself in public duties. There was no Jean to telephone at supper time to persuade him in her effective way to stop working and to go home. There was no Jean even to make going home worthwhile. So unbearably lonely and full of memories had the spacious Thurmond apartment become that Strom decided to rent it. He then moved into a small one-bedroom apartment on another floor of the Potomac Plaza. When he finally did leave the office on these bleak winter nights the Senator took with him a briefcase of material. After eating again at the Senate restaurant if the Senate were in session or at some hotel on the way home, he would read until the late hours when he drifted off to sleep.

Thus did the painful winter wear at last into spring.

With spring, fortunately, came the important business of running for reelection, and politics during the fascinating election year of 1960 became a timely diversion to Strom Thurmond. No major candidate rose to oppose him in the South Carolina Democratic primary. The only opposition was the token candidacy of R. Beverly Herbert, a prominent but elderly attorney of Columbia, who ran on a one-plank platform—that Thurmond and other southern senators were not "making the case" for segregation. Strom Thurmond, on his part, limited his campaigning to weekends to avoid interference with pressing Senate matters. During those appearances he made his appeal to voters on the basis of his record covering all major issues, not just that pertaining to civil rights. Thurmond won, as expected, with a huge majority of the vote, 273,795 to 32,136. The Republican Party offered no further obstacle in the November general election, so the individualistic junior Senator from South Carolina was back in the Senate for a second six-year term.

Having been the first man in history to be elected by write-in vote to the United States Congress, Strom Thurmond had begun his Senate career in unique fashion, and he was due to continue it in unique fashion. Upon taking his seat in 1955, he had held the balance of power that enabled the Democrats to organize as the Senate's majority party, thereby forcing members of his party to be nice to him despite the 1948 episode. Then, as a second-year senator, Thurmond had strode boldly into territory customarily reserved for the "inner circle" by taking the initiative in the Southern Manifesto. Next, he had resigned his hard-won seat in 1956 to fulfill an unnecessary campaign promise and had won unopposed reelection to the last four years of the term. Once back in the Senate, he had carved out still another special place in history for himself by establishing a new filibuster record. Two years later he had endured the grief of his young wife's death. He had risen from personal sorrow to win in 1960 his second Senate term, a term that would prove even more eventful than the first.

During the first six years on the national political scene, Strom Thurmond had gained the public image of an ultra-conservative, a maverick and a loner. Such an image was only partially accurate. An examination of the Senator's record in important areas reveals really a surprising difference between fact and image.

For instance, on issues involving a larger Federal role in American life, as indicated by actual votes on legislation in 1959–60, Thurmond was 100 per cent opposed, but so were Byrd and Robertson of Virginia and Dirksen of Illinois. In voting for measures promoting greater economy, Thurmond was tied for fourth place in 1957 by Williams of Delaware, Byrd of Virginia and Dworshak of Idaho. He was exceeded in voting for "economy" by Robertson of Virginia, Curtis of Nebraska and Frear of Delaware. The year 1958 found Thurmond still in fourth place in the Senate on economy.

From press accounts, one might conclude that the individualistic South Carolinian was far and away the most errant Democrat in the Senate. How often did Strom Thurmond oppose his own party in Congress? In 1959–60, he was 65 per cent in opposition but was exceeded by Lausche of Ohio and Byrd of Virginia. In 1960 Thurmond's opposition dropped to 59 per cent, and he was exceeded again by Lausche of Ohio and by Byrd of Virginia, and this time tied by Holland of Florida.

His voting record also shows that Thurmond was among the most consistent in supporting the traditional Republican-Southern Democratic coalition. In 1959–60 he supported it 94 per cent of the time and was exceeded only by Virginia's Robertson and by Stennis of Mississippi. He was tied by Curtis of Nebraska and by Harry Byrd.

Despite his public image as a "maverick," Thurmond's voting record reveals him as among the most consistent also in standing with his fellow southerners. In 1957 he was with them 91 per cent of the time. Exceeding him were only Russell of Georgia and Ellender of Louisiana. In 1958 Thurmond was with them on 93 per cent of the pertinent roll calls, and he was exceeded that year only by Stennis. In 1959 Thurmond was highest in support of southern unity. In 1960 he was exceeded in this area only by Stennis, Ervin and McClellan. He was tied by Byrd of Virginia and by Ellender.

In actuality, then, Strom Thurmond was not as far out and alone as his reputation had him. The fact that what Thurmond did, he did openly and boldly, causing his actions to stand out so publicly, probably was a major factor in creating his special—and somewhat misleading—image. Too, the newsmaking events of the times were most often those that reflected the fighting, non-conforming aspects of the man's nature.

Furthermore, what Thurmond did, he did with all of his considerable vigor. He made numerous speeches in and out of the Senate; he appeared every now and then on national television; and he started an outspoken newsletter that, in the opinion of many, was the meatiest thing on Capitol Hill. He stated unequivocally his position on issue after issue—before he needed to and more strongly than he needed to. Thurmond's technique constantly put him on the record when, instead, he could have sidestepped, but such was his way, and it was this "way" that made him sought-after, colorful copy in the press.

What did not make the news were the numberless hours spent on quiet, wearying, but necessary committee work. Senators had early discovered they could rely on Thurmond to listen for endless hours to dull yet essential testimony. Through the years they proceeded to saddle him with special subcommittee work—among other reasons, to make sure that at least one senator would appear for the less appealing hearings and, too, because this senator always did his work. Even on uninteresting assignments, there were no half measures with Thurmond.

The South Carolinian had begun his Senate career in

1955 by serving on the Commerce Committee (a membership he was to hold through 1964) and on the Government
Operations Committee and Public Works Committee. In
1957 he was removed from Public Works and placed on
Labor and Public Welfare. After two years of the independent Thurmond here, organized labor screamed for his
removal, so in January 1959 he was transferred to the Armed
Services Committee, which, because of his military background, had been his heart's desire from the beginning. He
also was taken off Government Operations at this time. It
was on the Armed Services and Commerce committees that
the bulk of Thurmond's tedious, quiet work was done in
his first term. During his second term, these would be the
committees which would earn him most of his headlines.

As the new administration shifted into high gear in 1961,
President Kennedy and everyone else were aware that Thurmond had supported Lyndon Johnson for the Democratic
presidential nomination and that when Johnson lost, Thurmond had done nothing for the ticket's election. In fact, he
hinted broadly that he had voted for Richard Nixon, though
he never came out and said as much.

Senator Thurmond, to the surprise of hardly anyone,
spent the first six months of his new term in frequent protest
and rebellion against the "radically liberal, socialistic program" of the new Kennedy Administration. The pressure was
turned on to conform, and the Washington cliché that one
has "to go along to get along" became more and more irri-
tating to him. The idea of knuckling under to a program
he abhorred was to the Senator like a red flag to a bull.
He disliked the concept of forcing people into molds—into
common equal classifications.

"I don't want to be a common man," he said emphatically.
"I want the freedom to be an uncommon man and I consider
myself an uncommon man."

Nevertheless, Strom Thurmond and the Kennedy Administration endured one another for some months with no more

warfare than frequent verbal blasts directed at the White House by the southerner.

One of the first and hottest blasts was a stern reply Thurmond made to presidential adviser Arthur Schlesinger, Jr., who had asserted in a debate with the editor of *National Review* that a welfare state is the best defense against Communism. An incensed Thurmond fired back, "not only is the welfare state no defense against Communism, but there is a serious question as to whether, in practical effect, the welfare state is even an alternative to Communism. Both in essence, are founded on the identical theories of state socialism and are equally antagonistic to the concept of private property. Under Communism all property is vested in the state; under the welfare state, the outward vestiges or title to property remain in the individual, but all meaningful attributes of property are exercised by the state through regulation. Welfare statism is like Communism in its mistrust of individual liberty and in its reliance on state control."

Open warfare finally erupted on Friday, July 21, 1961, a typically hot, muggy summer day in Washington. The day began with the usual routine. The Senator went through his morning ritual of fifty-nine push-ups and a vitamin-packed breakfast. He appeared at 9:00 a.m. in his office on the New Senate Office Building's fourth floor. Within minutes he received what he described as the shock of his Senate career.

An aide came in with a copy of the *Washington Post* and pointed out a United Press International story dealing with excerpts just "leaked" from a month-old memorandum from Senator J. William Fulbright (D. Ark.), chairman of the Senate Foreign Relations Committee, to Defense Secretary Robert S. McNamara. Thurmond took time right then to read the article. Suddenly he removed his glasses and rose from his high back leather chair. At that moment a one-man crusade began.

Thurmond promptly telephoned Fulbright's office but was unable to get the Senator. He said he wanted a copy of the memo discussed in the morning *Post* and in *The New York Times*. A copy could not be supplied was the reply. A Fulbright staffman very shortly appeared in Thurmond's door to explain things, and was promptly chewed into small pieces. Next, Thurmond wrote a letter to Fulbright and had it delivered to the latter's office, where it was not welcomed.

Now Senator Fulbright was annoyed. In a speech to the Senate a week and a half later he referred to the Thurmond communication as an "ultimatum demanding that he (Thurmond) be provided with a copy of the memorandum 'within the next hour.'"

"Aside from the fact that I had no copy of the memorandum at the time," the Foreign Relations Committee chairman added, "I was unwilling to open my private files in response to so impertinent a letter."

Actually, the letter from Thurmond was not at all impertinent. It began with a friendly "Dear Bill" and stated that the *Post* and *Times* articles "shocked and disturbed" him "very much." The letter concluded with the Carolinian's request, which read, "I am writing this letter to personally request that I be provided with a copy of this memorandum within the next hour as I would like to read its contents and possibly comment on it before leaving Washington after lunch." The letter reflected the newspaper report that the memorandum originated with the Foreign Relations Committee, rather than just the chairman.

Fulbright's reply began, likewise, with an informal "Dear Strom" and mildly explained his side of the matter. The letter was signed "Bill."

The tone of the written exchange between the two men was certainly within the bounds of senatorial courtesy and gave no evidence of personal animosity, as one might have mistakenly concluded from press reports.

Among the excerpts contained in the *Post* and *Times* stories, the particular points that had shocked Thurmond into action were:

That there was "considerable danger" in allowing the military to continue its present involvement in certain types of political campaigns in the United States.

That in eleven cases, listed and briefly described by the memo, "education and propaganda activities of military personnel" had been uncovered during the past year. That these propaganda activities might well become important obstacles to public acceptance of the President's program and leadership, if they had not already.

That the nature of the various propaganda activities had varied, but that running through all of them is a central theme that the primary, if not exclusive, danger to this country is internal Communist infiltration.

That the "thesis of the nature of the Communist threat often is developed by equating social legislation with socialism and the latter with Communism."

That "much of the Administration's domestic legislative program"... under such a philosophy would be characterized as steps toward Communism.

That "this view of the Communist menace renders foreign aid, cultural exchanges, disarmament negotiations and other international programs as extremely wasteful if not actually subversive."

That during the long haul of the Cold War, "radicalism on the right can be expected to have great mass appeal. It offers the simple solution, easily understood: Scourging of the devils within the body politic, or, in the extreme, lashing out at the enemy."

That an examination be called to deal with the relationships between the Foreign Policy Research Institute, the Institute for American Strategy, the Richardson Foundation, the National War College, and the Joint Chiefs of

Staff. That this examination should try to determine whether "these relationships do not amount to official support for a viewpoint in variance with that of the Administration."

That the parallel might seem "far-fetched," but that the revolt of the French generals is "an example of the ultimate danger."

In its story of July 21st, *The New York Times* said that on July 10th, only a short time following delivery of the memorandum, the Defense Department had announced new restrictions on speeches by top military men. Officers were instructed to discuss military matters and to steer clear of foreign policy. The *Times* said the directive had resulted from the Fulbright memo.

As reporters sought more information, Senator Fulbright undertook clarification of his document. He explained that it was not a Foreign Relations Committee memo, as the press had reported, but one drawn up by a committee staff-man for Fulbright's personal use. He had sent it as a confidential paper to McNamara and had sent a copy to the President. It was not intended to be made public, the Arkansas Senator declared, and he refused to make it public now, adding that he believed "someone at the Pentagon" had leaked its contents. In reply to reporters' requests for a copy, Fulbright said he did not know where they could get one "unless you get it from the Defense Department—they apparently have duplicating facilities."

"The point I wanted to make," Fulbright told reporters about his astonishingly frank document, "was that it is not the traditional role of the military to sponsor meetings weighted to one side of a political subject." The Senator added that he had no quarrel with military officers instructing their own personnel about the Communist menace but that "it is traditional that the military is not the agency that instructs the American people."

Not long after Fulbright's statements to the press, Strom Thurmond called one of his rare news conferences to express an opinion of the now-controversial memo. It was still early on July 21st when the South Carolinian faced reporters crowding around him.

The issue raised by the memo was not one of civilian control of the military, Thurmond maintained, pointing out that the examples of seminars cited by the memo were instruction sessions held for or by military reservists, not the general public. The memorandum was "a dastardly attempt to intimidate the commanders of the U. S. Armed Forces and prevent those commanders from teaching their troops the nature of the menace of world Communism," said the irate Thurmond.

As an Army Reserve major-general—and the highest ranking military officer in Congress—and also a member of the Senate Armed Services Committee, Thurmond had time after time voiced his belief in a strong, hard stand against every aspect of Communism. The Fulbright memo went against every grain of his fighting, uncompromising nature. To the Strom Thurmond of July 1961, as in earlier years, there were no grays, no inbetweens. He made judgments in absolute terms. Right was right, and wrong was wrong; and Communism was all wrong. Therefore, he believed in battling Communism as fiercely as possible with every sensible resource and with but one object in mind—to win. The idea of a foreign policy settling for stalemate or accommodation was abhorrent to him. It was this kind of "no-win" foreign policy (a phrase he coined) that he interpreted the Fulbright memo to reflect, and it was this very policy that he wanted to lay bare to the American people. Strom Thurmond also was not a man to keep quiet, especially when many people wished he would. He had always considered himself morally obligated to speak out and to take public stands on issues.

Continuing his blunt attack on the memo, Thurmond contended it "constitutes a serious blow to the security of the United States and is all the more alarming because the move originated, according to press reports, in a Senate committee." It states, he went on, that "the military is teaching troops that our defeats in the war against Communism are the results of appeasement and a 'soft attitude' by our own Government. I hope the charge is correct for it fortifies my belief that our military officers do understand the threat from Communism and are giving their personnel the truth, and knowledge of the truth is the only means by which our troops can be equipped to combat the Communist evil. If the military teaches the true nature of Communism, it must necessarily teach that Communism is fundamentally socialism. When socialism, in turn, is understood, one cannot but help realize that many of the domestic programs advocated in the United States, and many of those adopted, fall clearly within the category of socialism. Military leaders in this case are rightly teaching the truth, and as is often the case, the truth can and does hurt. It is important for the people to be stirred up about the threat of Communism."

"I am glad that the full Senate committee did not join in this damaging action," Thurmond concluded.

By Wednesday, August 2nd, Strom Thurmond had secured, as he swore on Friday he would, a copy of the Fulbright memorandum. The complete document alarmed him more than the excerpts. That afternoon Thurmond took to the Senate floor with a speech denouncing the paper and then inserted it into the Congressional Record. He did not name the author; he did not need to do so.

"It is a clandestine assault on the fundamental foundations of our republic. It is a smear campaign utilizing innuendo based on unsubstantiated allegations," he said. "I can well understand why anyone connected with this document would be fearful of public disclosure of the entire contents."

One of the passages in the complete memorandum that particularly outraged Thurmond was this:

In the long run, it is quite possible that the principal problem of leadership will be, if it is not already, to restrain the desire of the people to 'hit the Communists with everything we've got,' particularly, if there are more Cubas and Laos. Pride in victory, and frustration in restraint during the Korean War, led to MacArthur's revolt and McCarthyism;

Another which was the most infuriating to Thurmond, and which he was to quote over and over again in months to come, was the following:

Fundamentally, it is believed that the American people have little, if any, need to be 'alerted to the menace of the Cold War.' Rather, the need is for understanding of the true nature of that menace, and the direction of the public's present and foreseeable awareness of the fact of the menace toward support of the President's own total program 'for survival in a nuclear age.' There are no reasons to believe that military personnel generally can contribute to this need beyond their specific technical competence to explain their own role.

Making the first of many such demands, the South Carolina Senator told the Senate, "It is imperative that the Armed Services Committee immediately undertake a full scale investigation of this entire matter."

Fellow conservatives, Senator Karl E. Mundt (R-S.D.) and Senator Barry Goldwater (R-Ariz.) joined Thurmond in attacking the memo.

Senator Fulbright subsequently took the Senate floor to defend his position and to insert his own copy of the famous memorandum (identical to Thurmond's copy) into the Congressional Record. He was making the insertion, he declared, "to dispel the fears of those who have persuaded themselves that the memorandum contains material which is sinister, subversive, or sensational."

After mentioning Thurmond's "ultimatum" and "impertinent" letter of July 21st, the Arkansan remarked in his imperturbable drawl that he was "very much astonished at the interest in his criticism of propaganda activities by military personnel and was unaware the subject could "arouse great controversy." "There has been a strong tradition in this country that it is not the function of the military to 'educate' the public on political issues," he added, and went on to "thank" Thurmond, Mundt, and Goldwater "for disabusing me of my erroneous judgment that the principle of civilian control of the Armed Services is one which is accepted by all Americans."

Despite the repeated denials by Thurmond that civilian control over the military was an issue, it was to be raised repeatedly until finally laid to rest almost a year later by the committee's finding that "the best traditions of the military uphold this principle and the military profession has adhered to it, in letter and spirit, almost unanimously."

By the next day Thurmond's call for an investigation had the support of Senator Styles Bridges of New Hampshire, ranking Republican on the Senate Armed Services Committee. However, Senator Bridges was to die before the investigation could get underway. Insertion of the memo into the Record also brought calls for an investigation from a number of others, but Strom Thurmond was the man pushing hardest for an investigation that neither the White House, the Defense Department, the State Department, nor the Senate leadership wanted.

"Had Jean Thurmond lived," a friend of the Senator commented several years later, "it would have been right at this stage of developments in 1961 that she would have made her influence felt. I really question whether or not we would have continued this one-man crusade—which is about what it was—for the military muzzling investigation. It was something that was due to involve the highest officials of the Administration. Strom was walking into a situation where every card was stacked against him, and there was every likelihood that Strom Thurmond might not be able to emerge with his head still on his shoulders, politically speaking. Jean liked the Senator to be a statesman, but not

a figuratively dead statesman. Her natural caution and discretion would have come into play here."

There was no Jean Thurmond around in 1961, however,
and the Senator was as tenacious as a bulldog with a bone.
This time the bone was what he called the nation's "no-win"
foreign policy as reflected in the Fulbright memo. All the
battering the "powers" could throw at him couldn't make
Strom let go.

The tenor of the Carolinian's attack on the memo are
illustrated by these typical remarks:

"There are several far-reaching and radical recommendations in the memorandum. First, it would repeal or modify
the 1958 National Security Council directive which authorized the military anti-Communist seminars. Second, it would
increase censorship of military speeches. Third, it would
transfer the National War College from military to civilian
control. Fourth, it would even put unit level troop information and education training under civilian control. Fifth, it
would require graduate studies in the liberal arts at uni-
versities—perhaps at Harvard to give the officers a more
liberal outlook—as a prerequisite for promotion to high ranks.

"This document should be studied by every American,
particularly those who have the misapprehension that this
entire fight is one of civilian control over the military."

It took seventeen Senate speeches by Thurmond, what
news coverage he could get, and a resulting flood of mail
into Washington to stir the Armed Services committee into
action. Though press and citizen reaction were both pro
and con, the overwhelming sentiment was pro-investigation.
Whatever might have been the impact he was having on
the Senate, Thurmond was proving his ability to get through
to the American public. This was proven by the fact that
on the weekend before the Committee finally voted on
whether to hold the investigation, more than 17,000 telegrams were received by the Committee, of which only a
handful were against Thurmond's position.

Hearings were held by the committee on September 6th and 7th in connection with Thurmond's resolution before the group calling for a full investigation on the muzzling of military officers in their efforts to speak out on Communism. Defense Secretary Robert McNamara was the witness giving testimony on both days.

Thurmond's interrogation and McNamara's responses began on a harmonious note. The Carolinian prefixed his questions with a disclaimer of any motivations based on partisanship or personality. To McNamara, he said: "Mr. Secretary, before asking any questions, I would like to assure you that my questions, and indeed, my entire concern in this matter, do not arise from either a spirit of partisanship or of personalities.

"I personally am convinced that your goal is the highest national interest, and the direction of our Military Establishment to most adequately serve that national interest.

"I assure you further that my goal is identical. I am fully aware, and I hope others share my awareness, that the matter on which I have expressed extreme concern did not originate since you assumed the duties of the Secretary of Defense, although I must say that based on the evidence which has come to my attention, the activities which concern me have increased in scope and frequency during the past few months.

"I am seeking and urging an investigation by the Armed Services Committee not to impair your efforts but, on the contrary, in order that you may be assisted in more effectively carrying out your difficult duties," Thurmond concluded.

McNamara responded in the same tone, stating: "I do not believe there is any difference, as you yourself have indicated, between your objective and mine."

Although the exchanges remained free of personal antagonism, the differences between the two on the issues soon came boiling to the surface, and the Senator and the Secre-

tary really locked horns over the issue of identifying particular censors by name with specific speeches censored.

McNamara revealed the names of fourteen persons in
the Pentagon who censored speeches, but declined to
identify who reviewed any specific speech, and volunteered
to accept responsibility for changes made in speeches. He
acknowledged that State Department personnel also participated in the censorship of speeches, but he could identify
none of them by name.

Thurmond expressed the conviction that the censors were
changing the speeches to make them reflect the policy guide-
lines laid down by the Executive branch, and that the truth
of the matter could only be arrived at by questioning the
censors as to their reasons for making specific changes in
speeches.

From the very beginning, Thurmond made no effort to
conceal his real objective—to expose the Government's "no-
win" foreign policy to public view. The Administration was
just as determined to prevent such an exposure, and finally,
utilized the controversial doctrine of "executive privilege,"
rarely invoked by a President, to avoid being forced to
identify individual censors with their specific work.

Thurmond got a real break, when, in the course of his
testimony, McNamara mentioned that in searching for the
specific censorship actions which Thurmond had made public, it had been necessary to scan approximately 1,500
speeches in the files of the Pentagon censors. Thurmond immediately seized the opportunity to ask McNamara to fur-
nish copies of the 1,500 speeches to the Committee, which
McNamara agreed. Delivery of the speeches to the Committee was delayed, but with a helpful prod of the Defense
Department by Senator Richard Russell (D-Ga.), Committee Chairman, Thurmond got access to 1,500 speeches censored by the Defense and State Departments.

Finally on September 18, Strom Thurmond gave a
lengthy, major speech on the Senate floor in a climactic

effort to obtain an investigation. In his address, he summarized the basic issues, but more importantly, he repudiated with fact after indisputable fact much of Defense Secretary McNamara's testimony of September 6th and 7th before the Armed Services Committee. This piece of diligent research on the part of the Senator made a noticeable impact on the Senate and turned out to be the key speech of many by Thurmond that contributed toward approval of an investigation.

When the Armed Services Committee met to consider the question of conducting a probe, Thurmond was ready with a switch in tactics. Rather than stay with his Senate Resolution, he threw his support to a Committee Resolution which he had drafted. At this point, it was either a Committee Resolution or nothing, and the South Carolinian recognized that reality and acted accordingly. Thurmond's Senate Resolution would have required approval both by the Committee and the full Senate. Furthermore, the Rules Committee would have had to authorize funds, subject to approval by the full Senate. Congress was ready to adjourn for the year, and there was no time left for such drawn-out procedures. A Committee Resolution, moreover, would not have to go before the Senate.

Thurmond's Committee Resolution proposed to solve the money problem by turning the matter over to the Preparedness Investigating Subcommittee, a standing subcommittee with an appropriate budget of its own. After proper deliberation, the Armed Services Committee voted fifteen to one in favor of the Committee Resolution, after amending it. Senator E. L. Bartlett (D-Alaska) was the only dissenter. Strom Thurmond at last had his investigation but not before a hassle over semantics. The argument was over the phrase "study and investigate," which was amended to read "study and appraise." Some committee members felt that "investigate" implied crime and therefore opposed its use.

The issue over choice of words indicated clearly the

reservations committee members had over the idea of investigating a situation that involved a fellow senator—in this
case, Fulbright. As a matter of fact, this conflict with senatorial courtesy was considered by Thurmond to be the greatest single factor hampering approval of an investigation. The
new wording was interpreted by the group to mean the
same as investigate, so the practical effect of the change
was nil. An exasperated Senator Russell described the row
as a "tempest in a teapot."

As finally voted upon favorably, the resolution read:

Resolved: That a subcommittee of the Senate Committee
on Armed Services, to be appointed or designated by the
Chairman, be authorized and directed to study and appraise the use of military personnel and facilities to arouse
the public to the menace of the Cold War and to inform
and educate Armed Services personnel on the nature and
menace of the Cold War, and that such committee be
vested with the full subpoena power of the Senate Committee on Armed Services.

The Special Preparedness Subcommittee of the Armed
Services Committee, appointed on September 21 by Senator
Russell, was to begin its "study and appraisal," after several
postponements, in January of 1962, under the chairmanship
of Senator John Stennis (D-Miss.) Other subcommittee
members were: Stuart Symington of Missouri, Henry Jackson of Washington, E. L. Bartlett of Alaska, Leverett Saltonstall of Massachusetts, Margaret Chase Smith of Maine, and,
of course, Thurmond.

In the meantime, Thurmond did not let any grass grow
under his own feet or under the feet of anyone else connected with the forthcoming investigation. By the first week
in October, aides had plowed through all of the 1,500 censored speeches submitted by McNamara to the Senate
Armed Services Committee and had compiled a number of
deleted items that the South Carolina Senator promptly used

as the basis of many speeches he then was making throughout the country to present his case to the people. There were ten deletions in particular that he mentioned over and over as examples of unnecessary censorship, and their repetition was drawing shocked reaction. These were:

1. Communist conspiracy directed toward absolute domination of the world...
2. Soviet infiltration menacing this nation and extending throughout far corners of the globe...
3. The steady advance of Communism...
4. The Communist challenge...
5. On such theories socialism thrives...
6. Insidious ideology of world Communism...
7. Communism encompassing Marxism, Fabian Socialism, Socialism...
8. Soviets have not relented in the slightest in their determination to dominate the world and to destroy our way of life...
9. Nothing has happened to indicate that the goals of international Communism have changed...
10. Today in the face of the world-wide threat of international Communism...

Thurmond would then add, "This pattern of censoring out penetrating phrases on Communism is relatively consistent wherever such material is submitted. There appears to be complete consistency in the deletion of any use of the word 'victory' or the word 'war.' In each and every instance that I have found, such words were deleted and a substitute made therefor. Indeed, these are carried to rather ridiculous extremes. In a speech of a technical nature prepared for delivery on May 1, 1961, an official used the following sentence: 'The X-15 is the Man of War of the stable of research aircraft today.' The phrase 'Man of War' was deleted and the censor wrote in the margin, and I quote: 'Let's use another steed—Zev, Gallant Fox, etc., but not this one.' Even in this remote connotation, the term 'war' cannot be used."

Explanations of deletion of the word "victory" by the State Department were to add considerable fire to the controversy during the later stages of the hearings.

While the citizenry was left to stew over those points, Senator Thurmond was called to two-weeks active duty as a major-general—and at the Pentagon, of all places. He was assigned to a small ground floor office located two floors beneath Defense Secretary McNamara's office.

"Now, this is what I'd call real frustration," observed an acquaintance of the Senator's at the time. "There Strom is, right in the Pentagon, which he's been blasting on this military muzzling thing, and he's got to keep his mouth shut for two whole weeks."

Once those two weeks were up, however, Strom Thurmond was back on his speaking tours. The investigation was given the green light on September 20th and got officially underway on January 23rd, 1962. Thurmond made some eighty or more speeches in his effort to stop "muzzling of the military" and to reverse the "no-win" foreign policy against Communism. He spoke to audiences from coast to coast, his pace typical of the drive and physical stamina of this determined man.

Thurmond's bulldog tenacity and his constant bone-rattling of "no-win" foreign policy were paying off, even before the committee hearings started. Columnist Holmes Alexander pointed out on January 17th certain observable changes already taking place in the Pentagon. He wrote:

> . . . By his Senate floor speeches, by criss-cross tour of the nation in which he made scores of speeches and met thousands of concerned citizens, Thurmond has forced the Department of Defense to make sizable concessions. Here are some of the changes in Pentagon procedure for which the American public should be suitably grateful:

The blame has been fixed where it belongs. Evidence accumulated by Thurmond from Pentagon sources shows that the State Department really does the censoring of anti-Communist materials. The Defense Department merely goes along with the philosophy laid down by State. This, of course, reflects President Kennedy's own personal creed of how to deal with Communism . . .

. . . Censors have been instructed since Congress adjourned last autumn to inform the originator of a speech or book as to why deletions or changes have been made . . .

. . . Another large gain for the Senator, and concession by the Secretary of Defense is the set-up of an appeal procedure . . .

. . . For the first time in the cold war, the Defense Department has put forward a planned, service-wide troop instruction program on Democracy vs. Communism . . .

Officially, the investigation was to be divided into three phases of inquiry:

1. A study of the practices and procedures relating to the policy review or censorship of public speeches of military personnel for the purpose of determining whether they are established and administered properly and whether there have been abuses or improper practices in the administration thereof.
2. An examination of the military troop information and education program to determine the effectiveness of the existing program, the scope of the desired program, and the question of what could and should be done to strengthen the program and make it more effective.
3. A study of the proper role of military personnel in informing, educating, and alerting the civilian population as to the menace of the Cold War, including the participation by the military in Cold War or anti-Communist seminars and the military external information program in general.

Unofficially and fundamentally, of course, the Subcommitte was investigating the "unmentionable" subject of foreign policy.

"A broadly based study of foreign policy regarding our relations with Communist countries had never been undertaken by the Congress," Thurmond said some time after these particular proceedings, "and it was almost a certainty that the Senate Foreign Relations Committee would not be doing so as, after all, the State Department generally dominates the thinking of this committee, particularly with Fulbright as chairman. I was, in fact, using the issue of military muzzling under the jurisdiction of the Armed Services Committee as a way to expose our no-win foreign policy. I wanted to strip foreign policy of the various disguising cloaks and to lay it bare for the American people to view it for what it was. Foreign policy was my basic target, and the only way the Armed Services Committee could deal with it was through the effect on the military establishment. The Fulbright memorandum presented that opportunity."

Side issues kept cropping up so rapidly, however, that they were obscuring the major purposes of the investigation. For one thing, the probe had assumed the tones of a "conservatism versus liberalism" fight. Liberals—including the majority of the Washington press corps—tended, naturally, to gather in the Administration-Fulbright corner. Conservatives, on the other hand, grouped in Thurmond's corner. It goes without saying that the liberals were more powerful and that Strom Thurmond, with his history of states' rightism and opposition to national liberal programs, was pure poison to that community. A less rebellious, less outspoken senator —in other words, a less controversial figure nationally—might have fared better in the liberal press. Liberals already were tossing McCarthy labels at Thurmond but could not score a hit. They were waiting expectantly for him to make just one slip.

Another issue—and an important one—was the right of Congress to have free access to government records and to the uncensored views of personnel.

All in all, the Subcommittee hearings boded well to produce high drama when they at last began on January 23. The Senate Caucus room, site of the gathering, was filled to capacity as people awaited fireworks from the first major congressional hearing in some time. However, former President Dwight D. Eisenhower furnished the day's only surprise. Subcommittee Chairman Stennis opened proceedings by reading a long statement sent to him by Eisenhower. The contents raised a number of eyebrows, including to some extent those of Senator Stennis himself. In brief, the statement advocated letting the military speak out on Communism. The former chief executive wrote, in part:

... The entire nation, including the Armed Services, insists that in our free system military influence must be kept within proper Constitutional, legal, and administrative bounds. Moreover, as mentioned in my final address as President, we must watchfully mind the military-industrial complex for it tends to generate powerful economic and political pressures beyond the anticipations even of the participants themselves. But these are matters of proportion and sensible national leadership, requiring the same kind of continuing over-sight and perspective that other major power groupings in our society, including business, labor and government itself, require in the interest of keeping our system flexible, balanced, and free. In a half century of national service, I have yet to meet the American military officer who viewed himself as a budding Napoleon, or even a Rasputin, and I suggest it is worthy of note that in recent world history the three major dictators, Hitler, Mussolini, and Stalin, came from civil life. This fact does not warrant a general indictment of civilian

motivation, any more than one or two military extremists
might warrant the absurdity that all the military harbors
political designs dangerous to our Constitutional form of
government . . .

. . . Generally in the same connection, I question the
desirability of requiring the topmost government officials,
whether military or civilian, to submit their proposed public statements for what amounts to censorship of content
—as distinguished from security matters—prior to their ut-
terances. I am aware, in saying this, that procedures in
my own and in the Administration of my predecessor may
have functioned in this way. But, in thoughtful re-assess-
ment of this procedure, I incline to the view that when
responsible and respected officials feel compelled to submit to censorship, we are smothering the concept of
personal responsibility under practice of heavy-handed
and unjustified staff supervision . . .

Senator Stennis next read a statement from Robert A.
Lovett, who had been Secretary of Defense under President
Harry S. Truman. Lovett differed somewhat with Eisenhower on censorship, saying that both military and civilian
officials of the Defense Department "should hold their public
speeches to a minimum and in them deal largely with facts
in the area of their direct responsibility."

In regard to censorship, Lovett said, "If we are not to
have four military services going their divergent ways,"
speeches by Defense officials should be checked "at the
highest and most experienced level available."

When called upon, the recently retired Chief of Naval
Operations, Admiral Arleigh Burke, declared that "discussions of the nature of our freedom and the nature of the
enemy who threatens it are a general public responsibility,
with no distinction as to the clothes a man wears, the em-
ployer he serves, or the party for which he may, in ballot-

box secrecy, vote." Burke pointed out that this did not amount
to a military man becoming involved in "purely partisan
politics," and he added, "that area, every military man I
know would agree, is off limits to the man in uniform."

In his prepared testimony, Burke pointedly used many
of the very words and phrases to describe the enemy—"im-
perialistic, aggressive Communism"—that only a short while
before, when he was on active duty, had been censored from
his speeches.

Burke's appearance marked the beginning of a parade
of uniforms and stars, including General Lyman L. Lem-
nitzer, chairman of the Joint Chiefs of Staff; General Thomas
D. White, USAF (retired); Admiral George Anderson, Chief
of Naval Operations; General Frederick H. Smith, Vice-Chief
of Staff, USAF; Lt. General Arthur G. Trudeau, Chief of
Research and Development, U.S. Army; and General David
M. Shoup, Commandant of the Marine Corps.

The reactions of the senior military men to censorship
of their speeches, as reflected in their testimony, ranged from
"wonder at the motivation" of the censors to be "helpful,"
but none would admit that he had been "muzzled." To the
extent that dissatisfaction with the censorship was expressed,
it was attributed to the censor's individual judgment or
caprice. No senior official would admit that he could detect
any "pattern" in the censorship.

No sooner had the Joint Chiefs completed their testimony
on Tuesday, January 30th, than Senator Thurmond presented to the Committee censored speeches proving that
the Defense Department had censored the testimony of military men prior to delivery to at least three congressional
committees. In fact, Thurmond charged, the testimony being
heard by this very subcommittee was being reviewed beforehand.

The insult to Congress was compounded in Thurmond's
estimation no later than the next day when the Defense

Department again refused to identify censors who had reviewed specific speeches. Willis D. Lawrence, Deputy Director of Security Review, appearing before the subcommittee formally declined to name the man who reviewed
a particular speech by Lt.-Gen. Trudeau. Lawrence told
senators he was doing so on orders from Secretary McNamara. Significant information given by Lawrence did reveal
that the State Department "called the tune," as one person
expressed it, on military speeches dealing with Communism.
This fact actually was widely known, but Lawrence's testimony provided notable substantiation.

Senator Stennis reacted to the refusal by saying, "You
are, in effect, raising the question of executive privilege."
The subcommittee chairman added his assumption that
other Defense Department people would take the same position. He termed as highly important the issue of withholding information from the subcommittee and expressed his
intention to study the matter.

A letter from McNamara to Stennis followed Lawrence's
refusal to name censors, and the Defense Secretary reiterated
his stand. It would not be in keeping with sound principles
of management, he wrote, "to thrust on subordinate officials
burdens which are properly chargeable to me and my senior
associates."

The Justice Department had advised him, McNamara
said, that executive privilege could be invoked under the
circumstances. He added, "We would be most unhappy to
invoke formally the privilege in this inquiry."

A weekend meeting of Stennis, Thurmond, Saltonstall
and McNamara failed to resolve differences and thus to
avoid a showdown between Congress and the Executive
Department. The hearings subsequently remained in a state
of suspension for days while senators worked to break the
impasse.

Meanwhile, word "leaked" here and there from the Pentagon, which seemingly is as porous as a sieve at times,

that the censors did not want to be protected by McNamara.

Wrote Roulhac Hamilton, Washington correspondent for *The News and Courier* of Charleston, South Carolina, "One of the censors who is known to be entirely familiar with the attitude of his colleagues bluntly told a newsman that the censors to a man neither want protection by McNamara nor the senators. They were described as perfectly willing to answer any question and explain all of their actions."

Thurmond contended that the Administration did not dare let censors from either the Defense or State Department testify because the censors would have shown that they were reviewing speeches in accordance with policy and not from individual judgment or caprice, as various military officials had suggested.

On February 8th, President Kennedy invoked the doctrine of executive privilege and, in effect, clamped the lid on further meaningful information from both the Defense and State Departments relating to censorship. The subcommittee upheld the President. In addition, much of the press applauded the President's action. Later, during the Cuban missile crisis, the press raised a loud cry over "managed" news when information restrictions were applied to reporters. There was a different attitude than when a conservative southern senator was the target.

With the censorship phase of the hearings drawing to a close, Thurmond's efforts to prove that the censorship changes "were dictated by existing policy known to the censors but not known to the speechmakers or the public" appeared doomed. None of the military witnesses supported his contention in their testimony. The imposition of executive privilege precluded cross examinaton of the censors themselves.

When substantiation of the Thurmond contention did come, it came from an unexpected source—the State Department!

Almost as a matter of form, the Subcommittee had in-

structed both the Defense and State Departments to give
an explanation in writing for each of some 200 deletions
and changes in speeches made by censors in each of the
Departments, respectively.

When the State Department witness, Undersecretary
George Ball, first appeared before the Subcommittee, he
stated that he was not prepared to explain the reasons for
specific censorship actions. This led to a severe lecture by
Thurmond.

"You should have prepared yourself," Thurmond re-
proved.

Thurmond followed with a detailed interrogation of Ball
on U.S. foreign policy, centering around Thurmond's charge
and Ball's denial that the U.S. was following a "no-win"
foreign policy.

The Subcommittee session was concluded with a promise
by Ball to submit in writing an explanation of each censorship action. As it turned out, the most startling of the speech
changes was imposed by the censors in the State Department
rather than those in the Department of Defense.

When the State Department explanations were finally delivered to the Subcommittee, Thurmond at last had evidence
on which to base his conclusion that the censorship was
based on policy.

The most spectacular explanation submitted by the State
Department was directed at a speech in which the phrase
"victory on each of the four battlefields of the Cold War"
was deleted, and the phrase "defeat of Communist aggression" was substituted by State Department censors in the
speech of a military officer.

The State Department's written explanation for this
change was: "The word 'victory' has a militaristic and aggressive ring less suited than the substituted phrase to describing our national objectives. It implies an 'all or nothing'
approach leaving no room for accommodation."

Thurmond could now build his speeches, and even his

final report, on the State Department's own words, and he missed no opportunity to throw those words back at the State Department.

At this point there was nothing to do but proceed to the second and third phase of the inquiry. A less determined, less intense man might have been ready to give up his cause by now, but Thurmond was ready to do battle to his grave if necessary. The previous week, *Time* magazine had concluded a character sketch of Thurmond with these pertinent observations:

> Off the floor, Thurmond devotes himself to physical culture activities; he keeps barbells and a chest stretcher in his office, takes daily workouts in the Senate gym, and rides a bicycle. He abstains from whiskey, tobacco, coffee, tea, and even Coca-Cola, but he drinks prune juice with great gusto. "My God," says a Senate colleague, "the way he's going he ought to live to be 150." If he does, it is still doubtful that he will ever change his mind about any of his causes. For, as a fellow member of the Stennis subcommittee said last week, "Strom is very stubborn."

On the day that the President had invoked executive privilege, a storm had also erupted on Capitol Hill over the examination of thirty Marines by two committee investigators. Without the knowledge of General Shoup or of anyone on the Subcommittee, including Thurmond, two committee investigators had tested some Marines at the Washington Marine Barracks and Embassy Guard School on their knowledge of the Cold War. The questionnaire administered to the servicemen was conceived and prepared by G. E. Hartel, a retired colonel appointed to the subcommittee staff by Thurmond. The quiz was administered by Charles A. Byrne, on loan to the subcommittee from his position in the General Accounting office, and by Ben Kaplan, a temporary Thurmond aide working with the subcommittee in an informal capacity. According to J. Fred Buzhardt, Jr., the Senator's legislative assistant, some of the Marines "did very well;" some others did poorly. Questions ranged from elementary to difficult.

Regardless of motivation or results, the quizzing of Marines on the Cold War gave Thurmond critics an excuse to bombard him with cries of McCarthyism.

Wrote Robert L. Riggs in the *Courier-Journal* of Louisville, Kentucky:

> ... To those who watched the hearings for this three weeks, it seemed the South Carolina senator, who carried four states as the Dixiecrat presidential nominee in 1948, was making a special effort to do nothing that would justify anyone's comparing him with the rough, sarcastic, often sneering, and frequently insulting McCarthy.
>
> His questions were put in courteous though firm tones. His attitude toward witnesses was respectful. He even indulged in some pleasantries with one of his main targets, Arthur Sylvester, who, as assistant secretary of defense for public affairs, had the Pentagon censors under his wing.
>
> ... This foray into quizzing Marines was the one thing that brought back memories of McCarthy. It was too reminiscent of the activities of those remarkable young men, Roy Cohn and G. David Schine, to make anyone on either side very happy.

Senator Thurmond was in the midst of the storm swirling around the Senate floor over the incident. Not about to lie down and play dead, he rose to defend his aides and said he saw nothing wrong with the questionnaire. Somebody was trying to "make a mountain out of a molehill," he maintained. Thurmond told the Senate that the Pentagon's Arthur Sylvester had distorted and leaked the story of the Marine quizzing for the purpose of "besmirching and besmearing the Senator from South Carolina." The Administration was in this way, he added, "attempting to divert attention from the subcommittee hearings." He then blunted the attack on himself and got back at the Pentagon by bringing up the matter of a letter that had disappeared from the briefcase of a subcommittee investigator.

The *Sunday Star* of Washington, D. C., on February 11th, criticized both affairs, the quiz and the "stolen" letter, and gave balanced perspective to the situation by adding:

> If the staff members have erred, however, so has the Marine Corps. According to Senator Thurmond, a man in San Diego wrote a personal letter to the Senator's legislative assistant submitting information relevant to the "muzzling" inquiry. This letter was dated November 24, 1961. Four days later, a member of the subcommittee staff went to Marine Corps Headquarters carrying this letter in his briefcase. Someone surreptitiously opened the briefcase and removed the letter, which was passed on to General Shoup. The General, in turn, dispatched a tart note to the letterwriter in San Diego.
>
> Last month, Senator Thurmond asked General Shoup who had taken the letter from the staff man's briefcase. General Shoup, according to the Senator, replied: "I cannot reveal that information. The Secretary of the Navy has instructed me not to furnish that information."
>
> This is at least as extraordinary as the Marine quiz affair. Why should the Secretary of the Navy, or General Shoup, be covering up for someone who filched a letter having to do with subcommittee business from the briefcase of a subcommittee member?

There was one interesting aspect of the Marine quiz which went unnoticed by the press. General Shoup, Commandant of the Marine Corps, testified on January 30th. Asked whether or not the Marine Corps used the Code of Conduct wallet cards (by Pentagon order of 1955, all the services were directed to do so because of the Korean War prisoner-of-war experience), General Shoup replied, "Yes."

This answer came as a surprise, since staff investigators

had reported that Shoup, in an interview prior to his testimony, had characterized the Code of Conduct as "defeatist,"
and had said that the Marine Corps did not use the wallet
cards.

The quiz of the Marines took place on February 1st, the
day following Shoup's testimony. One of the questions asked
the Marines was about the Code of Conduct wallet cards.
The staff later revealed that the Marines knew nothing
about the wallet cards.

On February 2nd, the day following the Marine quiz,
and two days after he testified, the Marine Commandant
wrote a letter to Stennis, asking that his answer on the
wallet card be changed in the record of the hearing. Said
Shoup:

> ... During the hearing, Mr. Kendall asked me the follow-
> ing question: "Does the Marine Corps use the code of
> conduct wallet cards?" I answered "Yes," to that question.
> Upon looking into this matter, however, I discovered that
> I was confusing the Geneva Convention card which the
> Marines do use with the code of conduct card. The Ma-
> rine Corps has not issued wallet-sized code of conduct
> cards for the use of individual Marines. As I pointed out
> in my testimony, we do teach the code of conduct in all
> commands. The fact that the Marine Corps does not issue
> these cards should not be interpreted to mean that I have
> any reservation about the value of the code of conduct
> other than I stated before your subcommittee. ...

In Thurmond's view, the sequence of events was not
without significance.

Try, as they did throughout the hearing and particularly
in connection with the Marine quiz, opponents of Senator
Thurmond never did succeed in making the McCarthy label
stick to him. They failed because Thurmond did not make
the basic mistake that Senator McCarthy made. While Mc-
Carthy was charged with dealing in personalities, rudely

and roughly accusing numbers of people by name of being either pink or red, Thurmond dealt only with policy, and, though often baited, he did not accuse government officials of being Communists.

Another highlight of the investigation was the appearance of the controversial Major-General Edwin A. Walker. The general had been relieved of his command of the 24th Division in Germany on April 17, 1961, for allegedly violating the Hatch Act, which prohibits partisan political activity among government personnel. He was accused of trying to influence the votes of troops in his command prior to the 1960 Congressional elections. He himself traced his difficulties back to the hard anti-Communist "pro-blue" information program he instituted for the 24th division. (The Army report charging Walker with improper political activity at the same time cleared the general's "pro-blue" program.) His program, he said, was in execution of written directions from the National Security Council and the Army. The whole dispute arose following allegations by a publication called *Overseas Weekly,* which the general considered in bad taste, sensational, and detrimental to troop morale. He had sought in vain to ban it from distribution in his area. It was Walker's feeling that the publication had influence in high places and was out to revenge his efforts to ban it in Germany by accusing him of improper political activity, thereby bringing Pentagon wrath upon him.

General Edwin Walker had a distinguished military record behind him, and in the campaign to bring about the muzzling investigation, Thurmond had cited Walker's case as an example of suppression of the anti-Communist line. In fact, much of the press was billing the subcommittee hearings as "the Walker hearings" because the General was expected to be a star witness. Thurmond, meantime, insisted that the Walker case was only one incident and that it was a distortion to wrap the investigation around General Walker. The South Carolinian did not picture himself as

Walker's champion because he felt the appellation twisted his position, thereby inaccurately reflecting what he was trying to do.

Often mentioned by the press as an early defender of General Walker, Thurmond insisted that he was not. The Fulbright memo began the muzzling investigation, he said. Thurmond pointed out that publicity surrounding General Walker's case had been going on for some months prior to release of the memo. It was incidental, he contended, that his interests and Walker's merged toward the same goal, obtainment of an investigation.

It was Thurmond's contention, also, that the Administration wanted the hearings billed as "the Walker hearings" so it could point to what it termed a "political" general and say, "See, this is why we have to censor officers."

When the investigation was decided on, the General was invited to testify during the troop education phase of the inquiry. However, he resigned his army commission on November 2, 1961, and subsequently embarked on an anti-Communist crusade. Shortly after February 1, 1962, General Walker announced his candidacy for the Democratic nomination for governor of Texas. Thurmond forces were disturbed by this development. Since his resignation Walker had made bitter and extreme public statements.

Thurmond staff members were concluding more and more that Walker's appearance before the subcommittee would hurt the Senator. Strom Thurmond himself doubted that Walker's conduct could possibly affect him. If the General stumbled, only the General would be hurt, he thought. After all, he had met Walker for the first time in the fall of 1961 after the investigation had been approved. Walker had never been in a seminar, had never had a speech censored; his "pro-blue" program had been cleared. There was really very little the General would contribute to the hearings, Thurmond maintained. The Senator characteristically dismissed the Walker matter from his mind to concentrate fully on the policies of the Administration. Thurmond's staff did not forget about the General, however.

When the former soldier became interested in the Texas gubernatorial election, though, Thurmond was jolted. He and Goldwater met with Walker in Senator Tower's office. Vainly the three legislators tried to dissuade the General from political ambitions. This session was only the second time Thurmond talked with Walker. (The next time would be at the subcommittee hearings.)

Entrance into politics would distort the principles for which the General said he was fighting, Thurmond told him that day in Tower's office, adding emphatically, "You will be judged in a totally different manner if you get into politics."

Nobody changed the General's mind about running for office, and he did not change his mind about testifying. General Walker appeared on April 4 before the subcommittee and a standing-room-only audience. He fared all right that day despite the raking-over-the-coals he gave the Administration from top to bottom. The next day he was trapped by certain committee members into calling names. The mistake of naming people, coupled with the incident of allegedly socking an annoying reporter afterwards in the corridor, served in the eyes of many to undo him. Testimony he gave in defense of his anti-Communist troop education program and of himself became overshadowed by the sensational charges he made concerning what he termed the "collusion with the international Communist conspiracy" that he claimed was victimizing not only him but also the American way of life.

The second and third phases of the investigation were not concluded until October, but the real drama ended with General Edwin Walker's two days in the witness chair.

In all, the Subcommittee heard sixty-seven witnesses over thirty-six days of open hearings and submitted a report of some 90,000 or more words that included the majority view,

Thurmond's view and Bartlett's view. Thurmond's report alone contained 85,000 words. The amount of time consumed in preparation for witnesses was enormous. Even more astounding was the breadth of subjects covered at the hearings. It seemed as though any time somebody had a thought pertaining to any subject on the Cold War, the thought, for whatever it was worth, found its way into the voluminous transcript.

Conclusions by the Subcommittee and Senator Thurmond were in agreement on the second and third parts of the investigation. Thurmond summed up these aspects as follows:

On the second and third major parts of the investigation —education programs for U. S. Armed Services personnel on the nature of the enemy and our own system of freedom and the education of reservists and portions of the public through military participation in Cold War seminars—the investigating subcommittee was generally in accord. For instance, we agree that our military personnel should be given more and better training and education on Communism and also on our own system of freedom. We also agreed that the banned film, "Operation Abolition" should be made available to commanders for use in their troop education programs.

On the subject of Cold War seminars, we concluded generally that the seminar programs for reservists and active duty personnel, such as those at the war colleges, and the public seminars in which military personnel had participated, had served a very useful purpose except in a small number of instances. In other words, the point of agreement reached by the subcommittee on seminars virtually repudiated many of the points raised in the Fulbright Memorandum and in articles in left-wing periodicals warning against public and military Cold War seminars. The subcommittee did stress, however, the importance of qual-

ity control so that military personnel do not become involved in political issues in their own seminars or through
participation in public seminars.

Basic differences arose between the majority of the Subcommittee and Senator Thurmond on the first phase of the
probe—censorship. Yet even in this phase, the differences
were primarily of degree, intensity and detail, reflecting the
interest and energy put into the investigation by the participating senators. As might have been expected, Thurmond's report was characterized by greater intensity and
infinitely greater detail.

In general, the Subcommittee's conclusions on censorship
can be summed up in this paragraph from its report:

Although the Subcommittee is convinced that a system for
prior review and clearance of military speeches for policy
is altogether proper and desirable, the record of the hearings reflects that the actual operation of the present system has left much to be desired. Many of the changes
and deletions are justifiable grounds for perplexity. It
does not overstate the case to say that in many cases the
actions of the reviewers both in the Department of Defense and the Department of State have been characterized by ineptness, inconsistency, caprice, arbitrary personal judgment, and even irresponsibility. All of the
witnesses whose speeches had been altered in the process
of review testified that the changes reflected no detectable
pattern or policy and, indeed, that the only consistency
about them was the clear inconsistency. Many of the
changes simply defy logical explanation.

Strom Thurmond's overall conclusions on the subject are
contained in the following two successive paragraphs from
his report:

The conclusions indicated by the censorship actions
and the comments of censors emanating from the State

Department were reinforced and supported by the subsequent written explanations and oral testimony. This conclusion is that we have either a policy or a predominant attitude which can be summarized as follows: The U. S. foreign policy is containment of direct foreign military aggression. It does not seek victory over Communism, but only to deter aggression while seeking grounds for accommodation, so that the Communist-dominated territories will have the necessary time in which to "evolve" into nonaggressive, socialist states.

It is possible that censorship actions indicate only individual, although widespread, thinking among personnel involved in the censoring, rather than our official foreign policy. However, the distinction makes little difference in the net results, if such thinking dominates those who occupy positions of responsibility in the daily execution of our foreign policy.

In his own individual report, Senator Bartlett made these observations about the conduct of the investigation:

At the outset I had such substantial doubts as to whether this inquiry should be conducted that I voted against the authorizing resolution on September 20, 1961. I did so in the belief that the language of the resolution in one way or another might be construed as endorsing in advance the contention of some that the military role should be expanded to diverse new fields in our struggle against Communism. Also, at that time the atmosphere was electric, and I feared that the hearings could well be charged with emotionalism and might bring disunity in the land, at the very time when unity was most needed.

My fears in this regard proved to be without substance. My conclusion is that the hearings were useful, and will be productive. The very considerable success which was achieved was due very largely, in my judgment, to the judicial manner in which the inquiry was conducted. . . .

Like a cat with nine lives, Strom Thurmond had once again survived an impossible act of political derring-do. He survived because his conduct and the results of the inquiry, in the opinions of enough people (including Senate colleagues), essentially vindicated his stand. Thurmond came through the investigation a better known figure nationally and also a more controversial figure. He did, indeed, emerge with his head still on his shoulders. Not only was he still alive politically, he remained as outspoken and independent as ever, a fact the Kennedy Administration would in time discover.

VIII

Thurmond Fights On

THE lengthy, wide-ranging hearings of the military muzzling investigation began on January 23, 1962 and continued through June 8th. The final report was not made until October 19th.

Yet, these hearings had not even begun when Strom Thurmond started casting an anxious eye in another direction—toward Cuba. The South Carolinian who had "connections" in a number of key places, also had Cuban connections, and these led him to make his first statement on January 15, 1962, about a suspected Soviet missile build-up there. He was the first member of Congress to bring the matter to public attention, almost one year before the Cuban missile crisis. Nothwithstanding his preoccupation with the forthcoming subcommittee inquiry on muzzling, Thurmond took time that day to tell the Senate that Cuba "may soon have the capability to launch superbomber attacks against any point in the Western Hemisphere. There is substantial evidence now indicating that Mr. Castro is constructing mis-

sile launching sites and extending runways in Cuba." Sources
for the Thurmond speech were American naval personnel
at Guantanamo naval base in Cuba. They, in turn, had found
out from Cuban civilians working at the base and from
other sources of intelligence information that certain land
areas were being sealed off for what looked like the construction of missile sites. The January 15 Senate speech
served notice that Thurmond had another cause for which
he would campaign as soon as he had more time and information.

It was August 31 before Senator Thurmond picked up
the Cuban issue again in any really significant way. The
subject kept cropping up in day-to-day testimony at the
military muzzling hearings (reference to Cuba is found on
56 different pages of the transcript), but as yet the Senator
had not gone at it in his usual, crusading style. On the last
day of August, Thurmond took a firm grip on the Cuban
military build-up issue and began in earnest to harass the
Administration with constant warnings that very few wanted
to think about seriously at the time.

Thurmond announced that he had intelligence data that
"at least four intermediate range ballistic missiles" had been
installed in Cuba. He went on to advocate American expul-
sion of Communists from the island before Cuba could
threaten the United States mainland with an air or missile
attack.

"Recent reports strongly indicate that an undetermined
number of Soviet military forces have landed in Cuba," he
said. "There is also every reason to believe that the Soviets
have built or are building a space satellite tracking station
on the north coast of Cuba. The longer the U. S. waits to
expel Communism from Cuba, the more difficult will be the
job.

". . . If circumstances in 1960 and early 1961 justified
decisions by two administrations that a U. S. sponsored invasion of Cuba was essential," the Senator wanted to know,

"how can the far worse circumstances of today require less? Inaction can be justified at this point only by a no-win policy of paralysis."

By this time there were others in Congress asking questions about Cuba. Southern legislators were particularly concerned because their states were closest to Cuba and, therefore, the most vulnerable to air attack.

Representative L. Mendel Rivers of South Carolina, ranking Democrat on the House Armed Services Committee, as early as February 6th had told a closed door hearing of the group that Soviet "mobile missiles" in Cuba posed a threat. Rivers had more to say on the subject as the year progressed. He was joined by Rep. Edward Hebert of Louisiana and Rep. William Cramer of Florida in expressing anxiety over defense against missiles in the southeastern and Gulf states. Senator Kenneth Keating (R., N.Y.) was another who joined consistently in alerting the nation to the Cuban danger. Keating and Thurmond had access to some of the same intelligence sources, though each man operated independently of the other.

Keating, too, had made a statement on August 31st, about the arrival of Russian forces. He had word, he said, of Russian ships having unloaded troops, "not technicians," and they were "wearing Soviet fatigue uniforms."

Thurmond spoke up again on September 1st, saying, "There is substantial evidence that there are now at least four intermediate range ballistic bases in Cuba."

Just a few days earlier, President Kennedy had said, "it would be a mistake to invade Cuba," because an invasion "could lead to very serious consequences for many people."

"The United States has obligations all around the world," he said, "including West Berlin and other areas which are very sensitive and, therefore, I think that in considering what appropriate action we should take we have to consider the totality of obligations and the responsibilities which we bear in so many different parts of the world."

The President acknowledged that the Russians had expanded their "military advisory mission" in Cuba. "There certainly are technicians there. There may be military technicians," he said. He maintained, however, that he had no information of Russian "troops" having gotten to the island, in the sense that "troops" meant soldiers.

On September 5, Secretary of State Rusk and Secretary of Defense McNamara briefed both the Senate Armed Services and Foreign Relations committees about Cuba and other troublesome areas. Thurmond joined Senator Frank Lausche (D., Ohio) and Senator George Aiken (R., Vt.) in closely questioning the President's claim that Soviet rockets, missile-carrying torpedo boats and military technicians in Cuba were only "defensive."

"They're coming in by the boatload," said Aiken. "That's a hell of a lot of defensive weapons."

Senator Lausche charged "appeasement."

Thurmond reminded everyone of his recent statement about the four missile bases and the tracking station being constructed in Cuba. He added, "The Administration poohpoohed my charges then. Now the President, in effect, admits I was right."

Senator Hugh Scott, Pennsylvania Republican, advocated that a deadline be set by the Organization of American States and then "declare foreign military exports to Cuba to be contraband and subject to blockade."

Senator Sam Ervin (D., N.C.) said that the Monroe Doctrine had been violated by these Soviet arms shipments.

The President had admitted the landing in Cuba of antiaircraft rockets, missile-carrying torpedo boats and 3,500 Soviet military technicians. Yet, he said he saw "no evidence" of a "significant offensive capability" there.

The next day Thurmond made a speech on the Senate floor attacking the Administration's Cuban policy. He termed it an effort to reinterpret and to weaken the Monroe Doctrine to avoid a showdown over the Cuban military build-up. He added bluntly, "How can we expect our European or Asiatic allies to have faith that we will stand firmly by their side against the forces of Communism when we have not taken firm action on Cuba, which adjoins our shores. And the same question applies to other parts of Latin America."

Writing in *The Record* of Columbia, South Carolina, on September 18th, Professor Raymond Moore of the International Studies department, University of South Carolina, found himself in rare agreement with both Thurmond and Goldwater on the Cuban problem. Moore referred to the statements by those two conservative Senators in which they mentioned the great threat Cuba was to Latin America. He said in part:

> Readers of past columns will have noted that it has not been my practice, to say the least, to agree with Senator Goldwater or Thurmond on many issues. Their particular brand of "on to victory" militancy in foreign policy has frequently struck me as a vast oversimplification of enormously complicated and difficult problems.... Yet on Cuba, it seems to me that they are more right than wrong. ... in the long run, I think the Senators are essentially correct in their estimates of how serious the situation is. Since the disastrous Cuban invasion of last year there has been an understandable reluctance on the part of the U.S. Government to use force against Castro. Assuredly, there are grave risks involved in any such course of action, but there may be even graver ones, as Senator Thurmond suggests, if Castro is allowed to export his revolution.

On October 10th, Senator Keating of New York declared, "Six launching sites are under construction—pads which will have the power to hurl rockets into the American heartland, and as far as the Panama Canal Zone."

President Kennedy, who was busily campaigning across the nation for Democratic candidates prior to the 1962 Congressional elections, was critical of "self-appointed generals and admirals" and appeared resentful of Congressional demands for him to "do something about Cuba." He kept minimizing foreign policy, particularly Cuban policy. But suddenly he canceled his tour, returned to Washington and closeted himself with advisers. On October 22nd he took to national television and radio with his famous speech marking a dramatic switch in position on the Cuban situation. He relayed "hard information" which he said had come to him first on October 15. The information on missile sites confirmed what various members of Congress had been saying since January.

Washington correspondent, Frank van der Linden wrote in *The Journal* of Shreveport, Louisiana, on October 25th:

> The members of Congress who were "voices crying in the wilderness" last January, last February, last August, and even as late as early October now have the melancholy satisfaction of knowing they were right all along—and the Administration is at last going to "do something" to get those missile bases out of Cuba.
>
> The unanswered question is: Why did it take so long to get the "hard information" about the bases?
>
> Everyone knows that missile bases don't spring up overnight like mushrooms. They take months to prepare. Some day, perhaps, the Administration will explain its incredible delay in telling the truth about the Russian build-up in Cuba.

The Cuban problem was far from solved, however. As early as the last week of November, approximately a month after President Kennedy's confrontation with Khrushchev over missiles in Cuba, reports cropped up of Soviet reconnaissance planes overflying the southeastern United States. Thurmond and fellow conservative Senator John Tower (R., Tex.), were leading other members of Congress in bringing out in the open weeks-old rumors of Russian overflights.

These men were joined by others, Lausche and Keating to name two, in demanding an investigation of the rumors. The Scripps-Howard newspaper chain said on December 1 that it had verified the Thurmond-Tower evidence from independent sources and that the overflights were a fact despite official Pentagon denials. The newspaper chain suggested two reasons for the denials: (1) "It's embarrassing;" and (2) "We would like to wait until we shoot down one of the planes before telling the public." The following week Pierre Salinger, White House Press secretary, categorically denied the occurrence of overflights. The Scripps-Howard newspaper chain once more stood without a waver by the accuracy of its stories and recommended that Salinger acquaint himself with the facts of the situation.

In an interview on December 23rd with Frank van der Linden for *The News* of Greenville, South Carolina, Thurmond exploded again on the subject of Cuba as he pressed for the investigation which eventually was conducted by a subcommittee of the Senate Armed Services Committee.

"Cuba is a Communist fort today," Thurmond said. "Thousands of Russian soldiers are still there, with a tremendous quantity of weapons. We have reports that missiles and atomic warheads may be hidden in caves. Yet our Government has backed down on its demands for on-the-site inspections, the only way to make sure the missiles, bombers and other weapons have really been taken out, as the Russians claim."

The outspoken lawmaker had more to say on December 30. He declared: "Cuba cannot be allowed to stand as a sanctuary of Communism, and I would be in full favor of an invasion if it were necessary to clear the Communists out.

Thurmond fired his heaviest artillery of all at the Administration on February 1, 1963 when he made public in his weekly newsletter that according to Cuban statistics that had come into his possession there were between 30,000 and 40,000 troops in Cuba under the command of a Russian general. (This number was double the figure President Kennedy said were on the island.) The accompanying missiles, bombers and other arms, he stated, "indicates the presence of a complete Soviet army, and the inventory normally assigned to a Soviet air army."

To newsmen, the Pentagon replied sedately, "the information obtained by our intelligence has been and is being made public to the extent it does not compromise intelligence sources. If Senator Thurmond has proof of any kind to support the information he has released, which differs from official intelligence information, the Department of Defense would like to receive the evidence." However, the Senator refused to identify his intelligence sources.

Defense officials contradicted Thurmond's figure of 30,-000 to 40,000 Russian troops and questioned his contention that there were in Cuba missiles with ranges to 2,200 miles. On other items, in most cases, the Pentagon just changed totals and did not deny the presence of those particular weapons on the island.

Senator Thurmond and the Defense Department differed on the following statistics, according to United Press International:

Thurmond: Approximately 600 tanks.

Pentagon: Less than 400.

Thurmond: More than 2,000 artillery pieces.

Pentagon: Less than 2,000.

Thurmond: More than 1,000 mortars.

Pentagon: Less than 800.

Thurmond: Slightly less than 1,000 anti-aircraft missiles.

Pentagon: Less than 600 surface-to-air SAM missiles.

Thurmond: Nuclear-tipped frog missiles, with a 300-mile range.

Pentagon: The frog missiles in Cuba have a 50-mile range, with no evidence of nuclear warheads.

The Pentagon also minimized Thurmond's claim of "a

complete Soviet army" to "a complete Soviet division." It did not challenge at all, said UPI, the Senator's statement that Cuba has 150 cruise missiles, presumably for use against shipping, or that Soviet submarines are "resupplied in Cuba and call frequently at Cuban ports and bays."

Additionally, Thurmond charged that "in no instance were bare missiles revealed to our observers of Soviet ships leaving Cuba." Between 100 and 200 were estimated to be in "underground facilities," he said, and added that a recent shipment of "atomic warhead materials" to the island had been reported.

On April 21, a still perturbed Strom Thurmond set forth in a newsletter his own idea on what to do about Cuba. First, he said, "demand removal of all Soviet forces in Cuba —to be confirmed by on-site inspections. And if the Soviets don't get out right away, break diplomatic relations with the Soviet Union. If severing diplomatic relations doesn't get the Soviet forces out, then re-impose an air and naval blockade of Cuba. And in the unlikely event that these two steps fail, take direct military action in concert with other American states as a last resort." Needless to add, Thurmond's advice was neither welcomed nor followed by the Administration.

Finally, on May 9th, the Preparedness Investigation Subcommittee of the Senate Armed Services Committee made public an interim report on the group's extensive investigation into the Cuban arms situation. (After serving the previous year as special member of this Subcommittee for the muzzling investigation, Senator Thurmond was given a permanent seat on it in January 1963. Immediate investigation of the Cuban military build-up was Thurmond's first endeavor as a regular member of the group. He had furnished a memo on Cuba to the Subcommittee chairman just prior to the inquiry.)

Once again under the chairmanship of Senator John Stennis, the Subcommittee spent months questioning nearly one hundred witnesses, including the heads of all intelligence agencies. Senator Stennis presented the report on the Senate floor, and it is worthy of note that the Subcommittee, including Thurmond, was unanimous in its findings, which covered areas in which Thurmond's charges were denied by the Administration—ballistic missiles and the number of Soviet troops remaining in Cuba.

As to the continuing reports of strategic missiles in Cuba, the Subcommittee found that "strategic weapons may or may not be now in Cuba," and based this conclusion on "the lack of conclusive evidence." Indeed, the Committee revealed: "Photographic reconnaissance was unable to detect precisely how many ballistic missiles were introduced into Cuba. Prior to the Soviet announcement that forty-two missiles would be withdrawn, our photographs had revealed a lesser number. It could not be established, therefore, how many ballistic missiles were, in fact, introduced into Cuba." Noting the conflict between "refugee and exile reports" that the many caves in Cuba were being used for storage of missiles, and the "opinion" of intelligence analysts that the caves were being used for storage of other weapons, the Subcommittee pointed out that the latter "opinion" is "based to a substantial degree on the negative proposition that there is no hard evidence confirming the presence of strategic missiles in Cuba at this time."

On the subject of the number of Soviet troops on the island, the Subcommittee bore down on what it considered faulty Government intelligence information and, in effect, largely agreed with what members of Congress had been saying. The report revealed the following salient facts:

1. "On October 22, our intelligence people estimated there were 8,000 to 10,000 Soviets in Cuba. They now say that, at the height of the buildup, there were at least 22,000."

2. "The intelligence community estimated that approxi-

mately 5,000 Soviet personnel were withdrawn following the October confrontation. A net of 4,000 to 5,000
additional have been withdrawn since the first of the
year, our intelligence people say. However, because of
what is described by intelligence as 'technical reasons,'
the 17,500 intelligence estimate of those remaining is
unchanged at the writing of this report. At the least,
this indicates a low level of confidence in the original
estimate."

3. (Following an awesome list of the types of modern
   weapons brought into Cuba by the Soviets:) "We feel
   that the official estimates of the number of Soviet troops
   are questionably low when related to the large numbers of the weapons listed above.

4. "We conclude that no one in official United States
   circles can tell, with any real degree of confidence,
   how many Russians are now in Cuba and we are of
   the opinion that the official 17,500 estimate is perhaps
   a minimum figure."

The report contended that the Cuban problem, from
both political and military standpoints, should be given "the
highest priority by Government officials to the end that the
evil threat which the Soviet occupation of Cuba represents
will be eliminated at an early date."

For Thurmond, having the Subcommittee provide a
"substantiation" of his charges was not enough. In the many
speeches he continued to make on Cuba, he made it clear
that he would not be satisfied until "something was done
about Cuba." In such speeches, however, he now used the
Subcommittee Report to document the danger.

Very shortly after release of the Subcommittee Report
on Cuba, the whole matter of the Cuban threat lost the
limelight to another dramatic issue, the Nuclear Test Ban
Treaty. Strom Thurmond ripped into it with the same con-
centration and energy he had applied to the Cuban arms

problem. He got off to an early start on the question when the Preparedness Investigating Subcommittee began hearings on May 7, 1963, to deal with the proposed Test Ban Treaty. The group had been discussing for some months the whole field of test bans but got down to specifics in May when this one came upon the international scene.

On June 10 President Kennedy delivered a foreign policy address at American University in Washington, setting forth attitudes and test ban proposals that shook Thurmond deeply. Three days later, the Senator gave a major speech in the Senate to comment upon that address and to launch his own fierce opposition to the test ban agreement Kennedy had announced was in prospect. The President had "confirmed beyond any doubt," Thurmond declared, "that it is the United States' policy to accept the status-quo between the Communists and the free world and that if we hold onto the status-quo, the Soviet will evolve or change. The President stated that we should live together 'with mutual tolerance,' which is nothing more than formalizing the status-quo." It was this kind of policy, a policy of containment, stalemate and accommodation that Thurmond in the muzzling investigation and in public statements had accused the Administration of adopting.

In fact, in a 1962 speech following a trip abroad, Senator Thurmond had said, "U.S. policy on the world scene is viewed as being neutral toward our enemy, friendly toward the neutrals and unfriendly toward our friends."

The Senator had made a number of trips to foreign countries by then, delivering speeches in many of the nations he visited. His extensive travels, during the course of which he had met and talked with the officials of many countries, was an important factor in Thurmond's opposition to American policy. He had usually returned home in a state of aggravation over U.S. Government attitudes that made no sense to him. Thurmond's Latin American travels, for example, had convinced him that America should handle the

Alliance for Progress program differently. Instead of direct aid to governments, he favored aid with incentives to promote the development of private enterprise. He had been immensely impressed in Germany and in Japan by the individual initiative and imagination of the people in revitalizing their economies. The Senator thought the same kind of industriousness could be developed in Latin American countries.

As for President Kennedy's official revelation in that June 10 address of forthcoming nuclear test ban discussions agreed upon by Russia, Great Britain and the United States, Thurmond clearly stated his opposition. He was the first senator to do so. He was opposed for reasons that need no explanation where trusting Russia is concerned. He was also against a ban on testing in the atmosphere because the "United States needs to conduct nuclear tests in the atmosphere" to achieve and to maintain superior technical knowledge and weaponry in all phases of nuclear armament. America did not necessarily have parity, much less superiority in certain areas, he emphasized. Thus, a test ban treaty could work only to Russian advantage and to U.S. disadvantage.

Thurmond did more than just make a speech answering the President on June 13th, however. At the same time, he introduced a resolution which would have had the effect of putting the Senate flatly on record in opposition to a test ban treaty even before one could be signed. In explanation, Thurmond pointed out to the Senate that its constitutional power of "advice and consent" on treaties was only half met by "consenting" to ratification of treaties, and that it was necessary to act before the signing of a treaty if the Senate was to have any real say-so on the matter.

"The Senate has a responsibility to the American people to insure, among other things, that their security and rights are not impaired by a treaty," Thurmond charged the Senate. "This responsibility," he continued, "cannot always be completely fulfilled by waiting until a treaty is signed by the Executive Branch and formally sent to the Senate for consideration. If a nuclear test ban treaty is actually signed, the Senate will be told that regardless of how badly it would affect the interests of the country, a rejection of the treaty by the Senate would give the Soviets fuel for a major propaganda campaign."

The treaty was signed in Moscow on August 5th. On August 23rd, Thurmond spoke in the Senate against ratification and took Defense Secretary Robert McNamara to task for what he considered the latter's misleading testimony to the Senate Foreign Relations Committee on the treaty's behalf. The South Carolinian then carried with him all but two members of the seven-man Preparedness Investigating Subcommittee. The group released on September 9 its 5-to-2 unfavorable report on ratification. Moreover, as soon as the treaty reached the Senate floor that summer, Thurmond put full steam into efforts there to defeat consent.

The man's serious view of the matter was evident in the trouble he had taken to prepare himself for both the hearings and floor debate. A team of nuclear experts had gone to Thurmond's office regularly to give the staff what could be termed a course on nuclear physics and warfare. The staff, in turn, thoroughly briefed the Senator. He was able consequently to speak knowledgeably and technically in committee and Senate sessions. Altogether, he made five major speeches against the ban and participated fully in debate during those weeks the question was before the Senate. Thurmond's own prediction of June 13th, however, proved correct. Once the treaty was signed, the Senate was told that irreparable harm would be done if the Senate refused to consent to ratification. Despite the findings of the Preparedness Subcommittee that "serious—perhaps even formidable—military and technical disadvantages to the United States will flow from ratification of the treaty," the Senate consented to ratification on September 24, 1963.

How South Carolina's junior Senator, even with his vigor, found time to be everywhere at once was mystifying. His kinfolk often lamented the grueling pace he maintained. "I wish Strommy (which came out Strummy) wouldn't work as hard as he does. He gets so wrought up over the state of the country!" declared a perturbed relative, echoing the sentiments of other kin. "Well, I'm just trying to do what I can to save the country," was the Senator's standard reaction to concern over his health as he continued at full speed.

In addition to worrying over Cuba while participating in the military muzzling investigation, Thurmond had turned his attention in yet another direction—the mishandling of the nation's strategic material stockpiles.

President Kennedy told a press conference on January 31, 1962 that investigators had been checking into the government's multibillion dollar stockpile of critical materials. It was his opinion that there had been "excessive storage of costly materials" creating "a potential source of excessive and unconscionable profits."

"A thorough investigation is warranted," the President said.

The National Stockpile and Naval Petroleum Reserves Subcommittee thereupon went into action. At the time, this Subcommittee, under the chairmanship of Senator Stuart Symington (D., Mo.), consisted of only three members, one of whom was Thurmond. Three more were added "in order to better conduct the investigation."

Hearings on the stockpile situation, which got underway on February 23, 1962, were carried on simultaneously with those of the muzzling investigation and continued until January of 1963. The inquiry revealed shocking mismanagement which had resulted in huge wastes of government funds, appallingly excessive storage of various materials and scandalous profiteering by certain private companies, to say nothing of political pressures. In other words, since creation of the national stockpile by law in 1946, there had been much hanky-panky.

The fact that the stockpile was considered to be so closely

related to national security that its management was a guarded secret contributed substantially to the problem, it was felt by some of the Subcommittee members (including Thurmond).

The South Carolinian kept up with both the muzzling and stockpile inquiries, participating in all hearings as much as possible. He also had his own individual view to file on stockpiling as well as on muzzling of the military. In fact, the corrective bill that came out of the stockpile investigation was based primarily on Thurmond's view, which was considered especially geared to correction of the law. This bill passed the Subcommittee unanimously, then passed the Armed Services Committee unanimously and, finally, in early 1965, it passed the Senate unanimously.

Meanwhile, Senator Thurmond was off again toward still another area of concern—providing a defense against ballistic missiles, which, in turn, led to the darndest confusion the Senate had known in years.

"Who else but Strom would have been this determined?" remarked an acquaintance afterwards, recalling the parliamentary tizzy of the august Senate and the exasperation of certain colleagues.

Since 1960, Thurmond had been urging that the United States develop and deploy a defense against ballistic missiles. Each year when the annual military authorization bill came before the Armed Services Committee, Thurmond sought to have funds added to speed the development and production of such a system. In the hearings held in February and March 1963, in which the testimony covered all phases of defense posture, Thurmond interrogated Secretary of Defense McNamara exhaustively, particularly on the Nike-Zeus anti-ballistic missile system. The two men seemed fated in those days to knock heads at the mere sight of each other.

McNamara, representing the Administration, questioned the feasibility and desirability of producing an anti-ballistic system. He questioned whether a foolproof system could be built, and did not believe that the costs involved, the amount of which was in dispute, could be justified. Thurmond maintained that the system was feasible, as the Army maintained, and that the number of lives which could possibly be saved justified the expenditure.

The immediate issue was whether the United States should begin pre-production engineering on the Nike-Zeus system then under development. This step would be equivalent to a commitment to produce and deploy a system of some type. McNamara preferred to develop a more refined follow-on system, the Nike-X, before deciding whether to produce and deploy. Thurmond insisted that since it would take five years before the first units could be produced, it was urgent to make the decision then to save lead time.

Senator Richard Russell, Armed Services Committee chairman, went along with the McNamara view. On the authorization bill, the group first followed Russell in voting down by 9 to 4 the Thurmond proposal to include $196 million for pre-production engineering on the Nike-Zeus system. Having gotten three other committee members to go along with him on the first vote, the Souh Carolina Senator then got the committee to reconsider. By a 9-to-8 vote he won approval to include the Nike-Zeus funds. The committee reversal marked the first defeat Russell had ever suffered in that group. To say the least, the Georgian was displeased. He vowed to carry the dispute to the Senate floor and did.

Thurmond said the only way he could present his case to the Senate was to reveal classified information and to do that, the body would have to be called into a closed door session. On April 11th he proceeded to invoke a 169-year-old Senate rule to clear the galleries of visitors and of press representatives.

Policemen were stationed outside the chamber's closed doors—and had she been alive, Jean Thurmond would have been outside those doors, too. Unquestionably, she would have been just as disturbed and anxious over the outcome of this unconventional action by her husband as she was over his historic filibuster. She probably would have been standing in the corridor, conversing in her usual, gay way with either the policemen or with reporters. Outwardly, she would have been all nonchalance; inwardly, she would have been deeply concerned. She would have wondered what it all meant for Strom's future.

In truth, there was reason to wonder about these proceedings, for the Senate really was in a stew. Much discussion was taking place over procedure, as attachés were given secrecy oaths, and there was great scurrying about the place. The Senate had not been in closed door session since the war year of 1943. Some members and employees were so annoyed they could hardly contain themselves.

Nevertheless, Thurmond "educated" senators on the subject of anti-missile missiles and the broad range of the U. S. strategic power vis-à-vis the Soviet Union. He addressed himself not so much to the present picture but to the effect on the future of present and recent national security decisions. But his efforts on the pending vote were all in vain, as he knew they would be, because the Senate vote did not revolve around the actual merits or demerits of Thurmond's case. The vote really was on whether the heavily Democratic Senate would support a Democratic President and Administration, its "prized" Cabinet officer and its venerable Committee Chairman against the facts and logic of an unregimentable committee. The Senate could not vote against Russell, its Armed Services Chairman. After sitting for four hours and twenty-three minutes, the upper house voted down by 58 to 16 Thurmond's Nike-Zeus proposal.

"I hope we will not have to regret this action," Thurmond said upon announcement of his defeat.

Senator Mike Mansfield (D., Mont.), majority leader, and Senator Everett Dirksen (R., Ill.), minority leader, complimented Thurmond for trying. However, Mansfield added, "I hope there will not be another secret session of the Senate for another quarter-century."

A number of other senators remarked that the executive session debate was "impressive and revealing." Ohio's Senator Lausche was quoted in the press as saying he had learned more about the military posture of the nation from Thurmond's information than in his previous six years in the Senate. Senator George Smathers (D., Fla.) called the session "some of the most constructive debate I ever heard." Thurmond "opened some eyes," said Senator Thomas Dodd (D., Conn.). "For some strange reason," he added, "the responsible authorities have ruled against any procurement of the Nike-Zeus until it has been proved as a weapons system."

Acknowledging the applause and personal congratulations his speech had received, Senator Thurmond commented dryly and even a little wistfully, "Never have I seen so much congratulation supported by so few votes."

"I didn't expect to win," said the Senator about the lopsided vote against him. "I was opposed by an unbeatable combination: Dick Russell, the Armed Services Committee chairman, Defense Secretary McNamara and President Kennedy. But I achieved one major purpose by making the Senate meet in secret session: I aroused public attention to the alarming fact that we have no defense against an ICBM attack."

The victorious Russell remarked, "I will say it brought out the best attendance we have had in a long while. Senators are just like women, I guess. If you tell them you're going to divulge a secret, they will come and sit on the edge of their chairs."

Thurmond was roasted by many liberal publications for causing the secret session, yet later some of these same publications picked up information from the session through senators and jolted a number of readers with it. One choice tidbit—that the Russians had missiles already placed around Leningrad that could knock out Polaris-type missiles, or even ICBM's, under the right conditions—shook even members of the Administration.

Thurmond had not won the battle, but he had furthered his cause. The lopsided rejection of his all-out effort did not stop the tenacious southerner. In 1964 and 1965, he offered amendments in Committee to authorize funds to do pre-production engineering on an anti-ballistic missile system, but in each case failed to prevail. McNamara staunchly refused to go forward, even though the Joint Chiefs of Staff recommended unanimously that the system be built.

Persistence finally paid off for Thurmond. Again in 1966, the Joint Chiefs of Staff unanimously recommended authorization of funds for pre-production engineering on the Nike-X, but McNamara refused to request the money and opposed the move toward production even on the now very refined Nike-X system. Thurmond again moved to authorize the funds, and in April 1966, the Armed Services Committee backed Thurmond without a dissenting vote. This time the Senate, too, went along and the House of Representatives concurred. After six years of trying, Thurmond at last managed to have the funds authorized to begin pre-production engineering on a weapons system to defend the American people against an attack by ballistic missiles.

An opportunity soon arose for the Senator to do battle again, this time in behalf of the cause dearest of all to him—preservation of the United States Constitution, as he interpreted it.

The occasion was the introduction in Congress by the Kennedy Administration of the strongest civil rights bill in history. The bill had been drafted after the Negro rights demonstrations which began in Birmingham, Alabama, in the spring of 1963, and soon spread to other localities. The bill sought principally to break down the remaining barriers

of segregation and discrimination. Southern legislators contended that in guaranteeing Negroes certain rights of entry,
the bill was at the same time violating other rights just as
precious, such as private property rights. Though all the
southern senators opposed the bill, Strom Thurmond probably was the most vocal opponent. He had more chances
than many to be vocal since the Senate Commerce Committee, of which he was a member, conducted hearings on
the bill.

Despite the fact that liberal publications and liberal politicians wasted no opening in which to refer to Thurmond
as the ex-Dixiecrat candidate for president and as a segregationist, Capitol Hill had learned over the years that the man
genuinely believed in States' Rights and in a strict interpretation of the Constitution. During his tenure as Governor
of South Carolina, he had been considered a liberal, advo-
cating many progressive local measures. Later, he was
looked upon as an ultra-conservative senator for continuing
to espouse the same belief—that the states ought to be doing
what the federal government was doing more and more.

In 1957 when Thurmond made his record-breaking filibuster against the civil rights bill passed that year, many
observers felt he was doing nothing more than playing to
the grandstands. *Time* magazine had this occasion in mind
when it referred to the Carolinian's Senate career as being
distinguished "mainly for windiness." It was incredible to
Capitol Hill then that Thurmond was so concerned about
what he called "this unconstitutional legislation" that he
would talk against it passionately for 24 hours and 18
minutes.

Conviction notwithstanding, that well-publicized speech
fell largely upon skeptical ears. The man had been in Washington only two and a half years when he made his long
speech. Most people there really did not know the many
facets of his personality. They did not know that Thurmond
never did things in half-measure—that when he was for

something he was for it all the way, that when he was
against something, he likewise was against it all the way,
and that he would fight to the last breath for his stand. He
was all for the Constitution; and consequently all against
whatever in his opinion would violate it. Naturally, he found
himself against an increasing number of things as liberal
influence grew.

After the 1957 speech, colleagues heard the Senator
sound off so often and feelingly on what he thought was
desecration to the Constitution that it finally began to dawn
on them that he was in earnest. "Just listen to ole Strom,"
said a fellow southerner in the Senate during one such
oration. "He really believes all that stuff!"

It came as no surprise in after years, therefore, to learn
that the junior senator from South Carolina had bought up
a stack of booklets on the Constitution and was presenting
a copy to almost every visitor. The Senator was becoming
ever more concerned over the state of the nation and what
he termed "the definite path toward socialism" and the
"erosion of states' rights." He made a practice of reaching
into the closet of his private office and pulling out a green
and white copy of *What Everyone Should Know About the
Constitution: A Scriptographic Presentation*. The booklet contained twenty-four pages of cartoons, drawings and simple
explanations of the Constitution and of the Bill of Rights.
The publication clearly was designed for children of elementary school age. Along with a copy of the book, the visitor
would receive a patient, professorial lecture from Senator
Thurmond, who was anxious that everybody understand
and appreciate the American system of government. The
Senator also began stocking up on a companion red and
white publication entitled *What Everyone Should Know
About Communism*. Copies of this little book he kept beside
the ones on the Constitution and would give also to numbers
of visitors as he would go into a companion lecture on Communism. In fact, Thurmond habitually passed out pamphlets,

copies of old speeches and other informative literature to people who asked his position on one issue or another.

The day Strom Thurmond in all seriousness gave a copy of the child's booklet on the Constitution to United States Attorney General Robert Kennedy for the latter's edification, nearby faces promptly broke into broad grins. Capitol Hill knew by this time to accept such actions as "Thurmondisms."

That confrontation between Thurmond and Kennedy was a highlight of the Commerce Committee's hearings on the Administration's civil rights bill presented to Congress formally on June 18th.

As soon as the emotionally explosive bill was submitted, heated reaction came, as expected, from southern legislators. The section of the bill evoking the greatest anger and controversy was the one on public accommodations that would ban discrimination in hotels, lodging houses, restaurants and stores.

In order to avoid having the bill bottled up in the Senate Judiciary Committee, presided over by Mississippi's James Eastland, the Administration based its public accommodations proposals on the Constitution's commerce clause and sent the bill to the friendlier hands of the Commerce Committee. Thurmond was the only conservative southerner in the group and therefore the only opposition for the other pro-civil rights members to override.

The main thing the South Carolinian was able to do was to employ as many delaying tactics as possible and to grill witnesses in such a way as to point up what he and other southerners considered to be glaring faults in the bill and thereby to arouse public reaction against the legislation. The Senator proceeded with his task in the usual Thurmond way —with every ounce of his tremendous energy and unswerving determination. He closely questioned all Administration witnesses from Dean Rusk to Burke Marshall but his sharpest scrutiny of the proposals was in his questioning of the first witness, none other than the President's brother, Attorney General Robert Kennedy, who appeared on July 1st.

After making an opening statement in behalf of the bill, Kennedy submitted to questioning. Senators tried to pin the Attorney General down on specifics, such as what percentage of interstate trade did the bill mean by "substantial." "More than minimal," replied Kennedy, not offering much enlightenment.

The Administration did not want to regulate "social and personal relations," the Attorney General told legislators. Congress, therefore, might want to rewrite the bill to clearly exempt small family-run boarding houses. He added that this suggestion did not mean he favored a cut-off point which would "water down" the purposes of the ban. "As a practical matter," he said, "a cut-off might produce more difficulties than it would resolve."

The main point, Kennedy emphasized, was that the proposed law "would remove a daily insult to Negroes and I think we're going to pay for it for many, many years if we don't get this passed."

New York's *Herald Tribune* observed:

... The somewhat equivocal answers offered by the boyish figure in the witness chair of the caucus room—where he so often asked questions as counsel to the Senate Rackets Committee—proved the opening which Sen. Thurmond was seeking to press his segregationist case.

"I do not think it will be able to pass Congress," Sen. Thurmond said in opening. "I'm convinced the people are strongly against it."

Then for two hours the Southern Democrat, having passed an annotated copy of the Constitution to the witness, cited chapter and verse in an effort to show that "this bill goes directly against the Constitution and deprives a person of his property."

At times during this laconic exchange it seemed Sen. Thurmond had assumed the role of a Bible-school professor in some after-hours civics class, tutoring a reluctant pupil. This plainly made the Attorney General unhappy, but both men retained their composure and outward good humor.

What Thurmond handed to Kennedy, of course, was a copy of the child's booklet, *What Everyone Should Know About the Constitution.* With a worried frown on his brow, he said to the Attorney General—and Thurmond was completely serious—"Anyone can understand this, I urge you to study it."

Willard Edwards of the *Chicago Tribune* referred to the occurrence, saying:

> ... Kennedy has not been unaccustomed to mockery about his paucity of legal knowledge. He had heard his brother, the President, joke about the subject before a great gathering.
>
> But he and the senators present knew that Thurmond was not jesting. The senator from South Carolina is incapable of indulging in a gag. The great American practice of needling, friendly or otherwise, remains a mystery to him. When he is in a group which breaks into laughter at some witticism or wisecrack, Thurmond looks bewildered.
>
> "Bobby didn't know whether to laugh or cry," said an amused senator, recalling the incident. "He knew Thurmond was genuinely troubled about what he regarded as ignorance of the Constitution and was offering him in friendly concern, a juvenile instruction book on the subject.
>
> "It was almost impossible for him to take offense although he was being told, in effect, that he lacked a child's knowledge of the law of the land.". . .

Said Strom Thurmond afterwards, and just as seriously, the book was "really very good." Kennedy "needed it."

During their two-hour discussion, Thurmond and Kennedy went around and around on the issue of specifics.

Thurmond viewed both, the bill's language and Kennedy's attempted clarification of it, as entirely too vague. He had as little success as the other senators in pinning down the Attorney General. One of the most newsworthy portions of their lengthy conversation dealt with a theoretical barber shop at Fort Mill near the South Carolina–North Carolina line.

That dialogue went something like this:

Thurmond: Well, if two intrastate travelers visited a barber shop, it (the proposed law) would not apply?

Kennedy: You mean two intrastate travelers. Where is the barber shop?

Thurmond: Well, it is not connected with a terminal of any kind.

Kennedy: I doubt very much if it would.

Thurmond: Well, suppose fifty interstate travelers visited the barber shop. Would it apply?

Kennedy: Where is the barber shop?

Thurmond: It is off to itself; the same barber shop.

Kennedy: But it is getting closer to a highway.

Thurmond: Well, the barber shop is right on Main Street, and it is not connected with some other business.

Kennedy: I say generally the barber shops it would not apply to. If you get into a high percentage of people, if it's right on the border, for instance, between South Carolina and North Carolina, and people are always going over from North Carolina to come to the barber shop in South Carolina it might apply.

Thurmond: Well, I mean now, for instance, there is a little town, Fort Mill, between North Carolina and South Carolina. Now if two travelers went in the barber shop there in that town, and it is not connected with anything else, they came from North Carolina, they just stopped there to get a haircut and were going to South Carolina to spend some money, would that apply to them?

Kennedy: I don't think it would.

Thurmond: Well, suppose fifty stopped at that barber shop. Would that apply or would—

Kennedy: How many barbers does this barber shop have? I don't want to be facetious.

Thurmond: They might have only five barbers.

Kennedy: This is Mr. Murphy's barber shop.

The Chairman: In what period of time?

Thurmond: Say in one day, say fifty went in this barber shop in one day.

Kennedy: I would think he would have to come under it. I would think he would have to cut a Negro's hair. I don't think he could discriminate.

Thurmond: Suppose we cut that in half and only twenty-five say went from Charlotte down to Fort Mill.

Kennedy: All in one day?

Thurmond: In one day.

Kennedy: How many barber chairs?

Thurmond: The same five barbers.

Kennedy: And how many other customers does this barber shop have?

Thurmond: Would that make any difference?

Kennedy: Yes, a substantial degree.

Thurmond: Well, say half of them.

Kennedy: I think it would apply.

Thurmond: Well, what is your percentage now?

Kennedy: But I can't give you a percentage, Senator. You tell me what the story is.

On and on and on the barber shop matter went in the same vein, with approximately the same results.

At one point during the two-hour generally "good-humored sparring," as The New York Times described the conversation, Thurmond "asked what would happen if a restaurant owner decided to serve only 'red-haired secretaries.' Kennedy replied amid laughter:

"I think if he made it clear only red-haired secretaries, we might want to inquire why he wanted to do that."

The "red-haired secretaries" and the Fort Mill barber shop became almost as well publicized in the press as the theoretical "Mrs. Murphy's boardinghouse," often cited to illustrate provisions of the civil rights bill.

A sidelight of these hearings was the frequent haggling between Strom Thurmond and Senator John Pastore (D., R.I.). The latter occasionally presided as temporary committee chairman, and he and Thurmond disagreed heatedly over the way the southerner questioned witnesses before the committee. It was difficult to believe that the two men had worked compatibly on a five-year subcommittee study that resulted in 1964 passage of the important one-price cotton bill. For most of those five years, Pastore and Thurmond were the only members of the special Domestic Textile Industry Subcommittee to carry on the assignment. Amazingly enough, they were in complete agreement on three reports issued by the group during that time. Final enactment of the one-price cotton legislation recommended by this subcommittee as far back as 1959—and repeatedly urged in later reports—is credited for the current textile boom in the nation. However, to see Thurmond and the equally positive Rhode Islander at the Commerce Committee's civil rights hearings, an observer would never have guessed that the men had been able to join forces harmoniously for anything.

The civil rights hearings ground slowly through the autumn of 1963. When Lyndon Johnson succeeded to the Presidency upon John F. Kennedy's assassination in November, he put fresh impetus and his own special abilities behind efforts to pass the Kennedy civil rights bill. The House of Representatives responded first by passing on February 10, 1964, an even stiffer version of the bill than the one originally proposed by the Kennedy Administration. The House bill reached the Senate on February 17th. It was met head-on by an organized filibuster of southerners under Senator Richard Russell's leadership. The filibuster got underway in March and continued for weeks and weeks.

On March 18th, just prior to the filibuster's beginning, something else of note took place in a room off the Senate floor. Strom Thurmond engaged Senator Hubert Humphrey (D., Minn.), Senate whip and floor manager of the civil rights bill, in a nationally televised debate over the bill on the "CBS Reports" program. The Columbia Broadcasting System's national commentator, Eric Sevareid, was moderator.

When the network first approached Thurmond about the debate, he referred representatives to the southern leadership. If no one were interested, then he would undertake it, agreed the South Carolinian, who had never been one to turn down a challenge. No one else appeared interested, so Thurmond came forth to match oratory with one of the most effective speakers on Capitol Hill. To compensate for Humphrey's "glibness," as Thurmond aides termed the Minnesota Senator's debating ability, staff members briefed Strom Thurmond from A to Z and back again on provisions of the bill. When the southerner went before the cameras at 7:30 p.m. on March 18, he therefore was ready for battle. In fact, he knew the civil rights bill better than its floor manager. Whereas Humphrey spoke eloquently, but in general, of the need for such a bill and, in general, of its provisions, Thurmond spoke factually, citing titles and section. The latter's thorough knowledge of the bill enabled him not only to acquit himself well in the debate against a formidable opponent but to impress other colleagues as well.

Thurmond still had not said his last word on the subject. Before final passage of the bill by the Senate in the summer of 1964, he proposed thirty-six restrictive amendments—all of them rejected. Later, the Supreme Court upheld the law's constitutionality. Once again, Thurmond went down to defeat on a legislative issue, but true to form, he fought to the last vote.

As a matter of fact, the Carolinian still wasn't ready to give up his struggles for the southern cause. On a related, secondary matter to the Civil Rights act, Strom Thurmond went into action again. This incident did not affect history—presumably, at least—but it made the headlines, frustrated news photographers almost beyond endurance and enlivened Capitol Hill.

It involved two Democrats on just another hot, dull July 9th in Washington. One Democrat, naturally, was Senator Thurmond of South Carolina. The other was Senator Ralph Yarborough of Texas. The men were southerners, good friends, fellow members of the Senate Commerce Committee, and both were sixty-one years old. There, similarities ended.

Thurmond had refused to enter the Commerce Committee room the previous day to bring the number of members present up to a quorum so that a vote could be taken. The name of former Governor LeRoy Collins of Florida was before the group for approval as director of President Johnson's new Community Relations Service, a position dealing with racial disputes and mediation. The South Carolina Senator strongly opposed Collins' appointment because of a recent speech Collins had made in South Carolina—a speech regarded by a number of southerners as grossly unfair and insulting to white southerners.

With no quorum present, the Committee chairman, Senator Warren G. Magnuson (D., Wash.) postponed the voting until the next day. Two days earlier Thurmond had put Collins through his paces for three hours. When balloting time came, however, Thurmond remained in the corridor. Now on Thursday he again stood outside the room to prevent a quorum.

When Senator Ralph Yarborough arrived and observed

that the group would have a quorum if he could get Thurmond inside, he playfully pulled the Carolinian toward the door, saying, "Come on in, Strom."

Strom responded by pulling Yarborough away from the door. "I'll make an agreement with you, Ralph," said Thurmond. "If I can keep you out, you won't go in, and if you can drag me in, I'll stay there."

The Texan dismissed the challenge as a joke at first, but when the Carolinian pressed the issue, accepted. "A friendly agreement," both afterwards termed the arrangement.

The two men then handed their coats, pens, pencils, papers and Yarborough's eyeglasses to an unhappy Thurmond aide standing in the hallway. They pulled and pushed each other briefly, then Thurmond grabbed Yarborough's legs, threw him to the floor and pinned him there. Thurmond let his opponent up again for another round of shoulder-to-shoulder scuffling before throwing him once more. The trim, 170-pound Thurmond kept the paunchy, 190-pound Texan pinned for at least five minutes. Meanwhile, reporters and photographers came running. Capitol police thwarted all picture-taking efforts, causing the most disappointed cameramen in Washington. Reporters, however, observed every grunt, puff and hold for posterity. A Thurmond aide frantically pleaded with his boss to stop before the incident became publicized, but to no avail. While Yarborough lay on the floor, struggling occasionally to get free, Thurmond, perched atop the Texan, kept saying, "Tell me to release you, Ralph, and I will." Yarborough could not consent to preventing a quorum, so he stayed on the floor, answering with a grin that he was waiting for his second wind.

About this time Senator Lausche came along on his way to the committee meeting. "Gentlemen," he leaned over to warn the "aging wrestlers" (as one reporter described them) "you're both risking heart attacks." His advice, too, fell on deaf ears.

At last, someone told Chairman Magnuson what was taking place, and he came to the door. "Stop that!" Magnuson roared. "Get up off that floor!"

"I will have to yield to the order of my chairman," said Yarborough.

Both men obediently rose to their feet, retrieved their belongings and entered the meeting. Senator Lausche's presence assured a quorum, so Thurmond went in to vote no against Collins, who won approval anyway by a 16-to-1 vote.

Later, Thurmond and Yarborough, looking like sheepish little boys, faced television cameras to laugh off their ten-minute combat. Discretion prevailing, they refused to re-enact the scene for photographers. Even so, the incident was national news on television that night and in the press that afternoon and the next day.

It was all in jest, Thurmond smilingly assured reporters about the Thurmond-Yarborough wrestling match. "I told him I'd let him up any time he asked me to. We had a mutual agreement."

The two senators were officers in the same Army Reserve unit, but Thurmond had received the benefit of more recent training. "I had a weight advantage," said Yarborough, "but he had the advantage of that guerrilla training. He took a judo training course and guerrilla warfare course down at Fort Bragg, N.C. that I'm not familiar with." He had done some wrestling in his younger days, added the Texan, but this "wasn't exactly a wrestling match; this was a quorum match."

The combat was a half-serious, half-joking affair that got a little out of hand.

One Thurmond acquaintance commented, "Just as you begin to think for sure that nothing is ever funny to Strom, he comes up with something like this to show he's human after all."

Senator Thurmond's staff did not shrug the matter off quite that easily. Advisers lectured him for two weeks. Sophisticated Carolinians simply would not smile upon wrestling, they told him firmly. Just as they thought they were getting their point across during these various talks, an approving constituent would telephone to say, "That was great, Strom! You really showed that liberal!"—and all would be undone for a while. Staff members were able to persuade only one brave citizen to suggest personally to the Senator that perhaps wrestling was not the most appropriate way to prevent a quorum.

Meanwhile, Senator Yarborough was being smothered under shipments of Wheaties from Texas.

Having thoroughly entertained Capitol Hill with their physical prowess, the two United States senators returned to the serious issues of the summer of 1964.

Daring to defy all the odds for causes in which he believed, Strom Thurmond still somehow emerged alive each time. He seemed to possess a charmed political life. It was a political life he had been risking at intervals for years, to the uneasiness of friends. But rather than conform after those many skirmishes, the junior Senator from South Carolina was about to rebel on such a scale as to put his past "sins" of rebellion in the shade.

IX

The Rebel Finds a Home

Partial groundwork for Strom Thurmond's next rebellion—his dramatic, perilous, political realignment with the Republican Party—was laid during the summer of 1964 in California.

When the National Republican Convention at San Francisco nominated the country's best-known conservative, Barry Goldwater, for President, a situation began to evolve that would ultimately result in a major decision of Thurmond's life. The completing groundwork for that decision was to be laid a month later at the National Democratic Convention on the east coast.

In mid-July Senator Barry Goldwater of Arizona won the Republican presidential nomination. His opposition had been too inept to stop his nomination, but it was able—along with mistakes Goldwater himself made and along with an invincible Lyndon Johnson—to start his campaign on a steadily downward path beginning with his acceptance speech.

The hopelessness of the Goldwater effort was not obvious

immediately, but even if it had been, Strom Thurmond's decision would have been the same. After the nomination of the Senator closest to all men in Congress to his own conservative philosophy, the South Carolina legislator fell strangely quiet. Deep down he sensed the beginnings of a choice he would have to make. He openly praised the Republican ticket but added nothing about his own plans. As far back as 1961, Thurmond had expressed his conviction that there ought to be a political realignment of liberals in one party and conservatives in the other, but he had since let the matter drift as far as he was concerned.

The two had gotten to know each other back in 1957 and 1958 when Thurmond and Goldwater were fellow members of the Senate Labor and Public Welfare Committee. They developed mutual respect for each other's honesty and courage. They found that except on civil rights issues, they voted alike. Race issues, declared a political observer in recent years, were not good criteria by which to judge an officeholder either a liberal or a conservative. All southerners, including even Senator Fulbright, had a negative record on civil rights. Any other course would put them out of office. A man's real leanings, therefore, had to be ascertained by his record on other legislation. It was on these other issues that Goldwater and Thurmond were practically twins. In some ways the Arizonian was more conservative than Thurmond. Both adhered to a strict interpretation of the Constitution. Moreover, Goldwater had helped Thurmond in some of his Senate fights, like the one to get the muzzling investigation. In effect, there had developed a feeling of kinship between the men.

On the other hand, Thurmond also had a high regard for Lyndon Johnson's ability. When the latter succeeded to the presidency upon John F. Kennedy's death, Thurmond stated for the record, "Our country owes a great debt of gratitude to the late President for his foresight and vision in selecting as the man to succeed him in office, in the event of such a tragedy, one of the most experienced and capable leaders I have ever known."

However, President Johnson, in Thurmond's eyes, began soon to turn definitely in a leftward direction. The new President "rammed" through Congress an even stiffer civil rights bill than Kennedy's proposed one and, in Thurmond's opinion, continued to pursue a "no-win" foreign policy.

These matters had the Carolinian concerned, but the last straw was Lyndon Johnson's choice of Hubert Humphrey as his running mate. To Thurmond, such a choice meant one thing: Johnson intended to go—not middle-of-the-road —but strongly liberal. Humphrey had been a founder of the liberal Americans for Democratic Action and had been a militant liberal in his Senate career. The announcement of Humphrey at the August Democratic Convention in Atlantic City as the man to fill the vice-presidential slot was too much for Thurmond. He had no personal animosity toward Humphrey. In fact, he regarded the Minnesota Senator as "clean and a straight shooter" and their personal relations were pleasant, but politically, ideologically, they were poles apart.

Thurmond had managed not to attend the National Democratic Convention by going to Europe as a Senate delegate to the Interparliamentary Union meeting. Upon his return, though, wheels began to turn.

He decided that there were three choices open to him: (1) he could keep quiet; (2) he could endorse Goldwater but remain a Democrat; or (3) he could endorse Goldwater and go Republican.

In late August-early September, Strom Thurmond and his administrative assistant, Harry Dent, took a leap-frog journey over South Carolina to discuss the situation with key people. Ninety per cent of the persons contacted were solidly for Thurmond's keeping quiet.

"But you do not have a moral obligation to take a public stand," insisted one influential figure.

"We do think there is a moral obligation," reiterated both Thurmond and Dent.

"I don't see it," once more asserted their host.

One friend warned by someone beforehand of the nature of the Senator's visit, greeted Thurmond and his aide at the door with "No! no! no!"

To go Republican would mean political suicide, people told him.

When Thurmond told James F. Byrnes that he was seriously considering going Republican, Byrnes' eyes widened in astonishment. It took a moment for the elder statesman to speak, but when he did, he declared emotionally, "Well, I'd have to say that is a bold move and you are a man of real courage!"

But why could Thurmond not just keep quiet and ride out the election, Byrnes wanted to know. Because Lyndon Johnson was not the kind of politician to let somebody keep quiet, his visitors replied.

Byrnes then added, "You do what you think is right, and I know you will."

"And I will," Thurmond said.

Intending in his own mind to go the whole way to the Republican Party if he did anything at all publicly, Thurmond was impressed, nevertheless, by the overwhelming opposition of his friends. He was moved, actually, to reconsider the idea.

The night after his return to Washington, Senator Thurmond went out with Dent and another staff member for dinner, and as they ate, he made up his mind. He could have used his currently ailing gall bladder and his physician's advice for immediate surgery as an excuse to sit out the autumn, but Thurmond did not choose to sit out this campaign.

"I know what I have to do," he said.

He decided to draw up a tentative statement, and told

his aides to secure an appointment for him with Goldwater. The next day Thurmond's office was humming with momentous activity that concerned not only the Senator, but the state he represented as well. The staff contacted Dean Burch, National Republican Party Chairman, through whom Goldwater appointments were obtained and Saturday afternoon, September 12th, was set as the time for Thurmond to see Goldwater at the latter's well-protected Washington apartment.

Mrs. Goldwater received Senator Thurmond and his aide, Harry Dent, at the door that Saturday and led them in to see her husband. After a brief exchange of pleasantries, Thurmond proceeded with his customary directness to the main business of the visit.

"I have three choices open to me," he told Goldwater. "I can keep quiet, I can come out for you but remain a Democrat or I can come out for you and go all the way to the Republican Party. I'll do what will help you most."

Without hesitation, Barry Goldwater answered, "I very much want you to come out for me, and I want you to go all the way and change parties."

"Will this help you the most?" pressed Thurmond.

"That's right," replied Goldwater.

"Well, that's along the line I've been thinking," said Thurmond. "I think what you're doing is important to the country, and I want to do what I can to help you. I've prepared a statement saying that I'm coming out for you and that I am switching parties. Read it and see if you approve."

The Republican presidential nominee took the statement and carefully read it. "Don't change one word," he said on finishing it. "That's one of the finest statements I've ever read."

Reflecting on the presidential race, Goldwater commented, "I'm going to present it [his views and his candidacy] to the American people, and if they don't want me,

I'll just go back to Arizona and operate my ham radio."

This note of pessimism that Goldwater let slip struck Thurmond and Dent clearly. They realized immediately that the Arizonian felt his cause had little hope of success. The conversation then drifted to other topics, but before he was ready to leave, Thurmond asked Goldwater to call Republican officials in South Carolina and to talk with them through J. Drake Edens, state chairman. Thurmond got to his feet and walked to the door, then turned around and shook hands with his host. "Well," he told Goldwater, "I'm going to do it. I'm going to go all the way and change political parties." This statement was the first official declaration on Thurmond's part that his course of action was set.

They shook hands again, and Goldwater said eagerly, "Fine! I'll go ahead and call Edens today or tonight."

Thurmond added that he would make his television announcement to South Carolina on Wednesday, September 16th, so he could be on hand the next day for Goldwater's rally in Greenville, South Carolina.

After leaving the Goldwater apartment, Thurmond and Dent promptly went on to their office to set machinery in motion for proclaiming the historic decision. Dent telephoned Dolly Hamby of Bradley, Graham and Hamby, an all-woman advertising firm in Columbia, South Carolina and asked her to arrange television time for 6:15 p.m. Wednesday. Dolly Hamby, a veteran of previous Thurmond political undertakings, promptly did.

In the meantime, Lady Bird Johnson invited Thurmond to go on the "Lady Bird Special," a campaign train tour she was planning to make through the South.

Thurmond reportedly answered, "I appreciate the invitation, Lady Bird, but I'm having to make some fundamental decisions right now."

The wife of the President was quoted as having said then, "Strom, please don't do anything that would make us dislike you."

Thurmond was quoted as replying, "Lady Bird, I like you and the girls, too, but your husband and I don't agree on too many fundamental decisions."

Having thus gotten himself thoroughly out of grace at the White House, he flew down to Greenville on Monday, the 14th, to attend the funeral of industrialist and former U.S. Senator, Charles Daniel.

While in South Carolina, Thurmond was cornered by friends who had heard disturbing rumors about his switching parties. Please, begged one and all, don't do it—you will ruin yourself. Indignant kinfolk, of the opinion that they had not been consulted properly on the matter, expressed their unfavorable sentiments without delay. "No, Strom, no!" was the chorus he heard all over Greenville as one person after another pleaded with him, but they might as well have tried pleading with the mountains in the distance.

Just before boarding his plane for the return trip to Washington, Thurmond checked by telephone with his office to ask if the news release announcing his party-changing decision had been mailed.

"Well, we've got all these copies of the statement here and ready," said Harry Dent, who then chided, "but I didn't know whether or not you might want to make a change."

"What change?" barked the Senator. "Mail 'em!"

For better or for worse, another of Strom Thurmond's political rebellions was now irrevocably in motion.

Paradoxically, the rebelling Senator was in opposition to the Democratic Party on relatively fewer of the issues before Congress at this time than he had been during the previous two years. During 1961–62, he was the Senator most often opposed on party unity issues with an 80 per cent opposition record; during 1963–64, his rate of opposition dropped to 65 per cent, second to Senator Lausche, who had bucked the party on 68 per cent of the issues.

From a close examination, one might even have concluded—from the bare voting record alone—that Strom Thurmond was mellowing. From 1959 through 1962, he voted 100 per cent against a larger federal role in American life. The Senator's opposition rate on this question fell to 87½ per cent during the 1963–64 sessions.

There were other significant indicators in the statistics, however. Thurmond was always consistent in support of matters in which southern unity was involved. In the 1959–60 period, he was second only to Stennis in consistency with the majority of southern senators, and in the 1961–62 period, he was the most consistent in voting with a majority of southerners. In the years immediately preceding his change of parties, he ranked in fourth place in this category.

Most significant was Thurmond's consistency in supporting the traditional Republican-southern coalition. In 1959–60, Thurmond had supported the coalition 94 per cent of the time, and in the 1960–61 sessions, his percentage rose to 96. In 1963–64, his support of the Republican-southern coalition slipped, percentage wise, to 90 per cent, but only one senator, Ervin (D., N.C.), supported the coalition more frequently, and he only by one percentage point.

Regardless of what cold, unanalyzed statistics did or did not show about Thurmond's political unhappiness, his mood showed plenty, and he was ready to act.

On Tuesday night, September 15, the Columbia Broadcasting System's Walter Cronkite news program broke the story. CBS reporter Paul Nivin had been poking around Capitol Hill a month earlier for news and had more or less routinely included Thurmond. To his amazement, he found Thurmond open and frank in revealing the serious thoughts he was at that time giving to changing political allegiance. Nivin stuck with the Senator and came up with the "hard" story the night before Thurmond flew to Columbia to speak on television to the citizens of his state.

Looking as serious and as intense as he had ever looked —and with good reason, it would have to be acknowledged —Thurmond sat before a giant photographic backdrop of a smiling Barry Goldwater and faced the cameras. Gesturing frequently with outstretched hands, a typical mannerism he employed for emphasis even in conversation, he made his case. He appeared dedicated already to the task of exposing what he considered to be the evils of the Democratic Party and of extolling the virtues of Goldwater.

This speech probably was the most important one Strom Thurmond had ever made. In stating point by point his reasons for leaving the Democratic fold for that of the Republican Party, he revealed as much about his own philosophy and character as it was possible to do in a fifteen-minute address. In so doing he also tore the hide off the Democratic Party. This speech included all the issues he was to use as the basis for subsequent talks on Goldwater's behalf. He updated his campaign speeches with reference to the latest events but always returned to the fundamental points he set forth in his address to the people of South Carolina on Wednesday night, September 16. It was the same statement that Strom Thurmond had shown to Goldwater. In it he said:

My Fellow South Carolinians:

It has been wisely said that "For evil to triumph, it is only necessary that good men do nothing." Particularly is this true in time of crisis. Seldom before in the history of our Nation have we faced so great a crisis.

The people of South Carolina have placed me in a position of trust in the National Government. From this position, I have observed at close hand the conduct and factors which have brought about this crisis. I would, therefore, be most derelict in my duty were I at this time to remain silent.

I have no choice but to speak openly, frankly, and fully to the people of South Carolina on the crisis that confronts us.

The Democratic Party has abandoned the people. It

has turned its back on the spiritual values and political principles which have brought us the blessings of freedom under God and a bountiful prosperity. It has breached the trust reposed in it by the people. It has repudiated the Constitution of the United States. It is leading the evolution of our nation to a socialistic dictatorship.

The Democratic Party has forsaken the people to become the party of minority groups, power-hungry union leaders, political bosses, and big businessmen looking for government contracts and favors.

The Democratic Party has used the Government as a propaganda machine to distort the truth and deceive the public to the extent that a sub-cabinet official can publicly defend the Administration's "right to lie" and remain in office, unrebuked.

The Democratic Party has invaded the private lives of the people by using the powers of government for coercion and intimidation of individuals.

The Democratic Party has rammed through Congress unconstitutional, impractical, unworkable, and oppressive legislation which invades inalienable personal and property rights of the individual.

The Democratic Party has encouraged lawlessness, civil unrest, and mob actions.

The Democratic Party has violated its trust by using the power of government to suppress information on scandals and corruption of its leaders in government and party offices.

The Democratic Party has succored and assisted our Communist enemies through trade and aid at the expense of the American people.

The Democratic Party has established and pursued for our government a no-win foreign policy of weakness, indecision, accommodation, and appeasement.

The Democratic Party, as custodian of government, faltered at the Bay of Pigs and in the Cuban crisis of

1962—at the very moment when victory was at hand—and thereby forfeited Cuba to Soviet domination, subjected our nation to the peril of an armed enemy camp ninety miles from our shores, and opened the doors of the hemisphere to Communist subversion.

The Democratic Party, as custodian of government, has sent our youth into combat in Viet Nam, refusing to call it war, and demanding of our youth the risk of their lives without providing either adequate equipment or a goal of victory.

The Democratic Party now worships at the throne of power and materialism.

The Democratic Party has demonstrated a callous disregard for sound fiscal policies and practices.

The Democratic Party, while hiding behind the deceitful gimmick of a darkened White House, has increased deficit spending and squandered, at home and abroad, billions of hard-earned dollars taken from the American people.

The Democratic Party has utterly disregarded the disastrous effects of the resulting inflation on people with fixed incomes, such as retirees, pensioners, Social Security beneficiaries, and those who have their savings invested in insurance.

The Democratic Party, as custodian of government, has adopted the practice of taking your money by taxation and then using that money to attempt to buy your votes.

The Democratic Party is attempting with alarming success to change the Congress from an independent body representing the people to an amen chorus for Presidential proposals.

The Democratic Party has endangered the security of the nation by negative decisions of military preparedness, preoccupation with bilateral and unilateral steps toward disarmament, and by use of the military services domestically as instruments of social reform.

The Democratic Party has attempted to degrade and downgrade our men in uniform in order to discredit their warnings of the grave dangers to our society from the Administration's weak and senseless defense policies.

The Democratic Party has nominated for Vice-President a key leader of the Americans for Democratic Action, the most influential socialist group in our nation.

The Democratic Party has encouraged, supported, and protected the Supreme Court in a reign of judicial tyranny, and in the Court's effort to wipe out local self-government, effective law enforcement, internal security, the rights of the people and the States, and even the structure of the State governments.

The Democratic Party is converting our Constitutional Federated Republic into the same type of disciplined and submissive servant of an elite power group as it has made of the Democratic Party itself, as all who watched the Democratic Convention on television can bear witness.

The top leaders of the South Carolina Democratic Party have chosen to abandon the traditional independence of the State Party, and to lead the people of South Carolina down the road to serfdom mapped by the National Democratic Party. The party of our fathers is dead. Those who took its name are engaged in another reconstruction, this time not only of the South, but of the entire Nation.

If the American people permit the Democratic Party to return to power, freedom as we have known it in this country is doomed, and individuals will be destined to lives of regulation, control, coercion, intimidation, and subservience to a power elite who shall rule from Washington.

Fortunately, for those of us who cherish the traditional freedom entrusted to us by our forefathers, there is another choice this year. Although the party of our fathers is dead, the principles of our forefathers live now in the cause of a presidential nominee. The man who has gained the Republican nomination for President against all the odds and opinion polls, and who now has control of the Republican Party is one who believes in and abides by our Constitution. He has demonstrated his fidelity to freedom, independence, and the Constitution by his actions and his votes in the United States Senate. I personally know him to be able and responsible. He is an honest man of courage and conviction, who trusts the American people to hold the reins of government and rule themselves.

I cannot foretell what success will reward Senator Barry Goldwater's efforts to return the National Government to its Constitutional role and our Nation to its rightful place of strength and respect in the world. Nor can I predict with certainty how long those ideas and ideals of Senator Goldwater which I share will prevail in the councils of the Republican Party which he now leads. I do know that we have a fighting chance under Barry Goldwater's leadership and that we are welcomed to his banner.

I know also that the course for the Democratic Party has been set toward socialism and arbitrary rule. I know further that the Democratic Party's line of succession is Hubert Humphrey and Robert Kennedy, with Walter Reuther and Joseph Rauh pulling strings behind the scenes.

I have worked within the framework of the Democratic Party, because experience proves it necessary to work within the framework of one of the two national parties to be effective. I have, nevertheless, maintained independence of judgment on issues and have conscientiously tried to represent the people of South Carolina, seeking to protect their rights and freedom. I shall always maintain my independent judgment and action and put the people of South Carolina first. To do this in the future I must work within the framework of the Goldwater Republican Party.

For me, there is no alternative. The future of freedom

and constitutional government is at stake, and this requires that I do everything in my power to help Barry Goldwater return our nation to constitutional government through his election to the Presidency. This also requires that I join him in his fight, successful as of now, to make the Republican Party a party which supports freedom, justice, and constitutional government.

It will be a long and hard struggle, with many battles to be fought. At this time, one objective takes precedence over all others—electing Barry Goldwater President. As we give the Presidential race our undivided effort, I hope all our people, and particularly our young people whose future hangs in the balance, will join this cause with enthusiasm.

To my friends who have conscientiously advised me against this step, because of a sincere belief that I could best serve the country by following a course designed to keep myself in office, I can only say that I fully realize the political risk involved in this step and that my chances for re-election might, because of this step, go down into oblivion. But in the final analysis, I can only follow the course which in my heart and conscience, I believe to be in the best interest of our State, our country, and the freedom of our people.

I have chosen this course because I cannot consider any risks in a cause which I am convinced is right.

During the address, "Strom Thurmond (D., S.C.)" flashed across the screen. Two-thirds of the way through, two lines appeared reading "Strom Thurmond (R., S.C.)," and television audiences saw South Carolina history in the making before their very eyes. The ferocity of the speech and the astounding boldness of Thurmond's action were breathtaking. Viewers were left with a feeling of stunned limpness. People could not help reflecting, too, on the irony of events. Only four years earlier Thurmond had thrown his full support to Lyndon Johnson's effort to secure the Democratic nomination. Now, he was throwing his full weight against Johnson.

Even Thurmond's critics—and he had a number of them —were forced to credit him at this point in his life with great political courage. To jump from a winning team to a losing one and to risk one's own neck in the doing required mettle and an undauntable spirit. Whatever else one might have criticized about Thurmond over the years, one had to respect him for the honesty and grit he showed in this instance.

An acquaintance of the Senator summed him up this way, "You may dislike Thurmond's style and his personality; you may disagree with his views, you may question his judgment—especially now—but there are certain qualities you cannot take from him. These are his unimpeachable integrity and his unsurpassable courage that shine through everything he does—even his mistakes."

After the television appearance, Senator Thurmond and his aide, Harry Dent, went to dinner at a local restaurant. There, he got the first sampling of reaction. A group of airline pilots from all over the State was meeting in a private room. Upon learning that Thurmond was in the building, the men invited the Senator to speak to them and applauded him.

The next morning Thurmond and his administrative assistant sped to Greenville on the first leg of an exhausting campaign sweep through the South. Making his first public appearance as a Republican, Senator Thurmond introduced Goldwater at a noon rally of some 25,000 people on the Greenville-Spartanburg airport grounds. He used a speech composed in 1960 to present the Arizona Senator for the George Washington Award of the American Good Government Society. The speech still seemed to fit, in Thurmond's opinion, so he quoted it for this occasion.

"Knowing the southern people as I do," he read from

the four-year-old introduction, "it is my opinion that if he should be selected as the nominee of either major political party, he would carry the South. If elected, he would make a great President...

"Here is a man who has stood consistently against the tide of centralized government, Communist appeasement, fiscal extravagance, state socialism and submission to the tools of internationalism..."

Goldwater then told the partisan, cheering crowd what he thought of the newest Republican on the party roster.

"There is no way in the world that I can comment adequately on the action Strom Thurmond took yesterday," he said. "It defies words. It was an action that requires courage of the finest sort. I want to pay my respects to a great American, Strom Thurmond, who took one of the most courageous political actions I have ever heard of in the history of our country, and I am sure this action is going to redound to his eternal credit and to the benefit of Americans who put freedom above everything else."

After the Greenville rally, Thurmond and Dent boarded the Goldwater airplane for the campaign flight through Louisiana and Texas. Thurmond appeared with the presidential candidate on the podium at the afternoon engagement in Shreveport, Louisiana, and found that afterwards people were mobbing him as well as Goldwater to offer their best wishes. As soon as the Shreveport doings were over, the Goldwater entourage flew on to New Orleans for a motorcade and a large rally that night in the Sugar Bowl stadium.

It was after midnight when Thurmond and Dent reached their New Orleans hotel room. The exhausted 34-year-old Dent fell on his bed, too weary to shower or to do anything more than find a place to lay his head before falling asleep. The 61-year-old Thurmond, who had spoken at each of the strenuous rallies during the day and had shaken scores of hands, was not about to abbreviate his nightly routine. He showered, brushed his teeth and did push-ups and other exercises before retiring. The clock alarm was set for 5:30 a.m. so the two men could catch another motorcade, this one to the airport to board the Goldwater plane for the trip to Texas. When the alarm rang in the early morning, Dent looked over to see if his boss had heard it, but the Senator was already up and was on the floor doing another series of push-ups. The sight was unbelievable to the young assistant still summoning energy to lift himself out of bed.

(On Thurmond's sixty-first birthday the previous winter, an Army friend, a colonel from the Pentagon, came by the office to extend good wishes to the Senator. He was a big, well-developed man and fellow devotee of physical culture with whom Thurmond often played tennis. "Happy birthday, Senator!" he said, adding humorously, "Now, let's see if you can do sixty-one push-ups." In the face of such a challenge, the Senator promptly shed his coat. Before the astonished colonel and the equally astonished office force, Strom Thurmond breezed past sixty-one push-ups, stopping at last with seventy-five. "Actually, seventy-five are too many," confessed the Senator later, "but it was my birthday!")

Senator Thurmond and his aide left the Goldwater tour after stops in Longview and Dallas to return to South Carolina, where immense work was waiting to be done. By now reaction to Thurmond's change of party allegiance had hit the press, and there was no dearth of comment to be had without the asking. Messages coming into Thurmond's office were heavily favorable to his party realignment, but, of course, there was no way to judge the "silent sentiment" across the State, at least, until November 3rd. Some rather practical-minded observers tended to credit the party switch to realistic considerations—such as getting reelected—as much as to Thurmond's convictions.

"Crazy but courageous," pretty well summed up the feeling of southerners on Capitol Hill. Thurmond and Goldwater both had predicted other southern office-holders would bolt

Democratic ranks, but none did before the elections. In general, Democrats, on the state and national levels, were surprisingly restrained in their comments about Thurmond. Certain party officials and liberals over the nation said they were elated over the Carolinian's departure and proclaimed it good riddance.

National Democratic Party Chairman John M. Bailey growled, ". . . No man has used a party designation longer and served its principles more poorly than Strom Thurmond in the Democratic Party. I am sure his new party will find him ever the malcontent.

"His record demonstrates again and again that he stands with neither the traditions and dignity of the Old South nor the vigor and hopes of the New South. Thurmond's defection is hardly newsworthy since he has not supported a national Democratic ticket for twenty years . . ."

South Carolina Democratic Chairman Yancey A. McLeod was just as hot in his denunciation. He questioned Thurmond's wisdom, judgment and "moral right" to leave the Democratic party two years before expiration of his term. Thurmond was elected under the Democratic label by Democratic voters, he declared, adding, "The people of South Carolina were entitled to the representation for which he was elected. They have the right to make that choice."

South Carolina was now a two-party state, McLeod warned Democrats, and Thurmond has "thrown down the gauntlet of challenge" to every Democratic office-holder. "The Republican Party has moved in. The fight is now, not four years from now, with the result to be determined November 3rd." Democrats in the State would work all the harder because of Thurmond's desertion, McLeod maintained, and would "overcompensate" for any losses. President Johnson, he assured newsmen, "will win overwhelmingly."

There was some unhappiness in Republican ranks, too, over Strom Thurmond's move. Groans erupted from Repub-

lican liberals all across the country. One writer said it was
difficult to tell who was sadder—the Democrats or the Republicans.

Republican Senator Clifford P. Case of New Jersey made
it plain that he was unhappy. "The thing that bothers me
very much," he said, "is that I don't like to think that our
party is a hospitable place for a person of the segregationist
views of Strom Thurmond." The South Carolina Senator,
Case declared, "made a mistake if he thinks he is going to
be comfortable in the Republican Party."

On the other hand, Goldwater supporters, conservatives
in general and the party leadership welcomed the rebel
senator into the Republican fold, indicating they would try
to do well by him in Congress.

(Senator John Tower of Texas had volunteered even before Thurmond's official announcement to do all he could
in helping the Carolinian obtain good committee posts. He
said he would speak to Senator Everett Dirksen, Republican
leader of the Senate. The biggest loss Thurmond faced was
his approximate ten years of seniority as a Democrat. Senator Dirksen, at the beginning of the next session, did go to
bat for Thurmond. After much wrangling and juggling
within the ranks, Thurmond was given Goldwater's place
on the Armed Services Committee and the Preparedness
Investigating Subcommittee with no seniority loss and was
transferred from the Commerce Committee to the Banking
and Currency Committee, both groups being about equal in
status. In addition, he won a spot on the Republican Policy
Committee. Moreover, by virtue of his seniority on the Republican side of the Armed Services Committee, he became
an ex-officio voting member of the important defense and
military construction subcommittees of the Appropriations
Committee. In the meantime, Thurmond was assigned a
desk on the Republican side of the Senate aisle.

Once the dust of transition had settled, the attention of
the Thurmond forces turned to helping Goldwater carry

South Carolina and as many other southern states as possible. The Senator released his top aide, Harry Dent, for the campaign's duration to be assistant campaign chairman at state Republican headquarters. Dent's primary concern became the mapping of grand strategy and the scheduling of Thurmond speaking tours.

Campaign trips through the southern states with occasional return visits to South Carolina were lined up, with Thurmond's efforts concentrated in conservative areas.

Toward the last of September, the Senator joined a Republican "Truth Squad" trailing Democratic vice-presidential candidate Hubert Humphrey across the South "to set the record straight." On September 29, the paths of Thurmond and Humphrey crossed in Moultrie, Georgia. The irrepressible Thurmond, who had been blistering Humphrey regularly in every speech, took this opportunity to "welcome" him to the South. Thurmond walked briskly into the street to greet Humphrey good humoredly and to shake hands as the latter's motorcade passed. The incident made a lasting impression on the midwesterner, who commented about it quite some time after the election. He was surprised that Strom Thurmond would have anything to do with him under campaign circumstances in the deep South.

Having welcomed Humphrey and having "set the record straight" in Georgia, the South Carolinian was off to other politicking for Barry Goldwater. In fact, it was the opinion of at least some observers that Thurmond was doing a better job of selling Goldwater to southerners than was the Republican candidate himself. Whenever the two men spoke at the same rally, Thurmond, like an old-fashioned revival preacher, would work his audience up to an emotional peak, ready to walk the sawdust trail, only to see the excitement subside under the casual, almost folksy style of Goldwater. One man in Charlotte, North Carolina, sent a contribution of $1,000 to national Republican headquarters and remarked that since he was forking over money he felt free to offer advice. Tell Goldwater, he said, to step aside and let Thurmond do the speaking for him.

Even Thurmond was surprised at the response he received in his southern stumping tour. He spoke on a number of television programs and was covered in many southern newspapers, thereby reaching a large "invisible" audience, as an accompanying reporter described it. The big surprise, however, was the size of the "visible" audiences the Senator drew on his sweep through Virginia, Tennessee, Texas and Alabama. In city after city local arrangers of Thurmond appearances were surprised at the number of people who turned out to see and hear the controversial political phenomenon called Strom Thurmond.

Leverne Prosser, covering the trip for Charleston's *News and Courier*, wrote:

... His [Thurmond's] unseen but measurable audience was tremendous but his visible audience was nothing less than spectacular.

From the beginning it was evident that Thurmond was going to fare well on his trek through the Tobacco and Navy country of Virginia, hills of Tennessee, flatlands of Texas and states rights conscious Alabama.

At Petersburg, Democrats for Goldwater planned for about 150 persons "at the most" to fork over $25 each to hear Thurmond talk ... More than 450 persons showed up ...

At Norfolk, even the most optimistic of Goldwater supporters expected about 2,000 persons to turn up at Norfolk's spacious Center Theater. More than 6,500 came and cheered wildly ...

... Thurmond was supposed to be quietly brought into Nashville ... and whisked off to his hotel ... His 1 a.m. arrival was unpublicized but more than 200 Vanderbilt students were out yelling, "We want Thurmond." They got him. He not only talked to them then but insisted that he be taken to the school where about 1,500 students showed up to applaud him the next day.

In Memphis, the Democrats for Goldwater prepared for 200 persons at a fund-raising dinner at $25 a head. More than 500 showed up . . .

. . . (It was thought that) Thurmond could have some influence on the traditionally strong Democratic stronghold Houston suburb of Pasadena.

He did. About 150 persons—most working men in their shirt sleeves—were expected to pay $2 each for a plate of cold cuts, potato salad and some "down to earth" political oratory from Thurmond.

More than 600 came and gave him a standing ovation when he said, "The Democratic Party left me, I didn't leave it. I still stand for the same principles I stood for when I went to Washington 10 years ago . . ."

The last two weeks of the presidential campaign were reserved on Thurmond's schedule for South Carolina. There, the contest also had shaped up as a prestige battle between Thurmond and his old foe, Senator Olin Johnston, a consistent Democratic Party loyalist for his entire career. Thurmond's defection from the "party of his forefathers" merely inspired Johnston to work harder. He was rejecting other speaking invitations, he said, to concentrate on South Carolina.

"I'm going to devote my time to my people," Senator Johnston stated. "I may sleep a little from time to time," he told a state Democratic organizational meeting, "but you are going to find me most of the time until election day on the battlefront, where I think I should be."

With those words ringing in their ears, Thurmond forces knew they had to carry South Carolina for Goldwater, and carry it by a respectable margin, or Thurmond's political future would be in trouble. The two weeks before election day, therefore, were devoted to what could be termed a "Thurmond blitz."

Strom Thurmond, only a little grayer and older-looking than the last time he had been on the campaign trail was still as fit (with the exception of his uncooperative gall bladder which he simply was ignoring for the time being) and full of fire as he ever was. Endowed with more endurance than most men half his age, he turned on all his steam. He seemed to be everywhere in the State at once, averaging from five to six speeches a day, and frequently exceeding that number. His busiest day was in the Pee Dee area around Florence, South Carolina, when he made fourteen speeches and toured several grocery stores. It was the first time in his life that Thurmond had ever campaigned for somebody else, and he was putting just as much heart into the effort as if he himself were running—which, in a sense, he was.

If Strom Thurmond spoke like a dedicated preacher on his out-of-state engagements, he sounded even more like one in his home State. He viewed the people of South Carolina as his own flock, and felt responsible for their welfare. He would survey his audiences from the rostrum as if he were, indeed, a revival preacher of old, looking sternly at a congregation in urgent need of being saved, then burst upon them with his own kind of hellfire-damnation sermon. Hardly pausing between words, he would condemn the Democrats, denounce the Administration, warn of certain disaster if the present national leaders stayed in office, exhort and entreat the audience to follow the path of enlightenment toward salvation—political salvation—by voting for Barry Goldwater, who could save the country and the Constitution.

These arguments would pour out in a steady stream as Thurmond gesticulated toward his listeners, first with one hand, then with the other, frequently with both, outstretched, pleading for understanding and conviction. He would lean

forward to thunder home a point and sometimes land a
solid whack on the speaker's stand for additional emphasis.
He knew how to lift up his audience and to carry it with
him as an amen chorus from argument to argument. When
he had finished, his "congregation" was convinced that salvation must surely lie with Goldwater, and they were ready
to accept the Arizonian as the nation's President. By election
day, November 3rd, South Carolinians had been so "blitzed"
by their junior United States Senator that they were at the
point of exhaustion.

Thurmond forces had also kept the pressure up in other
ways. They knew their state-wide campaign had peaked
the night the Senator came on television to endorse Goldwater and to change parties. The problem was to keep the
campaign from losing momentum too fast. They, therefore,
persuaded key figures in the State to announce for Goldwater at regular intervals. Plans worked out in such a way
that a personage was coming out for the Republican nominee every seven days or so. As one worker said, "We try to
peak every week."

The Democrats, meantime, had not been idle. They had
put their heavy artillery into the battle and figured on clinch-
ing victory with the biggest gun of all, President Johnson.
The President spoke at an October 26 night rally on the
State House grounds. He drew the largest crowd of the
autumn in South Carolina and had the situation looking
good for his side when the state Republicans pulled another
trick out of their bag. They had Barry Goldwater end his
pitch for southern votes at a televised indoor rally at Columbia on October 31. The program listed every pro-Goldwater celebrity the Republicans could snag and cram into
the limited time period. The rally then was beamed over
a regional hook-up to all the southern states.

The Columbia rally was the *coup de grâce* to South Carolina Democratic Party hopes, though the Democrats could
not very well admit the fact.

On the eve of election day, leaders of both parties in the State held news conferences to forecast victory for their respective candidates. Democratic State Chairman Yancey McLeod told reporters that Lyndon Johnson would take South Carolina by 25,000 to 40,000 votes. At his session with newsmen later in the day, J. Drake Edens, Republican State Chairman, predicted Goldwater would carry the state "by more than 25,000 votes."

While Barry Goldwater went down to a terrible defeat nationally, he made history by taking the deep South. He captured 58.7% of the vote in South Carolina, outdistancing the President by over 92,000 votes. It was the first time a Republican had carried the State since Rutherford B. Hayes did so in the Reconstruction year of 1876.

How was this historic feat accomplished?

Edens attributed the State victory mainly to "literally thousands of dedicated amateur citizen-politicians who have worked in the last four years to develop the finest organization this State has ever seen."

"In a sense," the Republican chairman added, however, "the contest in South Carolina was one between the philosophies and personalities of Senator Thurmond and Senator Olin D. Johnston." The vote was "a tribute" to Thurmond, he said, and to Congressman Albert W. Watson, who likewise had worked for Goldwater.

(On election night a photographer caught a glum Olin Johnston at Democratic headquarters as he sat, chin in hand, spectacles on and lips poked out, his whole expression seeming to ask, "How could this have happened?" For sometime after the election Edens would gleefully display at every opportunity that classic Johnston picture for which the Republicans had waited so long.)

South Carolina Republicans under Edens' chairmanship unquestionably had done a remarkable job of precinct organizing. They had conducted house-to-house surveys to spot the Goldwater vote, and on election day they saw to it that known pro-Goldwater voters got to the polls. Though this and other organizational work were excellently accomplished, would organization alone have been sufficient to carry the state for the Republicans?

Most independent observers, most of the press and Democrats themselves thought not, despite strong Goldwater feeling in South Carolina. The big difference between the Republicans coming as close as they did four years before (When Nixon lost the State to Kennedy by less than 10,000 votes) and the smashing margin of victory in this election was Strom Thurmond, they said almost unanimously. The one missing element in the Republican cause of 1960 was a big State personality to serve as forceful leader, campaign catalyst, effective articulator of issues and professional hand at the wheel. Thurmond supplied that in 1964. Even workers at Democratic headquarters conceded that they could not overcome the tremendous impact which Thurmond's realignment with the Republican Party made on the race. Not only was the initial impact telling, they admitted, but each time the Democrats thought they were getting the State situation in hand, Thurmond workers landed another blow somewhere.

Strom Thurmond had laid his neck on the block for Barry Goldwater in this, the most daring rebellion of the Carolinian's career. In so doing, he pulled off another miracle in an otherwise defeated cause. The balloting results in South Carolina not only saved Thurmond's neck, but they automatically boosted the Senator to the pinnacle of his career, though for how long no one would predict in the fickle world of politics.

Except for carrying South Carolina, Georgia, Alabama, Mississippi and Louisiana—an achievement attributed in part to Thurmond's efforts—and his own state of Arizona, Goldwater suffered one of the most disastrous losses in the nation's history. Many lesser Republican candidates, too, went down in the slaughter. Even if Thurmond had foreseen a

Goldwater defeat of such huge proportions, it would not have affected his plans.

The one influence that might have altered Strom Thurmond's action and, thereby, possibly the history of South Carolina was one that could not be exerted. It was the considerable influence of his deceased young wife, Jean, whom he adored.

What would Jean have done had she been alive in the summer and autumn of 1964?

One can only speculate, but it would be well to recall that basically she was a conventional person whereas her husband was not. She had little of his rebel spirit but instead tended toward group associations. Too, she was really more liberal than the Senator, a difference Thurmond confessed somewhat reluctantly. Moreover, Jean had a natural affinity for the Democratic Party, stemming from her father's long Democratic connections. Added to these factors would be the friendly relations she had developed with both Lyndon and Lady Bird Johnson during her five years in Washington. This whole combination of factors indicates it would have been a wrench to Jean for Strom not only to defy the national Democratic Party as in 1948, but to leave it completely. It would be reasonable to suggest that she would have had much to say. Whether or not she could have stopped the Senator is another matter. He is not a person easily dissuaded from a course he has set.

Who knows what might have been, had Jean lived to be with her rebel Senator during the momentous years of the 1960's? She did not live, though, and the sorrow of her untimely death, as well as the fullness of her life, is part of Strom Thurmond's story, a story unique in American history.